DUCKTOWN

BACK IN RAHT'S TIME

JULIUS ECKHARDT RAHT
who for nearly a quarter of a century was the outstanding figure of the Ducktown district.

DUCKTOWN

BACK IN RAHT'S TIME

BY

R. E. BARCLAY

THE UNIVERSITY OF NORTH CAROLINA PRESS

CHAPEL HILL

Copyright, 1946, by
THE UNIVERSITY OF NORTH CAROLINA PRESS

Printed in the United States of America by
VAN REES PRESS · NEW YORK · PJ

PREFACE

For no reason other than to learn something of the history of the region in which he has lived for over forty years, the writer entered upon the task of compiling this narrative early in 1936. And before he had completed it, he had spent over seven years in arduous toil and had traveled some three thousand miles in his car. Libraries and court houses in Nashville, Atlanta, Chattanooga, Knoxville, Cleveland, Benton, Blue Ridge, Murphy, and Ellijay were visited several times. Older citizens living in remote mountain coves, and in towns and cities throughout this section were visited and interviewed. Letters seeking information on the history of a Ducktown long since forgotten were sent out to all parts of this country and to foreign countries.

Old roads, trails, and other landmarks were sought out; graveyards lost in brambles and undergrowth were found and their fading tombstones studied for names and dates. Aged and disintegrating newspapers, maps, documents, and all sorts of periodicals were perused and handled with the tenderness shown by the devout research worker.

The prize stroke, however, and the one which made it possible to expand this narrative to book length, was the discovery by the author of a great mass of accurate, detailed records, documents, and letters, all bearing upon Ducktown and the surrounding region from the 1840's to the early 1900's. The bulk of these records consisted of Captain J. E. Raht's personal papers. There were letters addressed to him and copies of his own letters which he had secured by the wet-press method. In this tremendous volume of relevant and rare papers and correspondence had been preserved a record of an important segment of Ducktown's early history, as well as a remarkable though disconnected narrative of Captain Raht's own life. Here indeed was material which, when added to that collected through the author's own efforts, made possible an authentic portrayal of almost every phase of life and activity at Ducktown throughout the period from its settlement until the closing of the mines in 1878.

During this first period of Ducktown's mining activity Captain Raht was for nearly a quarter of a century the outstanding figure in the district. Following resumption of mining twelve years later, it became a stock phrase of older residents of Ducktown to refer to things and events of the former period of activity as having taken place "back in Raht's time." It was a fitting expression, and a made-to-order title for a book that would someday be written on this unique region.

Bound up in this imperishable phrase are history, legend, and stories of early settlers, speculators, miners, mining companies, merchants, mail carriers, roads, schools, and churches—each of which played a leading role at Ducktown in the years preceding the present era. Forgotten though many of them may be, they were once of flattering importance.

The history of the present era of the Ducktown district is still in progress, since the Ducktown of today had its birth, or resurrection, with the coming of the railroad in 1890. It is the era previous to 1890, which extends back into the 1830's, about which so little is known and which it is the purpose of this volume to bring to light.

ACKNOWLEDGMENTS

Grateful acknowledgment is made of the assistance rendered by Mr. H. C. Parmelee, Editor of *The Engineering and Mining Journal,* in uncovering articles on the bessemerizing of copper matte in old files of the *Journal.*

Acknowledgment is also made of assistance and information furnished by the Post Office Department, Washington, D. C.; J. N. Houser, Vice President and General Manager, Tennessee Copper Company, Copperhill, Tennessee; Mrs. John Trotwood Moore, State Librarian, Nashville, Tennessee; L. A. Styles, Superior Court Clerk, Blue Ridge, Georgia; L. H. Park, County Court Clerk, Benton, Tennessee; Willard C. Holden, Ordinary, Ellijay, Georgia; J. D. Clemmer, Benton, Tennessee; Mrs. Pope T. Singleton, Copperhill, Tennessee; and numerous individuals who furnished the author with many interesting accounts, both factual and legendary, of life and times in and around old Ducktown. Especially grateful is the author for the assistance rendered in this respect by the following individuals, all of whom spent many hours at different times in relating anecdotes and events, the learning of which would have been possible from no other source: William P. Lang, Cleveland, Tennessee; Dr. J. R. Nankivell, Athens, Tennessee; John W. Chancey, Ducktown, Tennessee; Joseph P. Vestal, Epworth, Georgia; and James P. Aaron, Mineral Bluff, Georgia. Of these five, the first four named have recently died. Of a total of thirty-nine older citizens of this region who were interviewed by the author, twenty-eight have since died. With them went first-hand knowledge of the early history of Ducktown and its environs that will never again be available.

I extend my appreciation also to William P. Lang; T. S. Weaver, Copperhill; Emory Verner, Ducktown; and E. D. Raht, Chattanooga, for furnishing valuable photographs to illustrate the book.

R. E. B.

Copperhill, Tennessee
December 7, 1945

CONTENTS

	PAGE
Preface	v
Acknowledgments	vii

CHAPTER

1.	Introduction to Ducktown	1
2.	The Cherokee Indians	7
3.	The Ocoee District	11
4.	Border Counties	15
5.	Polk County, Tennessee	21
6.	Settlement in the Forties	25
7.	Development in the Fifties	31
8.	Preparations for Mining	43
9.	First Decade of Mining	58
10.	Consolidations	77
11.	Ducktown during the Civil War	87
12.	Social Developments, 1865-1890	102
13.	Mining, 1865-1878	129
14.	The Board of Directors	159
15.	The Trial	170
16.	"The Richest Man in Tennessee"	185
17.	Raht, Friend and Citizen	229
	Appendix	253
	A Note on Sources	267
	Index	271

ILLUSTRATIONS

Julius Eckhardt Raht	Frontispiece
	Facing Page
A Present-day View of the Copper Basin's Barren, Eroded Hillsides	50
The Copperhill Plant of the Tennessee Copper Company	50
A Portion of an Old Surveyor's Map of the Ocoee District	51
Diagrammatic Representations of Three Original Ore Formations of the Ducktown District	66
Diagrammatic Representation of Ore Formations	67
Map of Mining Properties	80
An Old-Fashioned Water Wheel	85
Hoisting Ore by Means of the Windlass	114
The Whim as a Device for Hoisting Ore	115
An Old Map of the 1870's Showing the Central Portion of the Ducktown District	130
The Old Copper Road through the Ocoee Gorge	131
McKinney's Mill, Chestnut Gap, Georgia	131
William L. Raht's Patent	150
J. E. Raht's First Warehouse and Store at Cleveland	154
The Isabella Smelting Works in 1875	Between Pages 154 & 155
A Rare Old Bank Note Issued by the Ocoee Bank, Cleveland, Tennessee	155
A Sociable Interlude at the Polk County Mine	155
Old Burra Burra Furnace Sheds at McPherson	178
Prospecting for Ore with a Diamond Drill	178
Interrogatories of the Receiver	179
The Cleveland National Bank Building	194
The Old Church and School Building at Isabella	194
The J. E. Raht Residence in Cleveland, Tennessee	194
Ocoee Street, Copperhill, Looking East	195
Receipt Exempting J. E. Raht from Military Service	203

DUCKTOWN

BACK IN RAHT'S TIME

CHAPTER 1

INTRODUCTION TO DUCKTOWN

TUCKED SNUGLY INTO THE SOUTHEASTERN CORNER OF POLK County, Tennessee, lies Ducktown, Tennessee's copper district which has been famous for nearly a hundred years. Known for some seven or eight decades simply as Ducktown, then for a number of years as the Ducktown Basin, but now more often referred to as the Great Copper Basin, or Copper Basin, this locality boasts a history and reputation unique in the annals of southern growth and development.

The area of the Ducktown Basin is approximately one hundred square miles, though the commercial and mining area covers only about twenty-five square miles. The state lines of Tennessee, Georgia, and North Carolina meet on a hill near the ancient church of Pleasant Hill, three miles east of the Basin's principal town, Copperhill. From there the Georgia-Tennessee state line runs diagonally across the Basin to Big Frog Mountain on the west. Several square miles of the Basin extend southward into the neighboring Georgia county of Fannin.

On the east, separating the Basin from Cherokee County, North Carolina, is Pack Mountain with an altitude of 3,500 feet. At right angles to Pack Mountain are Stansbury and Threewitt Mountains, forming the northern limits of the Basin and extending like huge brown backbones to Little Frog Mountain. From the north Little Frog Mountain, attaining a maximum altitude of 3,347 feet at Sassafras Knob, continues in a southwesterly direction and reaches to the Ocoee River on the northwest. The 4,300 foot summit of Big Frog Mountain forms the majestic skyline on the west. The mountainous chain continues around to the south by way of Hemp Top, Mule Top, and Flat Top. Far off to the southwest, beyond and rising above the jagged skyline of the "Tops," is the pale blue 4,137 foot summit of Cowpen Mountain. These mountains are the western spurs of the Blue Ridge Mountains. Their receding lines to the south make the southern limit of the Basin indefinite.

Three look-out towers of the Forest Service—on Sassafras Knob, Hemp Top, and Flat Top—are visible from the Basin. These towers serve as stations from which watchers keep a look-out for forest fires over a wide range of mountains in the region.

The area within the Basin is a mass of undulating, barren hills which, when viewed from the heights of the surrounding mountains, give it the appearance of an immense basin with a heavily wrinkled bottom. The barrenness is the result of damage done to vegetation largely in the roast-yard era from 1890 to 1904. During this period the trees were felled as fuel for the roast yards, and the heavy volume of sulphur-laden smoke from the smoldering piles of ore played havoc with the remaining vegetation. Erosion was a natural consequence. As this is a phenomenon of the history of the Basin of a period later than that embraced in this volume, its details will not be enlarged upon here.

Through almost every one of the narrow valleys in the Basin run streams varying in size from small rivulets to large creeks. Many of the larger streams figured prominently in the early history of Ducktown, especially the Ocoee River, which runs through the district in a northwesterly direction. The Toccoa-Ocoee River rises near Blood Mountain in Union County, Georgia. From there to the state line at Copperhill it is named Toccoa. Students of Indian history credit the name of Toccoa as being derived from Ta gwa'hi, meaning Catawba Place. An Indian village by this name is said to have once been located on the Toccoa River in what is now Fannin County, Georgia. Upon entering Tennessee the river takes the name Ocoee. This name, also of Indian derivation, came from Uwaga hi yi, meaning Maypop Place, from another Indian village once located near the confluence of the Ocoee and Hiwassee rivers in Polk County. The river, before leaving the Great Copper Basin, drains a vast expanse of the tri-state hill country.

Hot House Creek, which rises on the eastern side of Franklin Mountain in Cherokee County, North Carolina, empties into the Toccoa five miles south of Copperhill. Wolf Creek, which rises between Pack and Franklin Mountains, also in Cherokee County, empties into the Toccoa two miles south of Copperhill. On the south side of the river Sugar Creek, draining the hill country north and west of Blue Ridge, Georgia, flows into the Toccoa at Galloway, Georgia. Within the limits of the Basin in Tennessee six creeks empty their waters into the Ocoee River. From Pleasant Hill on the east to Little Frog Mountain on the west, the northern portion of the Basin is drained by Mill Creek on the east, Potato Creek in the center, and Brush Creek on the west.

The southern portion of the Basin is drained by Fightingtown Creek, Grassy Creek, and Tumbling Creek. Fightingtown Creek, one prong rising in Cash's Valley in the edge of Gilmer County, Georgia, and another prong rising farther to the west, weaves a serpentine course through Fannin County, Georgia, passes just west of Epworth, and empties into the Ocoee at Copperhill. Farther to the southwest are Grassy Creek and Tumbling Creek. Tumbling Creek empties into the Ocoee near the river's exit from the Basin between Big and Little Frog Mountains.

From the point where it knifes its way out of the Basin, the Ocoee once surged through a deep gorge for nearly twenty miles. Now, however, a concrete dam at Parksville gathers the waters into a placid lake that backs up to Greasy Creek. Midway of the gorge the once turbulent and beautiful waters are now shunted through a wooden flume to the Caney Creek powerhouse four miles down the river. Over this distance the bed of the river is nothing more than a gnarled mass of worn, deserted-looking rocks. And to add still further to the conquest of this once proud stream, the Tennessee Valley Authority completed in 1943 the erection of Ocoee Dam Number 3 just below the mouth of Tumbling Creek. From here the river is diverted by means of a tunnel through the mountains to a powerhouse some three miles down the river at the mouth of Little Gassaway Creek. The Ocoee Gorge, which was at one time a thing of scenic grandeur, now presents nothing more awe-inspiring than a dry river bed and some silent, mysterious-looking powerhouses.

The Gulf-Mississippi water divide in this region follows the top of the mountain range from Big Frog Mountain around by Flat Top, passes through Blue Ridge, Georgia, and continues thence in a generally easterly direction. The waters of the Ocoee, Nottely, and Hiwassee rivers rise to the north of this divide and eventually reach the Mississippi River.

Modern highways penetrate the mountainous Basin region. U. S. Transcontinental Highway Number 64 passes through the Copper Basin in an east-west direction. From North Carolina this highway enters the Basin at Angellico Gap. After leaving Ducktown on the west, the road traverses the entire length of the Ocoee Gorge on a roadbed that was first constructed in the early 1850's. Over this, the old copper road, copper was hauled out of Ducktown before and following the Civil War. Highway travel southward from the Basin is by way of Georgia Highway Number 5. The scenic route into the Basin from the north is by way of the Kimsey Highway over Little Frog Mountain. Maintenance of this road, however, has been neglected of late years and travel over it now is left to the discretion and daring of the motorist.

Railway service through the copper district is furnished by the Old Line of the Louisville and Nashville Railroad between Etowah, Tennessee, and Marietta, Georgia.

The population of the Copper Basin is approximately ten thousand. Copperhill serves as the metropolitan area of the district. The Georgia-Tennessee state line runs through the town and divides it into Copperhill, Tennessee, and McCaysville, Georgia. The population of these two towns and environs is approximately five thousand. The towns of Ducktown and Isabella, Tennessee, and Epworth, Georgia, are the other principal centers of population in the district.

In sharp contrast to the early days of mining at Ducktown when a dozen or more companies were engaged in the business, only one, the Tennessee Copper Company, is now operating here. Pig copper, sulphuric acid of different grades, iron sinter, zinc concentrate, copper sulphate, insecticides, fungicides, and a copper-furnace slag are now produced at the company's sprawling plants in the Basin. All of these, with the exception of pig copper, have been added to the products of the Ducktown industry since the beginning of the present era of operations in 1890.

The name Ducktown antedated by many years the first white settlers in this region, since the land was not thrown open to the white man until the latter part of the year 1838. Dr. Gerard P. Troost, first Tennessee state geologist, undoubtedly first brought to public notice the name Ducktown when he made a geological reconnaissance of the proposed Ocoee District in 1835. After exploring the gold region on Coker Creek in Monroe County, he desired to investigate the country between the Hiwassee and Ocoee rivers. He was forced to travel several miles into North Carolina before finding a fording place on the Hiwassee River. After crossing the Hiwassee, Troost "... crossed the NAUTLEE RIVER at NAUTLEE TOWN in North Carolina, and continuing westward crossed again the line of Tennessee, near the Indian village of Ducktown."

There is a satisfying amount of both legend and history in the origin of the name of Ducktown. Legend has it that the district took its name after an Indian chief named Duck who once ruled over this portion of the Cherokee Nation. Some of these stories go so far as to designate different sites of Chief Duck's village, where the glum old chief sat while Indian dances swirled around him. One story places the site of the village near the junction of Tumbling Creek with the Ocoee River. Another story is that the village stood at what is now Staffordtown, about one mile west of Copperhill, and that Duck was buried on one of the adjacent hills.

Turning now to recorded history for light on the origin of the name Ducktown, it is to be found in the Fifth Annual Report of the Bureau of American Ethnology. In the report a distribution roll of Cherokee annuities paid in the year 1799 shows the number of Cherokee towns in that year to be fifty-one. Included in this list of Cherokee towns are those of Ellijay, Tocoah, and Duck-town. Thus, long before Ducktown was inhabited by white men, it was an established town of the Cherokee tribe. For how long prior to 1799 it had been such is not known. In all probability, however, the town was one of the oldest of the Cherokee settlements in this part of the tribe's domain.

Authentic sources do not reveal an Indian chief named Duck. If there was a chief by that name, he probably remained in the seclusion of his mountain lair and did not venture out to war on white settlers. And if the good chief's social and civic activities among his clan led to the settlement's being named in his honor, then his reign must have dated back into the 1700's.

The names Cawoneh and Ducktown were at one time used synonymously. Cawoneh was the English version of the Cherokee word Kawa'na, meaning duck. Therefore, what to the Cherokee was Kawa'na was later to the white man duck. And from this came, or apparently so, the name Duck-town. With customary variation in the spelling of Indian words came Cowanee, from Cawoneh, or Kawa'na, the name of the Tennessee Copper Company's Cowanee Club at Copperhill.

Lying beyond Stansbury and Threewitt Mountains to the north of Ducktown is the Turtletown district, named, so it is said, after an Indian chief, Turtle. Turtle's name has not filled the pages of history that Duck's has. But the opposite should have been true had the domain of the two been reversed—which proves that events can sometimes make a man's name more enduring than he himself can.

From the earliest history of the Basin the name Ducktown has applied to the whole district. Early settlers were "going to Ducktown," whether to settle in the surrounding valleys or to work in the widely scattered mines. Within the Basin the present town of Ducktown was until recent years known as Hiwassee or Hiwassee Town. Since, however, the name Hiwassee for the town of Ducktown has fallen into general disuse, the more recent designation "Copper Basin" has come into use locally in order to distinguish the Basin as a whole from the town of Ducktown. The addition of the further descriptive word "basin" to Ducktown is of comparatively recent origin. It did not come into general use until well into the present century.

There has been nothing superficial or transitory about Ducktown. It was coming into prominence even before the present-day cities of Atlanta, Chattanooga, and Knoxville were anything more than promising trading communities. And so richly endowed was it in natural resources that it was soon deeply rooted in the soils of permanence. But Ducktown did not live alone. Men from beyond the seas and from the financial marts of this country came and left their marks upon the district—and went away with its marks upon them. Cornishmen came here on temporary assignments that later proved to be as permanent as the mines they opened. Curious natives came to see what was taking place, many of them staying on and leaving descendants who still people the community. The Civil War closed the mines for over a year's time, but not before many a Southern triumph had been scored—perhaps by reason of the copper which came from Ducktown. Lawyers, geologists, manufacturers, all felt the warming presence of this industrial community, and prospectors throughout the South dreamed of nothing more fortunate than being able to discover another Ducktown.

The district was dependent on its own resources and initiative and proceeded to evolve its own peculiar code of morals and ethics. It nurtured and perpetuated its own high-type citizenry. And into the twilight of industrial and commercial stagnation that followed the closing of the mines in 1878 went Ducktown's most adamant characteristic—an enduring spirit and determination to ride out every adversity.

CHAPTER 2

THE CHEROKEE INDIANS

DUCKTOWN REMAINED IN THE TERRITORY BELONGING TO THE Cherokee Nation of Indians until the last of a long series of treaties between the whites and the Indians was signed in December, 1835. That the early history of Ducktown may be as complete as possible, a short summary of the passing of this district into the hands of the United States government will be given.

When the English colonists first came into contact with the tribe of Indians known as the Cherokee, they found that these Indians held dominion over a tract of land in the southeastern portion of the New World embracing nearly 127,000 square miles. The Cherokee Nation embraced parts of the present states of West Virginia, Virginia, Kentucky, Tennessee, Alabama, Georgia, North Carolina, and South Carolina. The boundary line at that time extended from near Charleston, South Carolina, northwestward to the Ohio River. From the Ohio River it followed the Tennessee River into northern Alabama and then extended in a generally easterly direction, passing just north of the present site of Atlanta, back to its starting point. This was a magnificent empire for a tribe whose population seems never to have exceeded twenty thousand. But the stolid, pensive red man loved solitude, and he apparently wanted it in huge proportions.

Growth of the English Crown Colony at Charlestown and French territorial encroachments prompted Governor Nicholson of the South Carolina colony to enter into negotiations with the neighboring Cherokee chiefs for a treaty of peace and commerce. The first conference, held in the year 1721, marked the beginning of treaty relations between the Cherokee and the whites. Inconsequential though that first treaty was, the red man soon learned that the requirements of the growing colony called for other treaties. Gradually the pale-faced intruder, first the English and then the American, pushed the Indian back into ever-diminishing boundaries. Twenty-one succeeding treaties were signed. The last one, signed in the latter part of 1835, entirely invalidated Cherokee claims to lands east of the Mississippi River.

By the year 1819 the Cherokee had been deprived of all of his lands in Tennessee except the territory lying east of the Tennessee River and south of the Little Tennessee River. On February 27 of that year a portion of the territory extending down to the Hiwassee River was ceded to the United States. This territory was designated as the Hiwassee District. In the district the counties of Hamilton, McMinn, and Monroe were established that same year.

Included in the cession was Echota, the ancient capital of the Cherokee tribe. Echota was situated on the Little Tennessee River in what is now Monroe County, Tennessee. A distinct characteristic of Echota was the immunity it afforded those fleeing from barbaric justice. From this ancient site the Cherokee capital was removed and was re-established as New Echota near the present site of Calhoun, Georgia.

In May, 1830, Congress passed a bill nullifying all Cherokee titles to lands within the state of Georgia. The unfortunate tribe was again forced to seek a new site for its capital. The site selected was at Red Clay just inside the boundary of Tennessee and about twenty miles east of the present city of Chattanooga. Here the capital remained until the exodus of the tribe in 1838.

In December, 1832, the Cherokee country in Georgia was surveyed into ten counties: Lumpkin, Union, Cobb, Cherokee, Gilmer, Cass, Murray, Floyd, Paulding, and Forsyth. The county of Gilmer embraced what is now that part of Fannin County adjoining the Ducktown Basin. Thus that portion of the Basin lying south of the Ocoee River in Georgia became the legal domain of the white man in December, 1832.

As a consequence of the action of the state of Georgia in surveying the Indian lands into counties and extending her own laws throughout the territory, the once proud Cherokee Nation was left with a tract of land embracing but slightly more than five thousand square miles. A section of northeast Alabama, lower east Tennessee, and the southwest corner of North Carolina made up the territory left to the tribe. Factionalism over the question of selling its remaining territory to the United States and accepting lands beyond the Mississippi as future homes grew up within the tribe. The population of the tribe at that time was about seventeen thousand. Of this number nearly sixteen thousand, headed by John Ross, President of the Cherokee Nation, were opposed to moving to the West. The small minority led by Major Ridge favored bowing to the inevitable. It was Ridge who finally dealt with the United States commissioners.

The last treaty between the United States government and the Cherokee Nation east of the Mississippi was negotiated at New Echota in December, 1835. William Carroll, Governor of Tennessee, and J. S. Schermerhorn were the commissioners acting for the United States. Major Ridge and about five hundred of his followers attended the meeting as representatives of the tribe. The purpose of the meeting was well known, and John Ross and his followers refused to attend. The result of the conference was a treaty, the two most important features of which were: (1) that the Cherokee Nation cede all of its remaining lands east of the Mississippi River to the United States for five million dollars, and (2) that within two years after ratification of the treaty by the Congress of the United States the tribe retire to reservations beyond the Mississippi. The treaty was signed on December 29, 1835.

The Cherokee treaty was ratified by Congress on May 23, 1836. But other than occasional groups who began leaving soon after the ratification of the treaty, the Cherokee made no preparation to depart. The Indians who did leave were principally those who had favored the western move. In the spring of 1838, after it became apparent that the tribe did not intend to respect Major Ridge's treaty, General Winfield Scott was sent into the area with troops to expedite the evacuation. Thirteen stockades were erected throughout the Indian country for corralling the Indians. Among these were Fort Butler, which was built on the bluff across the Hiwassee River from Murphy, North Carolina; Fort Gilmer, erected in Gilmer County, Georgia; and Fort Cass, erected in McMinn County, Tennessee. From the stockades into which they were virtually driven during the summer of 1838, the Indians were assembled at three embarkation points. One of these was at Calhoun in Polk County. The other two were at Ross's Landing in Tennessee and at Gunter's Landing in Alabama. From these places the deportation took pl.ce over land and by water.

Many Indians escaped the dragnet of 1838 and remained in the mountains of Georgia, North Carolina, and Tennessee. Several of them remained in and around their old haunts at Ducktown for a number of years after the white settlers arrived. Indians lived on Fightingtown Creek near the present site of Epworth, Georgia. A small band lived on Tumbling Creek, and an Indian village remained on Little Frog Mountain near Cold Springs until well into the 1880's. The Kimsey Highway passes through the site of the old village on the mountain. Small, wiry peach trees, descendants of trees planted there by the Indians, can still be seen growing near the road.

Indians were hired by John Caldwell when work was first begun by him on the old copper road. And until the mines closed, Indians came down from North Carolina to cut cordwood for Pendleton Jones and other wood contractors in the Turtletown district. In a pamphlet, *Mineral Wealth of Township 2 and Fractional Township 1, South, in Polk County, Tennessee*, written by A. Chable and published in March, 1887, it was said: "A few years ago Indians now living in North Carolina, but formerly of Tumbling Creek in Tennessee, took a prospector from Kentucky to this place, and thus the locality has at least one of the characteristics of the ubiquitous Indian—an Indian Silver Mine." Periodic searches for this fabled silver mine are still made.

CHAPTER 3

THE OCOEE DISTRICT

IN TENNESSEE THE NARROW STRIP OF CHEROKEE TERRITORY secured by the New Echota treaty was established into what was termed a surveyor's district by an act of the General Assembly of Tennessee passed October 18, 1836. The territory was called the Ocoee District. Though the present counties of Bradley and Polk comprise much the larger portion of the Ocoee District, that portion of Hamilton County lying south of the Tennessee River and a strip along the eastern boundary of Monroe County are also included in the district.

Beginning at the point where the Tennessee River enters the state of Alabama, the boundary of the Ocoee District follows the Tennessee River up to the mouth of the Hiwassee River and thence up the Hiwassee River to near the present site of Wetmore. From there the boundary line follows a northeasterly direction along the divide between the waters of the Tellico and Hiwassee rivers to near Tallassee on the Little Tennessee River. It follows this river up to the North Carolina line, then follows south and west along the Tennessee state line back to the starting point on the Tennessee River.

The survey of the Ocoee District was made in 1837 by John B. Tipton, surveyor-general, assisted by John C. Kennedy, J. C. Tipton, T. H. Callaway, J. F. Cleveland, and John Hannah. The surveyors first established a basis or dividing line near the center of the district. The basis line ran from a point on the Hiwassee River at Calhoun, south twenty degrees west to the south boundary of the state. Ranges six miles in width were then run out in the district and were numbered progressively from one to seven both east and west from the basis line.

The ranges were next divided into townships six miles square. Townships in each range were to be numbered progressively from north to south. But if there were any connection between the order in which the townships were numbered and the way in which the act provided that they be numbered, it could not be found. Often there is no relation of numbers between adjoining townships within the same range. The townships were subdivided into 36 sections of 640 acres, or one square mile, each. The 36 sections in each township were numbered east to west alternately; number 1 being the northeast section and number 36 being the southeast section. Fractional townships and sections were treated as whole townships and sections in numbering. Thus the Copper Basin is situated largely in Fractional Township Four, south, in range five, east of the basis line.

The sixteenth section in each township was to be "reserved for the use of schools, in such township forever." But forever is a long time—too long, in fact, for township sections to be reserved for school purposes. Since passage of the act establishing the Ocoee District, the school section in practically every one of these townships has long since been disposed of, though they are the property of the citizens of each township and can be disposed of only through their consent. Section 16 in the Fourth Fractional Township at Ducktown, however, proved to be the site of one of the more valuable copper mines in the Basin, has remained the property of the citizens of the township, and has figured prominently in the history of Ducktown since 1850.

After the survey was completed the General Assembly passed an act on November 20, 1837, providing for disposal of the lands in the Ocoee District. The act provided that an entry taker's office be opened at Cleveland, Bradley County, from and after the first Monday in November, 1838. Luke Lea was named entry taker, and P. J. R. Edwards, register, of the Ocoee District. Ownership of land in the district was not legal until the entry taker's office began to operate.

The state took cognizance of the fact that even before the Ocoee District had been surveyed and provisions made for disposal of the lands many settlers had moved into the area and established themselves. Homes had been erected and farms cleared. Therefore, the act of 1837 provided that occupants should have priority of entry for 160 acres for three months at $7.50 an acre in order to include their improvements. At the end of the three-month period, an additional two months were allowed for entry of 160 acres at $7.50 an acre. Thus a settler had prior claim for three months to as much as 160 acres of land occupied by him. However, if the occupant had not purchased his claim at the end of three months, the land was then subject to entry within the following two months by anyone who was willing to buy it at the price of $7.50 an acre. Actually, the provision had the effect of putting a price of $7.50 an acre on all lands within the district for a period of five months from the date the entry taker's office was opened.

At the expiration of the first five-month period occupants had the same priority of entry for two months at the price of $5.00 an acre. An additional two months was then allowed for purchasing any remaining lands within the district at $5.00 an acre. Thereafter the lands remaining unsold were disposed of on the two-months-plus-two-months plan at $2.00, $1.00, $0.50, $0.25, $0.125, and finally, at $0.01 an acre.

The little frontier village of Cleveland enjoyed boom-time prosperity following the arrival of the entry taker. Most of the excellent farming lands on the Ocoee, Hiwassee, and Tennessee rivers had been occupied, and the occupants lost little time in entering their claims. Forty-seven grants were issued on the first day of the opening of the land office. Three grants were issued on Christmas Day, 1838—Santa Claus had probably neglected to drop 160-acre farms down the chimneys of three trusting pioneers the night before. During the first five-month period, which ended on April 4, 1839, a total of 510 grants were issued.

There was no rush to enter the lands beyond the mountains at Ducktown. This territory was remote, inaccessible, and not at all suitable for large-scale farming. A few quarter-sections here were purchased when the price was finally reduced to $1.00 an acre. Land grants at Ducktown were few, however, until the price dropped to one cent an acre. Land speculation, which was common in other parts of the Ocoee District, did not prevail in this uninviting section until men with "noses for metals" prowled through the hills some ten years later.

But the Cherokee had disappeared, the district had been surveyed and thrown open to settlers, and the white man was descending with a thud from Ross's Landing to Slick Rock Creek. The ore outcroppings in the vicinity of the old Indian village of Ducktown were lying exposed on the surface, and where the red man had trod in silence the white man was coming with a whoop. Things were going to be different.

Around the eastern foothills of the Frog Mountains was not the only place, however, where Fate was making preparations for the copper empire that was soon to be erected where Chief Duck had pitched his tents. In far-off Germany and Wales and in other distant lands were youths who were destined to find their way to Ducktown. Lads in their teens in Germany were being taught the technique of mining, and in Cornwall, England, they were hearing the miners' lingo as only Cornish miners could 'andle it. Much of the future history of Ducktown was to be made by these foreign youngsters.

CHAPTER 4

BORDER COUNTIES

THE THREE COUNTIES BORDERING DUCKTOWN'S HOME COUNTY of Polk were intimately associated with the early history of the copper district. These were Bradley County, Tennessee; Fannin County, Georgia; and Cherokee County, North Carolina. A brief outline of the history of each of these counties should, therefore, be found of interest.

BRADLEY COUNTY, TENNESSEE

Immediately following the Cherokee treaty of 1835 the Twenty-first General Assembly of the state of Tennessee, then in session, took action to bring the Indian country in Tennessee into the folds of the state. This was done by forming the territory, soon thereafter designated as the Ocoee District, into one large county named Bradley. Resolution Number 6, adopted February 10, 1836, appointed commissioners to lay off the county of Bradley into eight districts.

On January 20, 1838, two years after Bradley County was organized, the General Assembly named Cleveland as its county seat. In the meantime a post office had been established in the ambitious little village, on September 9, 1836, with Nicholas Spring as postmaster. Both in the post office records and in the act establishing the county seat, the name Cleveland was originally spelled as Cleaveland. The present spelling was adopted sometime later.

The village was named in honor of Colonel Benjamin Cleveland, a Revolutionary War hero. Cleveland served as a captain in Rutherford's Army in Rutherford's Indian campaign through the Carolinas in 1776. "Cleveland's Bulldogs," as his men called themselves, helped to demolish the British at King's Mountain.

Cleveland really began amounting to something in a cosmopolitan way when the East Tennessee and Georgia Railroad reached there from Dalton, Georgia, in 1851. The road was completed through to Knoxville in 1855 and in 1859 the short-line between Cleveland and Chattanooga was completed. The coastal cities of Savannah and Charleston were thus placed within rail distance of Cleveland.

The building of the railroad through Cleveland assured the continuance of mining operations just then beginning at Ducktown. Wagon road connections between Ducktown and Cleveland in 1853 resulting in a typical mining boom hitting Ducktown, and Cleveland was a principal beneficiary. Caravans of copper haulers, land speculators, mining officials, workers, and visitors plied constantly between the two places. Hotels, stores, and livery stables at Cleveland were the first to profit from the increased business originating at Ducktown, but as the industry at Ducktown became more stabilized, farmers of Bradley County disposed of many of their products there. The weekly newspapers of Cleveland were widely read in the copper district. Much the larger portion of mail to and from Ducktown was cleared through Cleveland, and the legal profession of the little town solved many of the problems that quite naturally arose over hasty land transfers at Ducktown. J. E. Raht, the dominant figure in the industry at Ducktown, established his home and office at Cleveland following the close of the Civil War. Until the mines closed in 1878 both Bradley County and its county seat profited much from the industry at Ducktown.

FANNIN COUNTY, GEORGIA

As we have learned, the Cherokee Indian country in Georgia was surveyed into ten counties in the year 1832. Gilmer was one of these counties, and Gilmer at that time extended up to the Tennessee line at Ducktown. The inaccessibility of Ellijay, the county seat, to citizens living in the northern section of the county made necessary the formation of a new county still farther up in the mountains. Especially did this become necessary following the opening of the mines in the Ducktown district when communities began springing up around the mines near Pierceville.

The county of Fannin was organized from parts of Gilmer and Union counties, by an act of the Georgia Legislature passed January 21, 1854. The act provided that until the county seat should be fixed by the inferior court the general elections and public business of the county were to be held and carried on at Joab Addington's store. The court soon afterwards selected Morganton as the county seat of Fannin. The name of the town honored the Revolutionary War hero, General Daniel Morgan.

In Fannin County, the name of an honored son of Georgia, James Walker Fannin, was perpetuated. Fannin, who held the rank of colonel, organized a company of Georgians in 1835 and took them to Texas in that year to aid the Texans in their war with Mexico. In an engagement at Coleta, Texas, in March, 1836, Colonel Fannin was compelled to surrender his force of about three hundred men to the Mexican force of about seventeen hundred men under General Urrea. The Texans surrendered as prisoners of war. Nevertheless, they were marched to the old mission church at Goliad, Texas, and on Palm Sunday, 1836, they were lined up on the plains near Goliad and massacred by the Mexicans.

Settlers were moving into what is now Fannin County along the upper reaches of the Toccoa River, along Cut Cane and Hemptown creeks, and down to Hot House and Wolf creeks in the early, 1830's. During the same time hardy pioneers were moving up Boardtown Creek from Ellijay, crossing the divide and filtering into the valleys south of the Toccoa along the headwaters of Fightingtown and Sugar creeks. A result of these movements was that the Georgia territory adjacent to Ducktown was settled, though sparsely, several years before white settlers occupied the Tennessee portion of the region.

The first of the roads cleared out in what was later Fannin County was the road between Blairsville, county seat of Union County, and Ellijay. It was along this route that the settlements of Hemp, Tacoah, and Blue Ridge were later founded. Another road extended from Dahlonega by way of Mechanicsburg, Lumpkin County, to Tacoah. It then extended down to Pleasant Hill in the vicinity of Ducktown. Still another road reached the Hot House settlement down the valley now followed by the Louisville and Nashville Railroad from Murphy to Mineral Bluff. South of the Toccoa River the road from Boardtown was extended into the region of Fightingtown Creek, and from there it was gradually cleared out by way of Rogers' Ferry to the village of Ducktown, or Hiwassee.

Long before the organization of Fannin County a post office had been established on the north side of the Toccoa River in the vicinity of the present site of Morganton. The office, named Tuckahoe, was established on March 15, 1837, with Benjamin Chastain as postmaster. The name of the office was changed to

Tacoah (also spelled Toccoa, Tacoa, and Tocoah) on December 12, 1838. It was changed again, this time to Morganton, on July 11, 1854. James Kincaid was the first postmaster at the Morganton office. The Blue Ridge post office, across the river from Morganton, was established on February 29, 1848, with Enos McClure as postmaster. This office was discontinued several times. It was last re-established on March 1, 1871. Until the railroad was built, the location of the office was dependent upon the residence of the postmaster.

CHEROKEE COUNTY, NORTH CAROLINA

In the southwestern corner of the state of North Carolina the Cherokee lands secured by the New Echota treaty were organized into Cherokee County by an act of the North Carolina Legislature in 1839. From the time of the treaty until the formation of Cherokee County, this territory had remained under the jurisdiction of Macon County.

The name chosen for the county seat of Cherokee County was Murphy, and the site selected was at the confluence of the Hiwassee and Valley rivers. The new county seat was named in honor of Archibald Deboe Murphey, a prominent lawyer of North Carolina. One of Murphey's outstanding accomplishments was his securing for the University of North Carolina in 1822 titles to lands in the state of Tennessee claimed by the University. Murphey and Joseph H. Bryan were sent to Nashville in that year to press the claims of the University, and it was because of Murphey's shrewdness as a legislative trader that the claims were allowed. It was fitting, therefore, that memory of him be perpetuated in the name of the county seat of Cherokee County. Through oversight the letter *e* was dropped from the name Murphey when establishing the county seat, and the error was never corrected.

Settlers in considerable numbers had moved into what is now Cherokee County even before the territory was relinquished by the Indians. A post office was established at the present site of Murphy, under the name of Huntingdon, Macon County, on February 23, 1835, with Archibald R. S. Hunter as postmaster. The name of this office was changed to Murphy, Cherokee County, on June 13, 1839. Hunter was said to have been the first white man to build a house in Cherokee County. The house stood not far from the place where Fort Butler was later erected on the bluff across the Hiwassee River from Murphy.

There was no hurry on the part of the state of North Carolina to dispose of the Cherokee Indian lands, and it was not until the latter part of March, 1842, that an entry taker's office was opened at Murphy. Unlike the Ocoee District in Tennessee where occupants had priority of entry, the Cherokee County lands were entered on a "first come, first served" basis. Immediately upon the opening of the land office, Drewry Weeks, the entry taker, was besieged by a riotous crowd eager to "enter" their lands. So great was the rush that the entry taker fled his office for safety. There was nothing to prevent a settler who had labored to improve his property from being dispossessed by another who could reach the entry taker first and claim the land. No doubt many a good Cherokee County citizen signed the entry papers with one eye on the records and the other on the door. But the county was soon effectively organized, and it was but a few years afterwards that western breezes were wafting the odor of burning sulphur into the nostrils of Cherokee County citizens living adjacent to the Ducktown mines.

Settlers moving westward from Murphy established themselves along creek banks from the vicinity of the town to the Tennessee line. By 1843 the population along Persimmon Creek was large enough to make a post office necessary. One was finally established on September 29 of that year near the place where the creek empties into the Hiwassee River. Benjamin Stiles was postmaster of the Persimmon Creek office.

Still later, and still farther westward, the Turtletown post office was opened on Shoal Creek, on December 23, 1847, by Elias W. Kilpatrick, postmaster. A mail route between Turtletown and Ducktown was inaugurated in 1853. Several decades later another post office named Turtletown was opened across the state line in Tennessee. Thus for a number of years there were two post offices by this name, one in Tennessee and one in North Carolina, separated by only some ten miles. However, the name of the Turtletown, North Carolina, office was changed in 1912 to that of Oak Park.

Another main line of settlement was along the route between Murphy and Ducktown. Across Angellico Gap from Ducktown, between it and Franklin Mountain, was the site of the Wolf Creek post office, opened on August 5, 1858, with Tyra A. Tatham as postmaster. And midway between Murphy and Ducktown was the Hot House post office, opened on February 23, 1877, with William A. Philips as postmaster.

The western portion of Cherokee County was, and has remained, sparsely settled.

Cherokee County's roads in the 1840's followed the aimless trek of settlers as they took up Indian lands along Persimmon, Shoal, and Hot House creeks, and down the valley in the direction of the present site of Culberson. Definite direction was given one of these routes, however, when the North Carolina Legislature of 1848-49 passed an act providing for the construction of the Western Turnpike from Salisbury to the Georgia state line by way of Asheville and Murphy.

Later on, after John Caldwell had opened his road down the Ocoee River from Ducktown, the North Carolina Legislature of 1854-55 amended its previous act and made Asheville the eastern terminus and the Tennessee state line at Ducktown the western terminus of the Western Turnpike. The road from Murphy to Ducktown thus became a state road, and wagon traffic between western North Carolina and lower eastern Tennessee, through the copper district of Ducktown, was for the first time made possible. The Western Turnpike figured prominently in the early history of Ducktown. Over this route "cotton rock" for the furnaces at Ducktown was hauled from Cherokee County, and mail carriers and other traffic plied back and forth over its winding course between the mines and Murphy. Although the designation Western Turnpike has long since passed into disuse, the general direction of the road has remained and now forms a link in U. S. Highway Number 64 between Ducktown and Murphy.

CHAPTER 5

POLK COUNTY, TENNESSEE

LIKE SO MANY OTHER COUNTIES WHICH CAME INTO EXISTENCE IN the formative days of our political sub-divisions, Polk County was created more for the sake of civic convenience than for anything else. Bradley County, which at that time embraced the greater portion of the Ocoee District, was simply too expansive for travel conditions of the day. It was extremely difficult for the citizens living in the eastern portion of the county to reach the county seat. With the rapid growth of population it soon became necessary to reduce the size of Bradley by dividing the territory into two counties. This was done in 1839, and the new county was named Polk. As the new county was formed of Bradley's eastern territory, it was unavoidably composed of but little level land and a great deal of mountainous terrain. For this reason it seemed obvious that Polk County, whose lot it was to fall heir to this unpromising portion of Tennessee, would begin its history with no illusions of future wealth or promise. Polk, however, was destined to and soon after its birth did, by virtue of its copper deposits, move into the front ranks of the wealthier and better-known counties of the state. It is to be regretted that the purposes of this volume preclude anything but a brief outline of the county's formative period. However, it can in all fairness be said that not a great many history-making events other than in its mining section occurred in the county during the period covered by this book.

The county of Polk was organized pursuant to an act of the General Assembly of the State of Tennessee passed November 28, 1839. With the exception of a narrow strip of some twenty-five square miles of land lying along the north banks of the Hiwassee River, which was taken from McMinn County, all the territory of Polk was taken from Bradley. Apparently it was deemed necessary to allot to Polk additional farming lands to compensate for the preponderance of non-agricultural lands within the county's borders. For this reason the narrow strip of McMinn County territory, embracing what is now the Wetmore and Patty sections, was given to Polk. In this annexed section was later developed the Wetmore, or Savannah, Farm, one of the richest and most prized pieces of farming land in Polk County.

The act authorizing the formation of Polk County provided that it be named in honor of James K. Polk, but recently elected governor of Tennessee, and that the county seat be named Benton, in honor of Thomas H. Benton, Senator from Missouri in the Congress of the United States.* In 1837 Thomas Hart Benton had endeared himself to Tennesseans by leading a successful fight in the Senate to have expunged from the records a resolution censuring President Andrew Jackson for allegedly having exceeded his authority in relation to the public revenues. Henry Clay had succeeded some three years previously in having the censure of the President spread on the Senate records. Benton had also served as a colonel in the War of 1812 while a citizen of Tennessee. This fact plus his loyal support of President Jackson undoubtedly accounted for his name being chosen for the county seat of Polk, since the county was organized soon after the signal victory in the Senate. A friend of Old Hickory's did not go unnoticed in Tennessee.

The village of Columbus, situated on the north bank of the Hiwassee River about four miles north of the present site of Benton, was the first settlement in Polk County. Columbus was already established when it was taken from McMinn County and made a part of Polk County. Settlers were rapidly taking up the farming lands in the valley between the Ocoee and Hiwassee rivers, but nowhere in this region had a settlement come to a head by the time the territory was separated from Bradley County.

* The following is an outline of the life of Benton as furnished by Mrs. Harvey A. Cragnon, Jr., President of Colonel Thomas Hart Benton Chapter, United States Daughters of 1812, Nashville, Tennessee: "Thomas Hart Benton was born in Hillsboro, N. C. in 1782 and was partly educated at the State University. He left before graduation, however, and removed with his widowed mother to Tennessee, where, twenty-five miles south of Nashville, they made their home, around which a settlement called Bentonville gradually grew up.

"He studied law with St. George Tucker, began to practice in Nashville, and was elected to the State Legislature in 1811. In 1815 he removed to St. Louis, Missouri, and was elected United States Senator in 1820 on the admission of Missouri to the Union....

"He became an ardent supporter of Andrew Jackson.... Benton opposed John C. Calhoun on almost every question, and they carried on a ferocious warfare in the Senate.... He was Senator from Missouri for thirty years (1820-1850)....Benton died in 1858 and St. Louis erected a beautiful statue to his memory."

The act of 1839, therefore, stated that the several courts of justice in Polk County were to be held at Columbus until a permanent seat of justice should be selected.

The county commissioners, John Towns, Jonas Hoyle, James Hawkins, Andrew Stevenson, Erby Boyd, John Williams, Allen Armstrong, Thomas Harper, and John F. Hannah, were authorized to hold an election on the first Saturday in February, 1840, for the purpose of selecting a site for the county seat. The result of this election was the choosing of McKamy's farm, the present site of Benton.

The first session of the county court was held at Columbus on May 4, 1840. Among other business transacted at this session, the court appointed John F. Hannah as county surveyor, assessed a poll tax of $37\frac{1}{2}$ cents and a state and county tax of 50 cents, and appointed three justices "to see and ascertain where a house can be had for the least expense suitable for to hold court in for Polk County, in Benton or Columbus, and report the same to the next county court." The county court continued to meet at Columbus until the first Monday in August, 1840, at which time the court held its first session at the newly prepared county seat of Benton. After the transfer of the county business to Benton, nothing of permanence was left to mark the site of the once important little village of Columbus.

Within a year after the Legislature had authorized the formation of Polk County, the full quota of county officials had been elected, the county seat prepared, and the tax rate fixed. A post office was established at Benton July 15, 1840, with Jonas Hoyle as postmaster. The office was established as Bentonville, but the name was changed to Benton on August 16, 1845. Whatever the destiny of this aggressive young county was to be, preparations were being made to meet it at the front gate.

Early road building in Polk County was largely a matter of individual needs and energy. Funds for public road building were scarce. Outlying parts of the county were connected with the county seat by articulated systems of roads first built between adjoining farms. Toll roads were numerous. These were built by individuals to whom the county court granted authority to erect toll gates and to use the tolls in paying the cost of building and maintaining such routes. Two important roads of that day, the Old Federal Road and the Stock Road, traversed the territory before Polk County was organized. The Federal Road was said to have been constructed by General Andrew Jackson during the war with the Creek Indians (1813-14) for transportation of troops and supplies into the Indian country in Georgia and Alabama. The road crossed the Hiwassee River at Columbus, passed through Benton and continued southward into Georgia. The village of Columbus was founded at the point where the road crossed the river. And no doubt the road was instrumental in the selection of a site for Benton, the new county seat. Henry E. Colton, a railroad promoter in this section, described the Old Federal Road in 1890 by saying, "It is one of the best pieces of engineering, in the selection of its route, to be found anywhere. Throughout its length from far up in East Tennessee, to Cartersville, Georgia, it is practically a level, and almost a positive straight line."

The Stock Road, also known as the Armstrong Ferry Road, was cut by Louis Armstrong. This road left the Old Federal Road several miles south of Madisonville, passed through, or near, Athens, Tennessee, and joined the Old Federal Road again near Old Fort, in Polk County. The road gained its name from the large droves of stock that were driven over it to southern markets.

Below the mountains Polk had its system of roads, rough and muddy though they were. However, travel by vehicle between the upper and lower sections of the county was not possible until the copper road down the Ocoee River from Ducktown was completed in 1853. Previous to this time connection between the two sections was by way of the old Indian trail over Little Frog Mountain.

Life below the mountains underwent but few changes during the following decades. But above the mountains strange and tumultuous scenes were destined soon to take place. Polk was to become known as a mining as well as a farming county.

CHAPTER 6

SETTLEMENT IN THE FORTIES

Ducktown, as we have learned, was inhabited by Cherokee Indians until the summer of 1838. Although a few white settlers had filtered into this remote region before the removal of the Indians, they were living on Indian lands with no right of title to the lands. These settlers were economically and socially but little better off than their red neighbors, for no white man owned land in the Ducktown region until the latter part of 1839.

There were no purchasers of Ducktown lands during the first year of the entry taker's office at Cleveland. The lands first selected by settlers in the Ocoee District were those suitable for farming purposes. There seemed to be no property east of the Frog Mountains worth the price of $7.50 an acre; nor were there any strips of potential farm lands in this region considered as being worth $5.00 or even $2.50 an acre. And as for the hills on which appeared large splotches of a metallic rust-like substance—they apparently created no excited curiosity or visions of hidden mineral wealth. However, when the entry price was reduced to $1.00 an acre on December 5, 1839, two of Ducktown's first settlers came to purchase lands on which to establish homes. John Rogers entered forty acres on December 23, 1839, and on February 8 of the following year John Davis, who came from Virginia, also entered forty acres. Rogers settled on the Ocoee River, and it was here that for three-quarters of a century the Rogers' ferry was operated where the old main road between Hiwassee (or Ducktown) and Ellijay crossed the river. Davis settled on the creek that still bears his name—Davis Mill, or Mill, Creek.

Until the departure of the Indians from this region, Ducktown had been a figurative red island in a white sea, and it was not until well into the forties that the white waves of settlers began to spill over in increasing volume into the hitherto forbidden territory. The pioneers of Ducktown were traditionally individualistic. They were not seeking sites upon which to erect empires of industry and commerce. Instead of joining in the westward caravans of settlers that had at that time extended the frontier line of the country to some three hundred miles beyond the Mississippi River, they preferred the seclusion of narrow valleys hemmed in by protecting mountains. An insight into the philosophy of the first settlers here was vividly portrayed by John Caldwell in a letter (quoted in Chapter 8) writen by him in 1855. Caldwell, who was prospecting for copper at Ducktown in 1849, saw the apparent wealth of the district and prevailed upon a gathering of citizens to assist him in opening a mine. Upon being told that the result would be to bring civilization to their midst, they replied by saying that it was from civilization they had fled, and that if it followed them here they would run again. Their desire for isolation would have been realized had they not unwittingly come to rest on immense deposits of copper.

So unpromising was the portion of Polk County above the mountains that it is not surprising to find an almost total lack of reference to this section in scattered accounts of the settling of the county. There was apparently nothing here to attract ambitious tradesmen, energetic workers, or farmers who envisioned expansive fields of waving grain. Hunting, farming along the narrow strips of creek and river bottom lands, and worshipping were the principal pursuits. The taxable value of all properties previous to 1850 was hardly worth the efforts of the tax assessor to reach the district and collect the taxes. Elections afforded periodical breaks in the solidified monotony at Ducktown. News of the outside world was brought into the district by returning jurors. Citizens living in the Ducktown and Turtletown districts were regularly chosen for jury duty. And the justices of the peace of the seventh and eighth civil districts were faithful in attendance at the monthly meetings of the county court. While there was an accumulation of news to bring back after each session of court, residents of Ducktown had little to report from their district when they plodded wearily into Benton.

It was only through their records of service as public officials that the names of a few of the first citizens of Ducktown and Turtletown were preserved to posterity. At the first election held in Polk County on March 7, 1840, James Ainesworth and L. L. Threewitt were elected justices of the peace and William Womble constable, in the seventh civil district. Womble soon resigned and was succeeded by Joel McClary. The latter, however, was unable to furnish a satisfactory bond, and he, in turn, was succeeded by G. W. Smith. John Davis, John McJunkin, and Solomon Stansbury were elected common-school commissioners in 1840. The circuit court jurors from this district in 1841 were William R. Witt, Walter Carruth, Russell McDonnel, John Davis, Seburn Rogers, James Bailey, Gabriel Deaver, James Ainesworth, and William Coleman. Some of Ducktown's first settlers were also among the first delinquent tax payers of Polk County in 1840: Howell Freeland, Jerry Pack, Cooper Prince, Jackson Prince, and L. L. Threewitt.

When the eighth civil district was formed in 1841 to include the central portion of Ducktown, John Davis and John Conner were elected justices of the peace and Young Davis was elected constable. The school-land commissioners for the Fourth Fractional Township in 1841 were Jesse Lemmon, David Jenkins, and William R. Witt. The eighth district judges elected in the March, 1842, election were William W. Hancock, John Davis, and Jesse Lemmon. Circuit court jurors from the seventh and eighth districts in the years 1842 and 1843 were L. L. Threewitt, Prestly Turner, Seburn Rogers, William Wiggins, Enoch Burnett, G. W. Smith, David Jenkins, and John Rogers. A. D. Merony was elected a justice of the peace and Enoch Burnett constable in the seventh (Turtletown) district, and Henderson Smith was elected a justice of the peace in the eighth district at the March, 1842, election.

Daniel Cooke, later the first postmaster here, was a justice of the peace in the eighth civil district in 1846, and was revenue commissioner at Ducktown in 1848. Another permanent family of the district was founded when Albert Styles migrated to Ducktown from Macon County, North Carolina, in 1846. In the same year William Kimsey came from Jackson County, North Carolina, and settled on Brush Creek about two miles west of the present town of Ducktown.

While the territory north of the Ocoee was being settled, log cabins were appearing in the forests south of the river along Grassy and Tumbling Creeks. Isaac N. Greer and David Dilbeck were two of the early settlers there. About 1850 Greer established a ferry on the Ocoee River, near the mouth of Tumbling Creek. The ferry was later operated for many years by George Barnes. The Hooper, Sutherland, Payne, Witherow, Chastain, Denton, and Beckler families were other pioneer residents of the territory.

One of the first permanent settlers south of the Ocoee, in what was then Gilmer County, Georgia, was Joseph Pierce. He first settled on Grassy Creek soon after the establishment of Gilmer County in 1832, but later moved and erected a grist mill on Fightingtown Creek about a mile west of the present site of Epworth. It was Pierce who introduced sorghum cane to this section. The Pierceville settlement was named for him.

Long before the Civil War there came into the present Epworth community Thomas Waters from Lumpkin County, Georgia, Pink Cochran from Gaddistown, Georgia, and David Vestal from Hall County, Georgia. Since that time much of the commercial, educational, and religious history of that portion of the Basin has been made by the Waters, Cochran, and Vestal families. Also into the Fightingtown district in this era came Archibald, Thomas, and Harbert McCay. Harbert T. McCay went across into Tennessee to marry Talitha Frances, daughter of Daniel Cooke, and was afterwards one of the leading merchants at Hiwassee.

Benjamin Burgess settled on the Toccoa River opposite the mouth of Wolf Creek. He was a large landowner, and was one of the few slave holders in this mountainous country. The Weese, Barker, Elrod, Mathews, Johnson, Galloway, and Millsaps families were other early settlers of this part of Fannin County.

The region along Hot House Creek and down to the Tennessee state line at Pleasant Hill was being settled in the early forties. Some of the first to move into that district were Thomas and Levi Wilson, Jasper Gilliam, William Harper, William Panter, John Johnson, and Thomas Anderson.

It is to be doubted that any of the first settlers at Ducktown were from Tennessee. The upper part of Polk County at that time was effectively shut off from the remaining portion of the county and state by a range of mountains through which there were no easy routes of travel. Tennesseans came sliding down the side of Little Frog Mountain into Ducktown when copper was discovered here several years later.

It seems that the first place in the Ducktown district that could be termed a settlement was Pleasant Hill. It is believed that a small country store was situated there about 1840. Provisions and other necessities were secured from Dahlonega by means of a two-wheel ox cart. Brush-arbor meetings were also held at Pleasant Hill. The discovery of copper at Ducktown a few years later drew the population to the center of the district. But for several decades afterwards the brush-arbor meetings, and the church building later erected by the Baptists, enabled Pleasant Hill to remain one of the chief religious outposts of the new Ducktown. It was one of the sturdy bulwarks which Satan had to hurdle on his way into the more congested district where he was sure to find a welcome.

Settlers moving into the territory just vacated by the Indians in the vicinity of Ducktown followed three principal routes. These routes were determined largely by the topography of the country and by old Indian trails. Streams were followed insofar as was practicable; mountain ranges were skirted and gaps were sought out for short cuts through natural barriers. The red man had built no roads. He traveled afoot in tandem formation and the narrow trail served as his highway. The Indian was early opposed to roads through his country, for roads meant wheels and wheels meant the hated white intruder and all his paraphernalia.

The first road to Ducktown north of the Ocoee River grew out of the Indian trail from Dahlonega, by way of Tacoah to the settlement at Pleasant Hill. The road was gradually cleared out to Potato Creek in the vicinity of the present site of Isabella. This was in the early forties. About the same time a road was being pushed through the Fightingtown region from Ellijay by way of Boardtown Creek and Bush Head Mountain. The settlements of Chestnut Gap, Madola, and Pierceville later grew up along this road. The road was extended to John Rogers' ferry on the Ocoee River, and from there it was completed to the Pleasant Hill road on Potato Creek. A second road from upper Fightingtown passed through Fightingtown Camp Ground (now Epworth), crossed the Ocoee River at James Dunn's ferry, and continued to the copper mines.

From North Carolina the first road was cleared out to Ducktown along Troost's old trail by way of Nautlee and Angellico Gap. This road later became a section of North Carolina's Western Turnpike. Roads into the Turtletown district from North Carolina were opened by way of Shoal Creek and the old State Line Church. No road had as yet been opened westward into Tennessee.

With many settlers living along the state lines of Tennessee, North Carolina, and Georgia, and with the nearest post office being at Tacoah, some twelve miles up the Toccoa River in Gilmer County, Georgia, a post office in the region became necessary, and one was accordingly established in the Ducktown district on June 14, 1848. This office, located on Potato Creek just north of the present site of Isabella, was named Culchote. Daniel Cooke was appointed postmaster. Culchote was served on a mail route that extended from Dahlonega, Georgia, by way of Mechanicsburg and Tacoah to Culchote, thence by way of Greasy Creek to Benton. John W. Walker of Dahlonega had the contract to deliver the mail on a schedule of a round-trip a week.

Postage stamps as they are known today were issued for the first time on July 1, 1847, only a year before the Culchote post office was established.

Throughout the decade ending with the year 1849 life at Ducktown went on in the most primitive fashion. What the settlers ate and wore were largely products of their own toil and ingenuity. Articles such as salt, brown sugar, soda, green coffee, calico, flannels, powder, lead, and rope were secured from distant stores at Ellijay and Dahlonega. Game was plentiful on the hills that now boast of only the hardy sparrow and an occasional itinerant lizzard. To the sick were administered medicines concocted from herbs and roots. Rustic romances culminated in marriage only when the prospective bride and groom and a preacher could be corralled at the same time and place.

The lyrical roar of the Ocoee was unbroken by the clangor of industry, and the scream of the panther went unchallenged by the scream of the steam whistle. From Pleasant Hill to Tumbling Creek, and from Turtletown to Chestnut Gap, the eerie note of the hoot owl was the nightly assurance to the pioneers that civilization was not on their trail.

CHAPTER 7

DEVELOPMENT IN THE FIFTIES

THE DECADE OF THE 1840'S CAME TO A CLOSE AT DUCKTOWN with a serene dignity becoming an era that had little to pass on to its successor. That decade, the first ten years of the white man's dominion over Ducktown, did not end with a veritable whip-crack as later decades were to do. It faded slowly and apologetically into the year 1850, which came in unostentatiously but which, before its close, ushered in a decade that proved to be the most interesting and the most exciting that Ducktown has seen. Shattered beyond repair was the quiet and peace enjoyed by those who had first moved into the district.

After the establishment of the first mail route through Ducktown in 1848 and after it became unmistakably apparent soon afterwards that vast quantities of copper ore were deposited in the district, Destiny began methodically weaving a pattern of civilization for the district that for design and quality had no counterpart.

Actual mining was begun at Ducktown in 1850. Two years later several companies were organized and charters secured for mining in the district. When the crackle of these official documents resounded throughout the land the slow trek to Ducktown was accelerated into a determined race. The California gold rush was still fresh in the minds of the people, and those who had missed it did not intend to pass up what might develop at Ducktown. Every element which entered into similar stampedes throughout the mining districts of the West in later years was present in the rush to Ducktown. Here was the scene of one of the most hectic scrambles of fortune-seekers ever enacted in the South.

In his report, "The Copper Mines of Ducktown," Eugene Gaussoin said, "... the high percentage of some of the parcels of ore taken out, created, after the first discovery of those mines, one of the wildest excitements recorded in the mining history." On a visit here in the year 1854, Richard O. Currey said, when looking down upon the district from Angellico Gap, "... at my feet, but a few miles distant, lay the rich mining region of Ducktown, the whole country thronged to overflowing with ardent speculators, while to the west rose the Frog Mountains."

The forerunners of the boom at Ducktown were the prospectors. Following the reports of their discoveries came the land buyers, some bent upon speculating, others upon risking their capital in one of the most financially hazardous enterprises in the world—mining. After the acquisition of promising tracts of land by those interested in legitimate investment, companies were formed and plans of operation mapped.

But the prospector, the speculator, and the investor were much in the minority. Hurrying over old Indian trails, struggling around knobs and through mountain passes where roads had but recently been made by cutting trees, or clearing roads as they traveled, came that mass of humanity upon whose shoulders the future of the district rested. It was they who were to clear the forests, sink the shafts, burn the charcoal, open the stores, minister to the needy, build the churches, drink the liquor, fight, pray, marry, and make of the place generally whatever they should choose. But always there was the possibility of a lucky "strike"; a lifetime was left in which to work should fortune be too fleeting.

>   Out of the pines of Georgia,
>   From the laurel of Carolin',
>   They came behind Buck and Bally,
>   In search of the copper mine.
>
>   The brush arbors were quickly deserted,
>   The saint and the sinner combined;
>   It was folly now to be bothered
>   By anything less than a mine.
>
>   Chief Duck and his tribe were hunters,
>   Little they cared for the ore,
>   They roamed the hills in their rompers,
>   And dreamed of the days of yore.
>
>   Where the trout had anchored in silence,
>   Where the Indian had lolled at rest,
>   The pioneers swarmed in a frenzy
>   For the spot that might prove best.

> They wielded their picks with ardor,
> They panned the streams up and down,
> And out of their vision and labor,
> Was molded the famed Ducktown.

The first permanent village at Ducktown was founded in 1850 around the first mine opened, the Hiwassee. The village, also named Hiwassee, was at first situated largely on the mining company's property. Adjoining this property was a tract of land belonging to Samuel M. Johnson. Some five or six acres of the Johnson land were purchased by J. C. Bell in 1855 and subdivided into lots which were sold during the next two years as the village grew away from the mining company's boundary. So solidly did the town take form that the main road through Hiwassee (or Ducktown) in 1855 was still the main street of the town of Ducktown in 1945. Villages and settlements sprang up around the other mines and throughout the district. None of these, however, kept pace with Hiwassee. This village grew into and remained the principal trading center of the entire region.

The Pierceville settlement was the principal gathering place for that portion of the region in Fannin County at the time Hiwassee was coming into prominence a few miles away. In addition to the mill and store operated there by Joseph Pierce, the Pierceville post office was established on February 19, 1853. Jeptha Patterson served as postmaster and also ran a store in the community. A bustling mining camp later grew up at Pierceville while the Mobile Mine and smelting works were in operation just prior to the outbreak of the Civil War.

Destined several decades later to be transformed into the social and educational center of western Fannin County was the old Indian village of Fightingtown. Later known as the Camp Ground, and now as Epworth, this sheltered retreat became the religious stronghold of early settlers in the vicinity. Old Fightingtown was a place of Indian celebrations, dances, and ball games. Its physical features were ideally suited for such occasions. A robust stream of crystal-clear water came from the ground in the midst of a grove of large trees. Nearby was a cleared stretch flanked by a gently sloping hill. From this hill the squaws, maidens, and papooses could view the ball games over the feather-bedecked heads of the gambling braves. In the wake of the shouting Indians at Fightingtown came the shouting Methodists and foot-washing Baptists. Camp meetings were held there prior to the Civil War, and from these meetings the place early came to be known as the Camp Ground.

Hiwassee began at once to assume some of the airs of regional leadership. Stores, churches, and other urban institutions were founded as the mining industry developed. Among the merchants of Hiwassee during this period were J. C. Bell, Erby Boyd, E. M. Kilpatrick, and Samuel W. and John Davidson. The latter two were brothers who had come to Ducktown from Haywood County, North Carolina, during the rush of the early fifties. The southern branch of the Methodist Church was the first to become established at Hiwassee. The Hiwassee Mining Company deeded a lot to this body on September 19, 1856. The building erected by the Methodists was also used by the Baptists. These two churches worked in close collaboration against the forces of waywardness that were rampant all around them.

The new mining camp was not without benefit of fraternal association. The Ducktown Masonic Lodge (Number 241) was organized at Hiwassee on June 23, 1855, and Robert I. Steele became its first Worshipful Master.

Hiwassee also had its newspaper, the Ducktown *Eagle,* before the Civil War. Little is known of this paper, other than through a few court decrees which were ordered to be published in its columns. The *Eagle* did not survive the Civil War.

Moving among the sick and the weary of the region, before Hiwassee was even a village, was Doctor J. D. Ketcherside. It is not known when he came to the region, but the good physician lost $32 on his first real-estate transaction at Ducktown. He bought 120 acres in section 3 of the Turtletown district from John H. Dyer, in January, 1852, for $332 and a month later sold the same land to James M. Cotter for $300. For the next twenty-five years this pioneer physician of Ducktown applied himself as assiduously to sections and quarter-sections of Mother Earth's epidermis as he did to the epidermis of the human body. But this absorbing pastime is not peculiar to the annals of the medical profession in the Copper Basin.

The next physician at Ducktown of whom there is any record was Dr. Augustin Gattinger, who was born in Munich, Bavaria, February 3, 1825. He attended the University of Munich from October, 1844, to February, 1849. For the part he took in a celebration in honor of George Washington, February 22, 1849, the authorities ordered Gattinger to leave Germany and make his residence in some country whose form of government was more to his liking than that of Germany. He left immediately, before his graduation, and turned his eyes to the land of George Washington. But before departing for America, Gattinger was married to Miss Josephine Dury. Upon his arrival in this country he made his way to Dalton, Georgia, the terminus of the Georgia and South Carolina Railroad, in June, 1849, and from there the trip was continued to Chattanooga by stage coach. After a "farming experiment" at Cave Springs, Gattinger moved to Charleston, Tennessee, where he remained until the year 1858 when he accepted a position as resident physician at the Ducktown copper mines.

Many permanent additions to the citizenship of the copper district resulted from the influx of workers and fortune seekers during the decade prior to the Civil War. E. P. McGee moved here from Hayesville, North Carolina, in 1858, and Joseph Chancey arrived at about the same time. Just prior to the war the Maughan family came to Ducktown from England, stopping first in Monroe County, Tennessee. The Maughans and another family were in Liverpool preparing to emigrate to Canada when a representative of an English firm that was trying to develop a silver mine on Pond's Creek in Monroe County persuaded the two families to come to Tennessee. Nothing came of the silver mine and Michael Maughan moved his family to Ducktown. Julius Quinn migrated to the copper mines from White County, Georgia in the late fifties, and Isaac H. Edwards moved there from Bradley County, Tennessee, and purchased the farm of James Dunn on the Ocoee River in 1857.

Mother England poured out her sons in lavish fashion for the great adventure at Ducktown, beyond the Atlantic. Beginning about 1853 Cornish miners and mechanics were requisitioned in large numbers by the companies endeavoring to develop the mines in Polk County. In the wake of the English parade through Ducktown in the fifties there were left John Quintrell, James Spargo, James Jory, James Nankivell, and James Phillips to contribute to the moral and economic stability of Ducktown in the decades that followed.

The wife of James Nankivell, according to the story told by her daughter-in-law, arrived in New York from England to join her husband at Ducktown just prior to the time of the Civil War. With her were her two children, James, Jr., and Annie. Shortly after leaving New York she overheard a fellow traveler on the train mention the name Ducktown. Weary from a long sea voyage, and in a strange land, the good woman could not but lose her natural reticence. She made known to the stranger her name and her destination and asked if he were acquainted with her husband at Ducktown. The stranger graciously introduced himself as E. M. Kilpatrick, a merchant of Ducktown who had been to New York to buy merchandise, said that he was well acquainted with James Nankivell, and very gallantly rendered every possible assistance to the mother and two children until they reached their destination. In later years two sons of the Nankivells, John and Octavus, married two daughters of the merchant, Lucie and Florence Kilpatrick.

An expansion of mail services became necessary in the 1850's because of the influx of settlers in the mining district. Another mail route, in addition to the one already in existence between Dahlonega and Benton by way of Culchote, was established through the new copper mining district in February, 1853. The new route extended from Turtletown, North Carolina, to Ellijay, Georgia, by way of Kimsey's Store and Hiwassee Copper Mines, Tennessee, and Pierceville and Santa Lucah, Georgia. The Kimsey's Store post office, located on Nigger Creek just west of Zion Hill Church, was established on November 18, 1852. The name of the Culchote post office was changed to that of Hiwassee Copper Mines on December 19, 1851, and again on July 21, 1854, to simply that of Copper Mines. The second change was accompanied by a change in location to the Tennessee Mine on Potato Creek. This office was discontinued in the latter part of 1859. Mail service between Ducktown and Murphy, North Carolina, was inaugurated in 1856. The mail was scheduled twice a week and was carried by two-horse coaches.

Despite the fact that the district was named Ducktown and its principal town Hiwassee, neither name was connected with a post office until several years after the mines were in operation. A post office to serve the village of Hiwassee was established under the name of Davidson's Store on June 29, 1857, but on July 15, 1858, the name was changed to Ducktown. With the discontinuance of the Copper Mines post office the following year, the Ducktown office became the hub of all mail routes in operation throughout this isolated region.

It is doubtful if there was an established school of any kind in the Ducktown region until after the opening of the mines. By the latter part of the fifties, however, the population of Ducktown had increased enormously and the general character of the population had undergone notable changes. In 1858 the scholastic population of Polk County was 3,118. Of this number of school children, approximately 1,200 resided in and adjacent to Ducktown. In addition to these, some two or three hundred children of school age lived south of the Ocoee in Fannin County, Georgia, principally in the vicinity of the Mobile Mine. Some attention was, of course, given the question of schools for this prolific district, but the facilities were meager and the flare for education had not yet taken root.

The first school house at Hiwassee stood near Davidson's Store just south of the village for several years. Here school was held for two or three months of each year during the prosperous times preceding the dark days of the Civil War. This was a subscription school, as were all other schools in the district during that period. School was also held at Isabella. This village was the center of the smelting works and ranked next in importance to Hiwassee. Charles Travena, an English preacher and school-teacher, is remembered as having taught there.

The first school in the Georgia portion of the present Copper Basin was held at Flint Hill. The Flint Hill building, used principally as a place of worship, stood about a mile north of the present site of Epworth on the Blue Ridge-Copperhill highway. The schools conducted for short periods each year at Flint Hill both before and after the Civil War were subscription, or pay, schools with fees charged for each pupil. Children unable to pay the fees were therefore denied the privilege of receiving a few weeks instruction each year.

A potential source of revenue for school purposes at Ducktown was the sixteenth, or school, section of the Fourth Fractional Township. Copper ore was discovered on this section and mining was done here by the Tennessee Mining Company for several years after 1850. An act relating to the school lands passed by the Tennessee Legislature on December 13, 1841, provided that the three school-land commissioners, who were also to be the common-school commissioners, were to conduct the school affairs in each township in the counties within the Ocoee District. All funds collected, together with the proceeds of the school lands, were to be applied to the support of common schools in the several townships. With a valuable copper mine on the Ducktown school section, it was expected that the educational fund in the Fourth Fractional Township would be handsomely augmented. But this did not prove to be true. No sooner was copper discovered on section 16 than there appeared the insidious head of litigation over ownership of the property. This law suit, which will be discussed further in the following chapter, was of such prolonged duration that as a source of revenue for schools section 16 was next to valueless.

Schools at Ducktown required teachers, money, and books; a copper industry required ore, money, and roads. Insofar as the native settlers were concerned, education was no pressing necessity and industrial works were of doubtful advantage. But insofar as religion and church buildings were concerned, these were different. Buildings could be erected by the devout from logs donated for that purpose. Itinerant preachers quibbled little over their remuneration, and there was no doubt concerning the Word and the reward.

The dates of organization of many of the churches in this section are not known. They were, for the most part, outgrowths of services that had been held in homes and in the open during the 1840's when the population was too sparse for permanent buildings. As the number of settlers gradually increased, services were held in groves and in brush arbors. The era of constructing buildings for purposes of worship began with the rapid increase of population following the opening of the mines. The first church buildings, of log construction, were the fountain-heads around which grew the limits and the names of many of the settlements at Ducktown.

The Bethlehem Baptist Church, erected near the site of the Culchote post office, was possibly the first native church in the central portion of the new mining district. At Zion Hill, four miles north of Hiwassee, the United Baptist Church was founded. L. L. Adams deeded one acre of ground, including the Zion Hill meeting house, to this church in 1851. The Baptists were both numerous and busy in the region south of the Ocoee River. Churches were established at Grassy Creek, Sugar Creek, Mt. Moriah, Lebanon, Damascus, and Macedonia. The Methodists worshipped at Flint Hill and Hopewell.

Social conditions during the first decade of mining at Ducktown were in a state of ferment. The population was a heterogeneous one, for to the native element were added English, Welsh, German, and other foreign nationalities, as well as many Americans whose ideals and customs were equally foreign to this remote region. Each panting ox team that came to a halt at one of the mines, and each coach that lurched into Hiwassee from the railroad at Cleveland, deposited individuals who had their own ideas of cultural and social values. Among these were miners, masons, carpenters, clerks, and a varied assortment of other laborers who were to move the wheels of the copper industry. The resultant admixture of different nationalities and customs was characterized by brawls, profanity, and nuisances. Much in the minority at first were the sober, industrious workers. A mining camp was in the making; repose and tranquility had but few champions. Boisterous days were inevitable. Many of those who came to Ducktown were rough and they were tough. They expected to work for a living and fight and carouse for a pastime. They were products of a shifting era and a strenuous industry. For several years there was a hilarious freedom of action in the much publicized copper district.

A vivid portrayal of the morality of Ducktown was written into a Chancery Court entry of June 1, 1857. Elizabeth Barker, guardian of the minor children of Patrick Nash, petitioned the court to allow her to sell sixty acres of land which had belonged to Nash near the Polk County Mine. Some of her reasons for desiring to sell the property were: It was not a suitable place in which to rear her wards as it adjoined the Copper Hill mines, at which place there was a great deal of drunkenness, fighting, debauchery, and other ill conduct; there was no school within reach; and there was but little tillable land on the sixty acres.

The ranks of the obstreperous were, however, being thinned perceptibly by 1860. The mining industry was becoming more stabilized, and an air of dignified permanence was supplanting the mushroom era of the previous decade. The unrestrained conditions at Ducktown were coming to an end, and for the following three decades the proud little village of Hiwassee took just pride in its moral excellence.

It is a singular fact that dances were never an accepted social function of the early settlers of this mountainous region. Stern religious decorum forbade the rollicking all-night shindigs that were so popular in rural communities elsewhere. The chief means of worldly diversion among the sacrosanct pioneers were occasional log rollings and corn shuckings. For purely feminine entertainment and relaxation quilting parties were much in favor. But protracted meetings, baptisings, wakes, and all-day singings were popular occasions for gatherings where gossip could be traded and the general welfare of each made known to all.

The population of Ducktown just prior to the Civil War is problematical. The population of Polk County in 1860 was 8,726. The number of inhabitants of the Ducktown and Turtletown districts, including the adjacent portions of Cherokee County, North Carolina, and Fannin County, Georgia, at that time was probably between five and six thousand. Much the larger portion of this number lived at Hiwassee and in the vicinity of the different mines. Approximately one thousand hands were employed by the mining companies at the outbreak of the war.

While the copper industry was the principal source of income for the large population that had grown up here, it should be interesting to peer through the smoke from the first furnaces in the district and witness some of the effects which the industry exerted on lesser lines of endeavor.

One of the first effects of the opening of the mines was upon land values in the district. Previous to this time real estate transfers in the vicinity had been few. The average price of land had increased but slightly over that at which it had been secured through state grants. Up to this time, too, the amount of property taxes paid to the county had been negligible. As preparations for mining went ahead, however, land values increased sharply. An illustration of how rapidly the land increased in taxable value after 1850 is given in a letter written by John Caldwell which appeared in the Nashville, Tennessee, *Daily Press and Times* of February 12, 1868. The letter said in part: "As regards revenue, I will illustrate. John Davis, of Ducktown, sold me 1200 acres of land on which he had never paid higher than five dollars in taxes. I immediately opened a mine on the property and the first tax bill I paid was $400.00.... The revenue in Polk County prior to the opening of the mines was a mere trifle, but since that time it has ranked among the wealthiest counties in the state."

With but few exceptions native residents of the Basin did not figure in land transactions involving mining properties. Until the beginning of industrial activity the natives were settled along the river and creeks where small farms could be cultivated. The copper deposits later discovered were invariably along the tops of ridges and in ravines. In one way or another ownership of these favored spots had fallen into more astute hands before their latent wealth became generally known. Much of this land was owned by individuals living outside the district, by men who had purchased the land as general enterers and who were willing to risk a penny for an acre of any kind of land. Since there was little wealth among the pioneers of Ducktown, the only opportunity they had of realizing profits from the wave of speculation that swept over the district was in prior ownership of some of the copper lands—which was seldom the case. There are, however, legends of sections and quarter-sections on which some of the richest mines were later opened being sold for cub bears and muzzle-loading shot guns.

But if the native residents had no lands on which copper was found, they had lands upon which food could be produced. And it took immense quantities of provisions for both man and beast as the rush to Ducktown continued. As the new mining district was dependent solely on wagon transportation for its welfare, the number of draft animals alone which had to be provided for was enormous. L. W. Gilbert said in a letter dated Athens, Tennessee, December 6, 1854: "There are some 500 teams engaged in the [mine] service, besides many others employed at the mines in hauling logs, boards, feed, etc. It requires no small amount of feed to support 500 or 600 teams, of 4 to 6 head each.... The mines furnish a good cash market for every kind of produce from the farm, besides employment for hundreds of men, and many hundreds of teams. One farmer told me today, as I was coming from the mines, that notwithstanding he had a good crop this year, yet he could not feed all the teams employed by the mines for a single night...."

Not only did the voracious market at Ducktown consume all the produce that could be raised on nearby farms, but farmers in Cherokee, Fannin, and Bradley counties profited much from this new outlet for their surplus commodities. Hogs, cattle, and sheep were slaughtered and hauled to the mines from distant points. Copper haulers returned from Cleveland with their wagons loaded with provisions. Other Ducktown industries such as grist mills, saw mills, carding and weaving, blacksmith shops, cobbling, cordwood, and charcoal also prospered. And it was said that Benjamin Taliaferro set up a shop at Hiwassee and turned out hats "that never wore out." A tannery was also established just west of the East Tennessee Mine.

Notwithstanding the fact that the little village of Hiwassee grew with great rapidity and many new business houses were opened, several of the mining companies in the district found it necessary to operate boarding houses and to permit certain of their officials to run commissaries for the convenience of their employees.

Many remarkable changes had been wrought at the remote region of Ducktown during the decade of the 1850's. Copper mines had been opened, villages and mining camps dotted the district, the population had increased enormously, roads had been built into the growing industrial center from all directions, schools and mail service had been established, and an air of permanent prosperity pervaded the community. And what was equally significant, Ducktown's fame as a rich source of copper had spread far and wide.

CHAPTER 8

PREPARATIONS FOR MINING

From the time of the discovery of copper at Ducktown in 1843 to the middle of the 1850's, the district passed through the various stages of prospecting, speculating in lands, organizing mining companies, and constructing roads in preparation for large-scale mining and smelting activities. Ducktown became early and widely known. There were two reasons for this: Good copper mines were scarce and therefore attracted much attention, and a large number of men both in this country and abroad were financially interested in the Ducktown industry.

The first information on the mineral wealth of the Ducktown region was embodied in Dr. Gerard P. Troost's Fourth Report to the General Assembly of the State of Tennessee in 1837. Troost reported the presence of hydroxide of iron at several places in the region between the Hiwassee and Ocoee rivers. Later, in 1857, Richard O. Currey, a Tennessee geologist, said that the hydroxide of iron which Troost told of seeing in this district was in reality outcroppings of the copper deposits at Ducktown.

Although Troost was primarily interested in what lay hidden beneath the surface, he was not unmindful of the rugged beauty of the country. He said: "This wild mountainous country, where the traveler is exposed to hard knocks, hard falls, hard resting places, and starvation, if his wallet is not stuffed with the needful for man and beast, is not destitute of romantic beauties. Standing on one of the summits called Bean's ridge, the sight recalled to my memory the Alpine scenery of Switzerland. It commands an extensive view over the Hiwassee valley, and I congratulated myself on seeing again some marks of civilization, after having wandered in the rugged, wild mountainous part of the Ocoee district. Before reaching the junction of the Hiwassee and Ocoee rivers, we have some fine level land on which a few farms are cultivated."

Troost probably never learned of the vast copper deposits over which he rode on his trip through the Indian province of Ducktown. In his last general report (the ninth, in 1847) to the General Assembly, he dwelt on the abundance of zinc ore in Tennessee. He recommended the importation of copper ore from Missouri to be smelted and refined in Tennessee, and the manufacture of brass by using Missouri copper and Tennessee zinc.

All during the decade of the 1830's prospectors searched the mountainous sections of western North Carolina, northern Georgia, and eastern Tennessee, and every stream was patiently and methodically panned. But it was gold, not copper or iron, that was sought. Even after white settlers had moved into the Ducktown district the prospecting was continued along the many creeks and smaller streams of the region.

It was during one of the many futile searches for gold that copper was first discovered at Ducktown. R. O. Currey, geologist, dramatized the discovery as follows: "In August 1843, a Mr. Lemmons, prospecting for gold found, on a branch in Section 9 which flows into Potato Creek, a reddish brown and blackish decomposed rock in which large crystals of a deep rich red color were abundant. The place of this discovery was later the sight of the Hiwassee Copper Mine. Mr. Lemmons was confident that here was the long sought-for gold mine. He, having no suitable vessel in which to place his precious metal, tied the cuffs of his coat with hickory withe and filled them. Slinging his treasure across his shoulder he made his way homeward, leaving his pan concealed in the bushes until next morning. He called in his neighbors—sent for whiskey—reveled and celebrated all night. The morning sun found not a ready laborer. That day the gold was examined again, and lo! its color was changed from the bright red, which was thought a sign of great richness, to a dark, dingy brown. This brought fears, and night stole the fortune of the day. The gold proved to be red oxide of copper in crystals." The ripple of excitement which followed Lemmon's discovery of copper soon subsided. The fruitless panning for gold went on, and the seclusion of the early settlers remained undisturbed.

A state geologist did, however, visit Ducktown soon after the report of the discovery of copper here. But, says Currey, so unfavorable was his report on the district that no attempt was made at that time to begin mining operations. The owners of the property did a small amount of exploration work by digging a trench up the stream where Lemmon had made his disappointing discovery, and several tons of ore were thrown out of the trench. Samples of the material were sent to Nichols Height, New York, for examination. The samples proved to be made up mainly of iron, but one piece of ore thought to be of little value was included in the shipment of samples and assayed 11 per cent copper. For men who had visions of a gold mine the report on the samples was poor encouragement and all work was suspended. Four years passed before the abandoned workings received further attention.

The next appraisal of the old Lemmon discovery was by A. J. Weaver (or Weber), a German mining engineer from the district of Werner, in April, 1847. He inspected the rock formations in the old trench and informed the owners, Thomas H. Callaway, J. B. Tipton, Ebenezer Johnson, Samuel M. Johnson, and T. C. Lyon, that huge deposits of copper lay beneath the surface. Arrangements were accordingly made whereby Weaver was to work the property and pay a royalty of one-fifteenth of the proceeds to the owners. Work was started on May 1, 1847. The lease was for four hundred acres in section 9.

Weaver shipped ninety casks of ore to the Revere Smelting Works at Port Shively near Boston. The dry weight of the ore was 31,210 pounds. The ore, shipped in two lots, assayed 32.5 per cent and 14.5 per cent copper, respectively. Weaver was in Boston when the ore was sold, and he never returned to his Tennessee lease. Gold mining, he said, was to be his first work. Early in 1848 he left for Mexico, and in a letter dated Fort Independence, Missouri, April 15, 1848, he explained that upon his return from Mexico he hoped to secure the aid of his friends in Boston and return to the mine in Tennessee. But Weaver fell by the wayside, a victim of hostile Indians, before reaching Mexico and thus ended the first mining venture at Ducktown.

The ninety casks of ore were transported out of Ducktown by mule-back. The route, which at that time was no more than a trail, was by Boardtown to Ellijay, thence across the mountain to the railroad at Dalton. This was six years before the copper road to Cleveland was opened. As the outlet to Cleveland had not at that time been contemplated, all hope of mining in the district was virtually abandoned.

At the same time Weaver was working his copper prospect, B. C. Duggar was erecting an iron forge near the mouth of Potato Creek. Duggar began the production of iron implements in the following year, not long before the Culchote post office was established in the district in June, 1848. All these were symptoms of the order from which Ducktown's first settlers had fled. But Weaver soon disappeared; Duggar was forced to seek elsewhere for iron ore containing less copper than the ore he was attempting to utilize; and the post office brought no improvement in roads or transportation methods. Nature herself seemed to be on the side of the settlers.

The undertow that was soon to drag Ducktown into the sea of industrial activity began growing in force in 1849. The story of the event that was to prove so momentous to the future of the district is fully described in a letter written by the leading actor in the scene. The letter is reproduced here in full as it appeared in Currey's *A Sketch of the Geology of Tennessee* (1857):

DUCKTOWN, 1855.

To Dr. R. O. Currey & C. A. Proctor,
GENTLEMEN:

I came to Ducktown in 1849, scouting for copper, and found some five or six tons in a cabin, 10 ft. square, on the property now known as the Hiwassee. I found the country unexplored; the school section, a property now worth a million of dollars, attracting little or no attention. Sat down in the woods to mature some plan to open and control the section. I owned, at that time, one twenty dollar bill. After three hours' reflection, resolved upon calling a meeting of the citizens of the township, and make a speech explanatory of the value of the School Section, and the importance of leasing it for mining purposes. Told the people that as soon as the mines could be opened, their condition would be improved, and that civilization, intelligence, comfort and wealth would be the inevitable results. At the conclusion of this remark, a speaker arose in the crowd and informed me that a large portion of the inhabitants had come here to get away from civilization, and that if it followed them, they would run again. After the speech was made, drew up a memorial to the Legislature praying the passage of a law authorizing the Commissioners to give a mining lease on the School Section. The memorial was signed by a majority of the citizens, and on personal application, the law was passed, and under it the lease was taken. In May 1850, commenced mining in the woods. In the same year, sunk two shafts, and obtained copper from both of them. The excavations made did not exceed twelve feet—at that depth the copper being found. Commenced mining at Hiwassee mine in 1851, in connection with S. Congdon, the agent of the Tennessee Mining Co.; built a double cabin, and taught Sabbath-School in the kitchen end of the establishment, aided by young Mr. Walter Congdon. We were tantalized by one of the miners, who exclaimed, on a certain occasion: "Good

God Almighty! does that old mud-sucker think he can worship Jesus and work a copper mine?" While this same miner was planning a way to pack copper ore out of the mountain on mules, I surveyed the Ocoee river, and determined to make a road eighteen miles through an impassable desert. I had no means but a strong determination to surmount every obstacle. Going to a Methodist camp meeting, I obtained permission to make a road speech, in the recess of divine service. The speech over, we took up a collection, principally on credit and payable in trade. This, however, served the purpose, and on the 6th of October, 1851, the work was commenced. On the first day, three hands worked; on the second, two; on the third, worked alone—public opinion, strong and powerful, being against the enterprise; on the fourth day hired a dozen Cherokees. Thus began one of the most important projects in the State—which was consummated in two years, at an expense of about $22,000.00. The Tennessee Company came early to help in the enterprise—but the Hiwassee held back till 14 miles of the road was passable for wagons. At the close of the first year, Robt. McCampbell was employed as the engineer of the road, after which I again turned my attention to mining.

(Signed) John Caldwell.

Caldwell was a citizen of Jefferson County, Tennessee, and was actively engaged in the mining industry at Ducktown for several years. The cabin he described finding, in which there were five or six tons of ore, had been erected by A. J. Weaver. An account of Caldwell's lease of the school section, with the resultant litigation over the property, will be given later. His principal contribution to the development of the Ducktown mines was the construction of the road from Ducktown to Greasy Creek.

There is something about a mining venture that will loosen the purse-strings of investors and speculators more spontaneously than will any other venture. Perhaps it is the lure of the unseen, the hidden possibilities. But the fact that the possibilities often remain hidden does not deter some from plunging in where others are staggering out.

For several years following the year 1848, Ducktown properties were in the forefront of mining speculation both in this country and abroad. At that time mining was one of the chief undeveloped industries in this land of fabulous resources. There was good reason to believe that as the population moved westward, and into the sparsely settled regions of the South, mineral deposits of great wealth would be discovered. And throughout the financial centers of the world men were ready and eager to embark upon such enterprises.

A writer in the *Mining Magazine* (1853), commenting on the apparent wealth of the new copper fields at Ducktown and on the mineral wealth of this country as a whole, said:

> The mining capitalists of the old world are ready to make unlimited investments here, if we can furnish grounds that will pay. Three hundred millions of capital employed in England in mining operations it taxed to support the crown, the nobility, the church, and the paupers, until, when the whole is footed up, twenty-eight shillings sterling is paid annually on every hundred dollars of working capital. In that country the weight of taxation, the depth of the mines, the weight of water to be raised, the exhaustible coal fields, and many other reasons, are operating powerfully to transfer the minning capital of England to the United States.

It was not long, following the receipt in Boston of Weaver's ore, until the first agent representing capital in interesting proportions arrived at Ducktown. In May, 1849, "a gentleman from the west," claiming to be an agent of English capital seeking investment in mineral lands, approached the owners of the property formerly leased to Weaver. Whereas the German had possessed but little money and had leased the property from the owners—who were to profit only if royalties were realized—it was a different matter with the roaming Englishman. The agent, William Warne, fresh from the fountains of wealth, was promptly and firmly taken in hand, and on May 14, 1849, Thomas H. Callaway, John B. Tipton, Samuel M. and Ebenezer Johnson, and T. C. Lyon sold the four hundred acres in section 9 to Warne for $30,000. This marked the first evidence of financial faith in the rusty splotches of terrain at Ducktown.

The next investment in mining property here was the Congdon purchase of the school section in 1850. By 1852 four mines had been opened at Ducktown. In that year samples of ore from one of the mines were sent to London, England, to be analyzed. Following the reports on the samples a company of London capitalists sent an agent to Ducktown to purchase any promising mining properties that might be found. In describing the agent's visit here a writer said: "The lands bought by Capt. G., who is the agent referred to, are to be paid for in July and November. For one lot in Georgia, he has paid $40,000.00. Three lots in Tennessee he is to pay for in this manner: To C. M. & K, $150,000.00 for 160 acres; to T I W D, $75,000.00 for 160 acres not opened; to D, $30,000.00 for a lot not opened. Both of these last lots present good evidence on the surface. A few years since the lands were entered at from 50¢ down to 1¢ an acre...." * Jeptha Patterson was offered $100,000 for his lands situated near Pierceville. $50,000 was to be paid in cash, and $50,000 in notes secured by the purchasers. Patterson rejected the offer, and probably spent the rest of his life in deep distrust of his own wisdom. With $50,000 in cash he could have purchased about all of the remaining lands in Fannin County.

As will be shown later, the first mining companies were organized in 1852. The following year saw the beginning of the land boom at Ducktown which lasted about two years. Capitalists or their agents from New York, Charleston, and New Orleans, and from England, visited the district in increasing numbers. It was during this period too that the throngs referred to in Chapter 7 flooded the new mining district. The options, leases, quit claim deeds, purchase agreements, and warranty deeds were executed with such frequency and fervor that they were often overlapping and confusing. The unhurried routine of the Register of Deeds' office at Benton was suddenly shattered. This official's records at once became the most important of all the county records.

Additional transactions of the period involving some of the better known mines were the following:

January, 1853: Thomas H. Callaway and Euclid Waterhouse sold the Callaway Mine to John M. Dow for $30,000.

April, 1853: Samuel Congdon sold the East Tennessee Mine to William Hickok and associates for $30,000.

July, 1853: Samuel Congdon sold the Mary's Mine to L. W. Gilbert, Charles Congdon, and William Hickok for $25,000.

April, 1854: A. H. Keith, John Caldwell, and the Mastin heirs sold the Polk County Mine to Polk County Copper Company for $60,000.

June, 1854: George Wood sold the London Mine to Warren Delano for $85,000.

July, 1854: Elias Davis sold the Isabella Mine to L. W. Gilbert for $25,000.

October, 1855: Thomas H. Callaway and Euclid Waterhouse sold the Eureka Mine to the Eureka Mining Company for $46,666.

There were numerous other lesser real-estate transactions in-

---

* The names of the individuals whose initials appear are not definitely known. It is questionable, though, that the transactions mentioned actually took place for the amounts stated by the writer. There is some value to the reference, however, because it reveals at least hypothetically the tremendous sums thought of in connection with mining properties at Ducktown.

volving Ducktown mining properties between the years 1853 and 1860. Those who participated in the larger deals were mainly Charles and Samuel Congdon, John Caldwell, L. W. Gilbert, J. V. Symons, William H. Peet, John Thomas, Thomas H. Callaway, Euclid Waterhouse, Samuel M. Johnson, H. B. Henegar, Lyman Denison, P. M. Craigmiles, Jesse H. Gaut, T. M. Mastin, J. E. Raht, John M. Dow, J. C. Bell, and John and Elias Davis.

While mining properties and other real estate were being bought and sold with speculative abandon, companies were being organized to develop the natural resources of the Ducktown district. Although many of these companies never progressed beyond the stage of incorporation, the amazing number that received charters was proof of the high excitement and fond hopes that centered in the district in the first era of activity.

The first company to be granted a charter by the state of Tennessee to engage in business in the new mining fields at Ducktown was the Cocheco Mining Company, incorporated January 23, 1852. The incorporators were Oliver Wetmore, Leonard Bostwick, William H. Wyles, William N. Bilbo, and A. O. P. Nicholson. (A. O. P. Nicholson was a former United States Senator from Tennessee.) The capitalization of each mine owned was not to be in excess of $250,000. This was to allow the directors to make a separate and distinct interest of each mine.

The second company to receive a charter was the Hiwassee Mining Company, incorporated January 28, 1852. The incorporators were Samuel F. Tracy, John M. Dow, Frederick O. Prince, Nathan T. Dow, and Alexander H. Freeman. The capital stock of the company was to be not less than $300,000 and not more than $600,000. The charter was for ninety-nine years and granted the corporation the right to explore for copper, iron, and other ores, minerals and metals; to mine, work, smelt, manufacture, and vend the same; to sue and be sued; to buy and sell property needed for carrying on the operations, providing "that the cost of all such real estate shall not exceed the maximum amount of the capital stock." The corporation was not to contract debts until $50,000 capital stock was paid in, no part of which was to be withdrawn or diverted from the business of the company, and was not to "contract debts at any time to an amount exceeding the amount of capital stock annually paid in."

The Culchote Mining Company was incorporated on the same day, for the same purpose, and under the same commissioners, as the Hiwassee Mining Company.

A present-day view of the Copper Basin's barren, eroded hillsides. In the foreground is Potato Creek and on the horizon is Little Frog Mountain. Ducktown can be seen far off, toward the right. Old mine workings are visible on both sides of the highway in the distance.

The Copperhill plant of the Tennessee Copper Company, one of the several units of the copper and acid industry now being operated by the company in the Copper Basin.

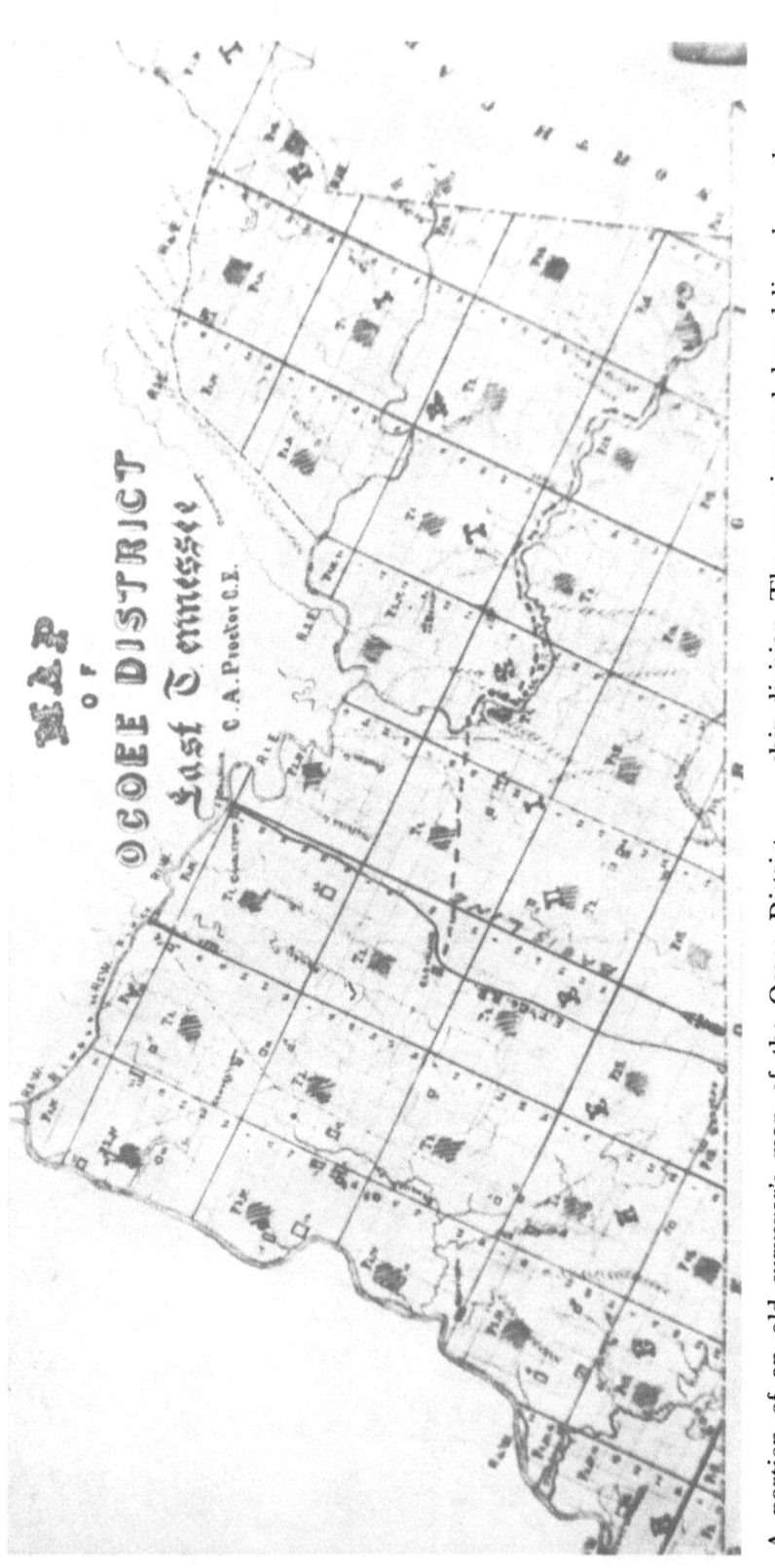

A portion of an old surveyor's map of the Ocoee District (drawn c.1856) showing township and sectional divisions. Ducktown is located in the extreme lower right-hand fractional township division. The superimposed dotted line shows the course of the copper road from Ducktown to Cleveland, a distance of forty miles, the only shipping outlet for Ducktown copper.

Two other companies received charters in 1852. On February 25 the Tennessee Mining Company and the Ocoee Mining Company were incorporated. The incorporators for the Tennessee Company were Charles Congdon, D. H. Arnold, Samuel Congdon, James S. Stone, and R. C. Greene. For the Ocoee Company they were William P. Tift, Lewis Legriel, John Caldwell, Samuel Congdon, and Benjamin C. Harris.

When the Legislature reconvened at Nashville in January, 1854, a long list of applications for charters by other mining companies at Ducktown were awaiting enactment. The charters granted were substantially the same as that of the Hiwassee Mining Company, with the capitalization of the corporations ranging from $100,000 to $1,000,000. The companies and their dates of incorporation are given in the accompanying table.

COMPANY	DATE OF INCORPORATION
Callaway Mining Company	January 18, 1854
Ducktown Mining Company *	January 18, 1854
Athens Mining Company *	January 18, 1854
Eureka Mining Company	January 18, 1854
Cherokee Mining Company	January 26, 1854
McCulloch & Glenn Copper Company *	January 26, 1854
United States Copper Company of Tennessee	January 26, 1854
Mary's Copper Company	January 26, 1854
Excelsior & Ocoee Mining Company *	January 26, 1854
Isabella Copper Company	January 26, 1854
East Tennessee Mining and Smelting Company	February 13, 1854
Polk County Copper Company	February 13, 1854
Waterhouse Mining Company *	February 13, 1854
Tennessee Smelting Company	February 28, 1854
Davis Copper Company *	February 28, 1854
New York & London Mining Company	March 1, 1854
Turtletown Mining Company *	March 1, 1854
Fillmore Mining Company *	March 1, 1854
East Tennessee & Maryland Mining and Smelting Company *	March 1, 1854
Union Consolidated Mining Company of Tennessee	March 1, 1854
Benton Mining Company *	March 4, 1854
New Jersey Copper Company of Tennessee *	March 12, 1854
Toccoee Mining Company (later called Burra Burra Copper Company of Tennessee)	March 12, 1854

* No records found of any operations carried on at Ducktown.

The incorporated companies had gone through the accepted formalities of organization and had received legislative sanction. But there were other companies in the district that were born with less fanfare and, presumably, with more modest plans of operation. One such company, composed of G. W. Middlecoff, J. C. Camp, J. L. Simmons, J. M. McGonigal, and A. McNabb, all citizens of Bradley County, was organized March 30, 1854, at Middlecoff's store in Bradley County under the name of Chatata Mining Company. A lease was secured on forty acres of Ducktown land belonging to Ephriam Prince, and each of the five members of the company contributed $10.00 for the purpose of hiring hands and securing provisions. Another tract of one hundred acres was later secured, for which each member paid an additional $25.

Another such company, known as the Walker Valley Company, composed of Isaac Day, John Goodner, G. W. Middlecoff, and N. G. Burgess, did some testing for copper on lands of Ephriam Prince. The outlook for this company seemed brighter, as each member deposited in the treasury $41.15. Feeling the pressure of larger, more formidable companies by which they were surrounded, the Chatata Mining Company and the Walker Valley Company combined their resources and determination into one company, called the Union Mining Company. History fails to record what happened to this company after that.

Allusion has been made to the degree of speculation that pervaded the Ducktown district during the land boom of the early fifties. That the word speculation is fittingly used is borne out conclusively when it is understood that much of the capital that was first invested here was invested wholly upon the strength of surface indications. While it is true that the gossan indicating immense copper deposits was present to a startling extent, such indications were often misleading—a fact which proved to be true at many places in western North Carolina and in Georgia. To ascertain the probable value of the Ducktown ore bodies, several of the men financially committed to the district secured the services of eminent geologists to examine their properties. Excerpts from some of these early reports will be given. However, it will be of help to the reader to have first a general understanding of the formation of the original ore bodies here. The following description was embodied in a report on the properties of the Polk County Copper Company by M. F. Maury, L.L.D., U.S.A., and Richard O. Currey, A.M., M.D., in 1859:

The out-crops of the gossan are very large, and this substance is scattered in huge blocks over much of the surface of your property. Aside from the frequent bunches or pockets of ore, the upper or soft deposit is known to be from 30 to 100 feet in width. The ore lies in true, well defined veins.

The gossan is the first rock into which the miner drives his shaft. It is a honey-combed, ferruginous residue of the original copper vein. Aqueous and atmospheric agencies have decomposed the more elevated portion of the ore, washing down the copper to a lower level, and forming not only thick beds of a peculiarly valuable deposit, but also frequent pouches or aggregations of the resulting oxide at some distance from its first position. It was the working of this gossan as an ore of iron that first led to the discovery of the better minerals below.

Under the gossan and from five to twenty feet below the surface of the ground, we strike the "black ore." It consists in different mines of the green carbonate, black and red oxides, and the black sulphuret of copper, the last variety appearing to be the most abundant yet mined. Of course this requires no deep or expensive mining, the workman with his pick detaching it with great ease. No better ore could exist. It is cheaply and quickly smelted without a wasting process. It is very rich, varying from twenty to sixty per cent of copper.

The black ores rest upon a shelf of mundic or lean rock. This is in the beginning a sulphuret or iron, intermixed with the yellow sulphuret of copper. In all the mining of this district this lower rock is found to increase remarkably in its per centage of copper as the shaft sinks deeper. But better still—says Prof. Currey: "In the Mary mine (and whatever may be said of it, is also true of Copper Hill upon your property), after cutting through the mundic, a second stratum of decomposed or black ore was brought to light, the extent of which has not yet been ascertained. In the Hiwassee and Tennessee mines the yellow ore under the mundic has been penetrated, proving to increase in richness. To the mining of this lower ore all the operations must at last come, and, however easy it may be to mine the decomposed ore, there is gratification in knowing that below there is a supply of the original yellow ore, sufficient for all time to come."

One of the first reports on the Ducktown mines was made by J. D. Whitney, United States geologist, who investigated the Cherokee and Beaver properties in 1853. He described the region as being heavily timbered with a variety of forest trees, but chiefly of white oak and other hardwood. Of the geology of the district he said: "The rocks at the mines are micaceous and chloritic slates, probably of Silurian age, but so metamorphosed as not to be referable to any subdivision of that system." Whitney reported only two great veins, or beds, extending through the township. He said that the veins were not true fissure veins, but were to be understood as "contemporaneous" or "segregated" veins. The two veins described proved to be the middle and western veins. The third, or eastern, vein, on which the Polk, Mary's, and Callaway mines were opened, was soon afterwards examined and found to be equally as rich as the other two.

Whitney said that the veins, or lodes, consisted of gossan, black copper, and the undecomposed deposits, flanked on each side with mica slate. And "the depth to which decomposition has extended is variable, as it is identical with the level which water is found." The water which ran from the mine excavations was strongly impregnated with copper. The iron tools of the workmen, when allowed to remain in contact with the water, would become coated with metallic copper. The black ore was being mined at the time of Whitney's visit in 1853. The yield was 15 per cent to 25 per cent copper. He estimated that "6,300 tons of this ore should be available per mile in length, worth, at present prices, $750,000.00." The ore was easily mined. Little or no blasting was required. Shafts sunk in the gossan for purposes of ventilation needed no timber supports. The black ore could be taken out with the pick and shovel, and was "so wide that several men could work abreast in the levels driven on it."

A distinguished and experienced geologist and mining engineer of London, England, named Bray, spent about two months at Ducktown in 1854 examining and exploring the district. He estimated that the mines here could produce at least 72,000 tons of ore annually. This, he said, would produce 14,400 tons of pure copper a year valued at $600 a ton. The total value produced would therefore approximate $8,700,000. This, less a "cut" of $1,700,000, would leave an estimated net profit of $7,000,000.

In the winter of 1854-55 the Ducktown district was visited by another English geologist, D. T. Ansted, M. P., F.R.S. His report dealt principally with the Tennessee, Hiwassee, Isabella, and Polk County properties. He said, "The country consists of altered talcose and chloritic schists, probably of Silurian date, alternating with hard micaceous grits and with other rocks distinctly crystalline of a poryphritic character." Ansted did not believe, as some did, that the black copper below the gossan and above the hard mundicy veinstone was the result of nature's process of leaching, but "...was a different and subsequent operation to that of segregating the veinstone itself."

PREPARATIONS FOR MINING 55

Another noted geologist, M. Tuomey, state geologist of Alabama, visited Ducktown, probably in the year 1854. Tuomey said: "The mines are situated at the junction of the Silurian and metamorphic rocks—or as Mr. Whitney suggests, the cupriferous slates may be altered Silurian strata." "The upper portion of the bed is composed of a porous, amorphous mass of red and brown oxyd of iron, the gossan of the Cornish miners, Iron Hat of the Germans, which is the residue of the ore after the copper has been dissolved out. Next is the bluish black altered sulphuret. The lower portion is of arsenical iron." Tuomey asked, "Now what is below the arsenical iron?"

All of the experimental shafts viewed by Tuomey were still in the arsenical iron portion and he prophesied that "should this arsenical iron terminate, at a moderate depth, then indeed may Tennessee boast of such mines as are not found in the history of mining operations."

Richard O. Currey visited Ducktown in 1854. Fourteen mines had been opened at that time, all yielding as he said, great profits, since they produced nearly one thousand tons of ore monthly at a value of about one hundred thousand dollars. He said further that the mines here were regarded as the most valuable property in the state and that "an idea of their value may be presumed when it is stated that one mine is now in litigation in the United States Court at Knoxville, and its value estimated at two or three millions of dollars." Currey gave an analysis of the ores taken from several of the mines, part of which is given in the following table:

MINE	KIND OF ORE	PER CENT COPPER
Culchote	Green Carbonate	21.5
Cherokee	Red Oxide	40.0
Polk County	Black Oxide	29.5
Isabella	Black Oxide	26.5
Hancock (London)	Red Oxide	44.0
East Tennessee	Black Oxide	20.5
Eureka	Black Oxide	24.0

Certainly there was reason for optimism on the part of those who had invested in Ducktown properties after reading the geological reports on the district.

Immediately following the resumption of mining activity at Ducktown after the close of the Civil War, the American Bureau of Mines made an extensive reconnaissance of the properties of the Union Consolidated Mining Company at Ducktown. Two members of the Bureau, Dr. Alexander H. Tripple and Dr. H. Credner, were charged with the personal reconnaissance and field work. This report, published in 1866, was the most complete report made on the district during the period following the war. Nevertheless, as enough has already been said on the geology of Ducktown as it was known at that time, it will not be necessary for the purposes of this volume to quote from the Bureau's report.

The fourth, but by no means the least important, phase of preparations incident to successful mining at Ducktown was that of developing the road system so that the ores could be moved out to a railhead and the necessary supplies and materials received back at the mines. When miners first appraised the road situation at Ducktown in 1848, they found three outlets—to Ellijay, to Dahlonega, and to Murphy. Virtually impassable in winter, these roads were but little better in summer for heavily loaded wagons. The Murphy and Dahlonega roads were useless in any case because they led to no railroad within hauling distance of the mines. Dalton, Georgia, the nearest railroad point at the time, was seventy miles distant from Ducktown, and could be reached only through the mountains by way of Ellijay. Ducktown was, therefore, unquestionably doomed to remain undeveloped so long as seventy miles of mountainous roads separated the district from the nearest railroad. That was the road situation at the beginning of 1850.

At that time the East Tennessee and Georgia Railroad from Dalton to Cleveland, Tennessee, was under construction and seemed to be nearing completion. Perhaps this led to an act that was passed by the Tennessee Legislature on February 5, 1850, authorizing Euclid Waterhouse to open a road from a point near the house of Elisha Dodson in Polk County to intersect with the Georgia road at some point between William Mills's house and the copper mines. William Mills, Elisha Dodson, and Abraham Lillard were named as commissioners to select the route and to see that the road was operated according to law. While it was not possible for the writer to determine the exact route selected for Waterhouse's proposed road, it is probable that it was along the banks of the Ocoee River where the copper road was later constructed by John Caldwell. It was the latter road through the Ocoee Gorge, completed in 1853, that assured development of the Ducktown mines. The East Tennessee and Georgia Railroad had in the meantime been built to Cleveland, and this combination of transportation systems placed the mines within forty miles of a shipping point. Caldwell's own story of the building of the road was related in his letter, previously quoted.

The next problem after the road was completed to Dalton was its maintenance. Some means of keeping up the repairs and bearing the burden of costs had to be devised. A company was organized for this purpose under the name and title of Ocoee Turnpike and Plank Road Company, and a charter of incorporation was secured on February 1, 1854. The incorporators were S. F. Tracy, A. E. Douglass, W. Delano, L. W. Gilbert, John Stanton, John Caldwell, J. Sloan, T. H. Callaway, D. C. Keener, S. Congdon, C. A. Proctor, and associates. The charter was for ninety-nine years, and the capitalization was $50,000.

Previous to completion of the road, it was economically feasible to ship only the richest of the black ores near the surface. The freight on a ton of this ore to Savannah, Georgia, was $24.50. Of this amount, $15.00 was taken up in the wagon haul from Ducktown to Dalton. And as the road to Dalton was passable only in the summer months, the copper industry was virtually reduced to a seasonal one.

No attempt had been made to develop the mines below the line of decomposition before the opening of the road to Cleveland. The new road made it possible to work the mines on a scale hitherto deemed financially impracticable. The distance to a railroad was shortened to forty miles, the transportation cost by wagon was reduced by about one-third, and shipments could be made the year round.

Ducktown's road system had been completed by the year 1855. North Carolina's Western Turnpike had in the meantime been diverted to the Tennessee line at Ducktown, and Murphy, Morganton, Ellijay, Benton, and Cleveland could now be reached from the copper mines. Although these roads were roads in much the same sense that log huts with dirt floors are dwellings, they remained practically in their original state of development for nearly three-quarters of a century.

Although Currey designated Weaver's attempts at mining in 1847 as marking the beginning of the mining industry at Ducktown, this venture did as little to permanently inaugurate the industry as did the small amount of work done in the trench excavations of 1843. It was not until seven years later that the first permanent mine, the Hiwassee, was opened. But by 1854 fourteen mines were ready to flood the markets of the world with Tennessee copper.

CHAPTER 9

FIRST DECADE OF MINING

SPECULATIONS IN MINING PROPERTIES, FORMATION OF COMPANIES, examination of the district by competent geologists, improving transportation facilities, and the actual opening of the different mines were contemporaneous events, all reaching their highest state of activity between the years 1850 and 1854. These preparations all had one objective in view—mining, the story of which can best be approached through discussion of the activities of the individual companies.

The Hiwassee Mine was opened by Thomas H. Callaway in August, 1850. It is to be doubted, however, that much ore was mined by Callaway. It seems likely that the work done by him was in the nature of explorations for the purpose of offering the property for sale rather than for the uncertainty of deriving profits from mining. Callaway and his associates had experienced difficulty in disposing of the mine. Weaver, the German who leased it in 1847, had deserted the district for more promising fields. Later, in 1849, the property was sold to the English agent, Warne, but no attempt was made at the time to open the mine. As a matter of fact Currey said that the result of Warne's purchase was the holding up for some two years of any further attempts at opening the mines at Ducktown.

The Warne mortgage which Callaway and his associates had been holding, probably with a great deal of anxiety, was assigned to the newly organized Hiwassee Mining Company in June, 1852. This company began mining operations at once at or near the scene of Lemmon's discovery, where Weaver had later made his abbreviated attempt at mining. The Hiwassee company was composed principally of northern capitalists who had invested their money at Ducktown in good faith. Samuel F. Tracy of New York was president of the company and was also president of the Sewanee Mining Company located near the present Tracy City, Tennessee.

FIRST DECADE OF MINING

The success of the Hiwassee Mining Company in its second year was fully detailed in the company's Second Annual Report, covering the period April, 1853, to May 1, 1854. As the report furnishes much information in condensed form that is not otherwise available on the early history of mining at Ducktown, it is reproduced here at some length:

RECEIPTS

Balance in the Treasury, per statement 1853,	$12,888.76
Sales of Ore, $404-\frac{1804}{2352}$ tons,	40,492.42
Received on account ore sold,	4,000.00
Drafts of the Gen. Agent, (Chg'd. in Expenditures)	15,593.45
Total,	$72,974.63

EXPENDITURES

Buildings—captain's house, boarding house, mill, cabins, ore sheds, stables, etc.	$1,895.60
Mules, oxen, horses, wagons, saddles, etc.	8,983.28
Machinery, grist-mill stores, castings for sawmill, crusher, etc.	610.37
Ocoee road, expended during year	5,078.67
First Annual Report, Prof. Leslie's Charge, etc.	983.94
Subscription for a church at Ducktown	100.00
Traveling expenses, and obtaining amendment to charter	615.54
Taxes, stationery, postages, advertising, assaying, cordage, charcoal, etc.	630.78
Iron & Steel, and track in mine	1,478.65
Candles, used and on hand	455.56
Powder & fuse, used and on hand	243.26
Lumber	1,002.37
Insurance on ore from Savannah	467.25
Carriage of materials and supplies	810.40
Transportation of ore—	
675 + tons gross by wagon to Dalton	12,109.04
357 + " " " " " Ocoee	3,267.64
R.R. freight and expenses on 2639 boxes and 194 bags	7,846.85
Freight from Savannah on 2439 boxes and 194 bags	1,358.60
Agency and commission, receiving and forwarding at Savannah	358.64

Labor, including mining captain's salary	6,382.41
Salaries for the year ending 1st May	1,626.75
Stable account	948.14
Teamster's suspense account	73.45
Interest	229.87
	$57,557.06
Balance on hand, cash, and bills receivable	15,417.57
Total	$72,974.63

ASSETS

Real Estate & Mining Property, at cost	$220,000.00
Buildings, at cost	2,874.34
Machinery, " "	655.37
Ocoee Road, expended by this Company	7,367.07
Horses, mules, oxen, wagons, etc.	10,538.75
Cash and bills receivable	15,417.57
2427 boxes of ore sold, now in Savannah and enroute from mine, will give, free of further carriage	41,500.00
To which may be added 150 tons of ore in store at mine, which will give, free of carriage	10,500.00
Total Assets	$308,853.10

LIABILITIES

Capital Stock, 60,000 shares at $4.00 paid in,	$240,000.00
Drafts of the General Agent, not matured, and due sundry individuals	15,593.45
Total Liabilities	$255,593.45
Showing a surplus of	53,259.65
Total	$308,853.10

The mine captain, John Harris, from the Lake Superior district, had been employed since June, 1853. In his report he stated that development work had been carried on at the Tracy, Green, and Delano shafts, all whim shafts, and that a new engine shaft was being sunk. Ore amounting to 1,100 tons had been taken out, and an additional 3,500 to 4,000 tons had been exposed to view. He said: "I can guarantee to take out 300 tons per month for the ensuing year, and continue all the necessary drivages, shafts, and explorations, provided I can procure 13 more good miners, not having had but 3 at any period." A contingent of fifty Cornish miners was enroute to Ducktown in July, 1854. No doubt their arrival relieved the acute shortage of good miners referred to by the mine captain.

The dividends promised the stockholders of the company had not materialized. The grade of ore had proved to be much lower than anticipated, and the general financial distress had added to the burdens of the company. Difficulties were many and varied, for "... ore shipments during November 1854 and February and March 1855 were small, and barely sufficient to meet expenses. This was for no lack of ore, but the other companies paid the ore haulers a higher rate than had been established, and the Hiwassee company would not join in this disastrous competition."

The erection of reduction plants for treating the ores soon became a necessity for the companies operating at Ducktown. The layers of black ores lying near the surface were soon stripped and the grade of copper dropped sharply as the red ores lower down were reached. It was one thing to pay transportation charges on ores assaying 40 per cent to 60 per cent copper, and quite another to pay the same charges on ores assaying 10 per cent to 20 per cent copper. The grade of the Hiwassee ores had become so low that the company, following the lead of the Tennessee and Eureka companies, erected smelting works at the junction of Burra Burra Branch and Potato Creek in 1856. The Hiwassee smelters were described as follows by Eugene Gaussoin: "On the Hiwassee smelter property the water [of Potato Creek] flows three feet deep through a race four feet wide, running first, at an old saw mill, a wheel of twenty feet diameter and four feet wide, used today for the working of a stamping mill of 8 heads, and then below a second wheel of 17 feet diameter running the blast machine adapted to two reverberatory and one blast furnaces. Besides a large English calcining furnace, large dressing, wood, charcoal, and roasting-sheds are erected there...." The cost of this plant was $12,131. The capacity of the four furnaces was four hundred tons of ore a month.

The Hiwassee Mining Company operated continuously from 1852 until 1859. As early as 1854 the company began considering plans for deep workings after the supply of black ores was exhausted. Several shafts were sunk on the property, the deepest of which was 352 feet. In addition to the smelting works, the Hiwassee company erected seventy-four buildings of both log and frame construction, installed a steam hoisting engine, assisted in the improvement of the Ocoee turnpike, made donations to the church at Hiwassee Town, and faithfully published its financial condition for each of the seven years of its existence. The Hiwassee stock was listed on the New York Stock Board and was quoted variously at about five, although the company never paid a dividend. Two calls for funds were made on the stockholders in 1859, one at fifty cents and one at ten cents on each share owned. The receipts for seven years totaled $330,011.59, which was at an average value of $48.55 a ton on 6,797 tons of ore mined.

In 1860 the Hiwassee Mining Company properties were purchased by a newly organized company, the Burra Burra Copper Company. The sale of the Hiwassee company marked the passing of one of the most progressive companies that operated during the first decade of copper mining at Ducktown. A brick chimney, marking the site of the first engine-shaft in the Basin, still stands on a hill near the highway intersection just south of the town of Ducktown. The chimney was erected by the Hiwassee Mining Company before the Civil War.

Opened by J. V. Symons in October, 1850, under very much the same circumstances and for the same purposes as the Hiwassee Mine, the Cocheco Mine never figured prominently in the mining annals of Ducktown. The Cocheco adjoined the Hiwassee Mine on the east, situated on the same ore body. Eugene Gaussoin was superintendent of both the Cocheco Mining Company and the Hiwassee Mining Company, and from his report on the district in 1860, it seems that the small amount of ore mined at Cocheco was smelted at the Hiwassee furnaces. Symons was actively engaged in land speculation at Ducktown during the early fifties, and as a result the Cocheco mine was only nominally opened until acquired by mining interests over a year later. The Cocheco property was included in the Burra Burra Copper Company purchase of 1860.

The Tennessee Mine (known now as the "Old Tennessee" or the "School Property" Mine) was opened by John Caldwell in October, 1851. This was the mine about which Caldwell made his speech to citizens of the district, which resulted in an act by the Legislature authorizing the school commissioners to lease the property for mining purpose. The Tennessee Mining Company, controlled by the Congdon interests of New York, took over and began working the mine in 1852. Previous to the formation of this company the Congdons had been actively engaged in exploration work at Ducktown under the name of Congdon Mining Company. Charles and Samuel Congdon were connected with the mining industry here for several years afterwards. Samuel Congdon was superintendent of the Tennessee Mining Company.

The potential source of funds for school purposes which this mine seemed to offer did not materialize. Though the school section property was mined, an extensive lawsuit was being carried on at the same time over the ownership of the land. On May 21, 1850, the township school commissioners, B. C. Duggar, Samuel Denton, and James Lemmon, leased section 16 to John Caldwell and J. V. Symons for a period of ninety-nine years. About the same time another group, composed of Thomas H. Callaway, Euclid Waterhouse, Samuel M. Johnson, John B. Tipton, and T. C. Lyon, described as celebrated land speculators, attempted to get control of the property under the legislative acts of 1844 and 1846 authorizing the sale of school lands. Their efforts were successful and the circuit court clerk sold the section at public auction on July 25, 1850. The purchase price paid by the group was $1,770. Thus the property had the distinction of being both leased and sold at the same time. Another incongruity in the matter was that the terms of the sale included a provision that the mineral interests were reserved to Caldwell and Symons, the lessees.

In the meantime, an injunction had been obtained by Caldwell and Symons to prevent the sale which was completed in spite of their action. Following the sale, however, bills and cross-bills were immediately filed by the disputants. While these were pending, Samuel Congdon arrived in the district from New York, learned the status of the titles, and thereupon bought both sets of claims for his principals, Charles Congdon and associates. $5,000 was theoretically paid for the lease, and about $17,000 or $18,000 for the title by purchase. Congdon reasoned that at least one of the parties had a valid claim to the property, and by purchasing both he would be in indisputable possession of it.

The Tennessee Mining Company was organized to work the sixteenth section, and the company agreed, under the terms of the lease, to pay to the school commissioners 7 per cent of the net profits. A small amount was paid in the years 1853 and 1854. After that the company's system of bookkeeping showed, erroneously it was later claimed, that no profits were realized.

On February 13, 1856, John Goodman and Yancey S. Bledsoe, having been elected school commissioners, filed an injunction against the Tennessee Mining Company and the individuals involved in the original transactions for the purpose of regaining possession of the property and collecting back rents. The bill charged that the lease was in contravention of an act of Congress passed February 15, 1843, the second section of which provided that the school lands should be leased for not more than four years, whereas the lease to Caldwell and Symons had been made for a period of ninety-nine years. The bill charged also that the sale was invalid because it had been made while the property was under lease and had been obtained by fraud.

The first decision in the case was made by the chancery court in favor of the defendants in August, 1858. After this decision the school commissioners appealed to the state supreme court at Knoxville, where, on October 21, 1858, the case was decided in favor of the commissioners on all points. The mining company and co-defendants then carried the case by writ of error to the Supreme Court of the United States. No decision was handed down at Washington until December, 1862, at which time the case was rejected because of lack of jurisdiction. The war prevented final disposition of the embattled case until December, 1865, when the decree of the state supreme court at Knoxville was put on the records. This resulted in the ownership of the school property being returned to the citizens of the Fourth Fractional Township, where it has since remained.

In commenting on the lawsuit, Captain J. E. Raht said that R. M. Edwards, attorney for the school commissioners, was awarded a fee of $20,000 by the court. Captain Raht's opinion was that if the courts allowed such fees to lawyers there would be no more "lawing" over the property.

For several years while the lawsuit was in progress work was being carried on at the Tennessee Mine by the Tennessee Mining Company. By the middle of the year 1854 there had been produced approximately 2,460 tons of ore, averaging 27.5 per cent copper. The development work consisted of about four hundred feet in shafts and one hundred feet in drifts. Several shafts, some of them of less than one hundred feet in depth, were opened on the rich ore body. The shafts extended only through to the hard quartzy veinstone that underlay the black ores. Until furnaces were erected it was not profitable, even with Caldwell's new road open, to produce ores assaying less than 20 per cent copper.

The Tennessee interests erected the first furnaces in the Ducktown district. Two furnaces were built on the banks of Potato Creek in 1854. The smelting works were controlled by the Tennessee Smelting Company, a Congdon corporation. The purpose of the company was to erect furnaces to treat not only the ores from the Tennessee Mine, but the ores produced by the other companies in the district. However, the operation of the two Tennessee furnaces proved a failure, either because of improper construction or lack of competent operators. This led the Eureka Mining Company to construct furnaces of its own in the following year, and the success of these furnaces was responsible for the Tennessee furnaces again being put in operation, this time with better results, in 1856.

The lawsuit over ownership of the school section forced the Tennessee Mining Company and the Tennessee Smelting Company to discontinue operations in May, 1858. The total production of ore at the mine from the time it was opened in 1851 until May, 1858, was approximately five thousand tons. From November, 1856, to April, 1858, a total of 1,780,261 pounds of copper was shipped from it.

For several years the activities around the Tennessee Mine rivaled those at nearby Hiwassee Town. The Copper Mines post office was located there from 1854 until the office was discontinued in 1859. There was also a commissary at the mine, as well as a large group of company dwellings and a boarding house. An inventory of the buildings and other improvements at the Tennessee Mine in 1857 showed:

> 3 First Class Dwelling Houses
> 39 Dwelling Houses for Laborers
> 1 Store, with Dwelling attached
> 2 Lumber Houses
> 1 Blacksmith Shop
> 1 Assay Office
> 3 Ore Sheds
> 2 Stables—Stalls for Mules, and Corn Cribs
> 4 Horse Whims and a Pump Whim
> 1 Water Wheel, etc., etc.

It was the intention of the Union Consolidated Mining Company of Tennessee to include the Tennessee Mine in its list of holdings when the company was organized in 1858, but pending litigation over the mine prevented this. The Union Consolidated utilized the Tennessee furnaces, but other than this the mine remained idle until after the Civil War.

As the word "whim" appears frequently in the following pages, what a whim was and the function it fulfilled will be explained.

In the early stages of mining at Ducktown the black ore, which could be removed with but little expense and effort, was carried from the mines on ladders. Windlasses were used when the shafts became too deep for ladders, and as the mines increased in depth the whim came into use. The whim was a mechanical device which hoisted the ore from the mine. A horse was connected with an upright drum situated near the shaft, around which the hoisting rope was wound as the animal walked in a circle. The ore bucket was lowered into the mine when the horse reversed his direction. Horses used in whim service often became highly trained; starting, stopping, reversing, and increasing their speed at given signals. With the exception of one or two steam engines installed in the late fifties, the whim was the most efficient method of hoisting at Ducktown prior to the Civil War. Whims continued to be used here to some extent until 1878. Mine pumps, too, were frequently operated by whims.

The Polk County Mine, opened in November, 1852, by John Caldwell, was the fourth mine opened at Ducktown. So strong were the indications of immense ore deposits on the hill on which this mine was located that it was named Copper Hill. At the time of the opening of the mine the property was owned jointly by John Caldwell, A. H. Keith, and the heirs of Thomas W. Mastin. Under this ownership it was worked to some extent until 1854. On April 6 of that year the mine was sold to the Polk County Copper Company, which had been chartered some two months earlier. Work was continued until 1856, when a lawsuit involving the right of the Mastin heirs to dispose of their equity in the property forced a suspension of operations. J. E. Raht served as mine captain during the first years of mining at the Polk County Mine. When the mine was closed in 1856, two thousand tons of ore assaying an average of 24 per cent copper, and two hundred tons of ore assaying an average of 18.5 per cent copper, had been produced. Work was not resumed at the mine until 1859 when the Polk County Copper Company was reorganized.

Much of the first copper-bearing material shipped from the Polk County Mine was scooped up from large shallow pits. It was possible to do this at several of the other mines in the district, but it seems that the decomposed deposits on Copper Hill were unusually plentiful. The open-pit method of copper mining, however, was never practiced at Ducktown other than in the very early stages of work at some of the mines when cuts and pits were preliminaries to deep shafts.

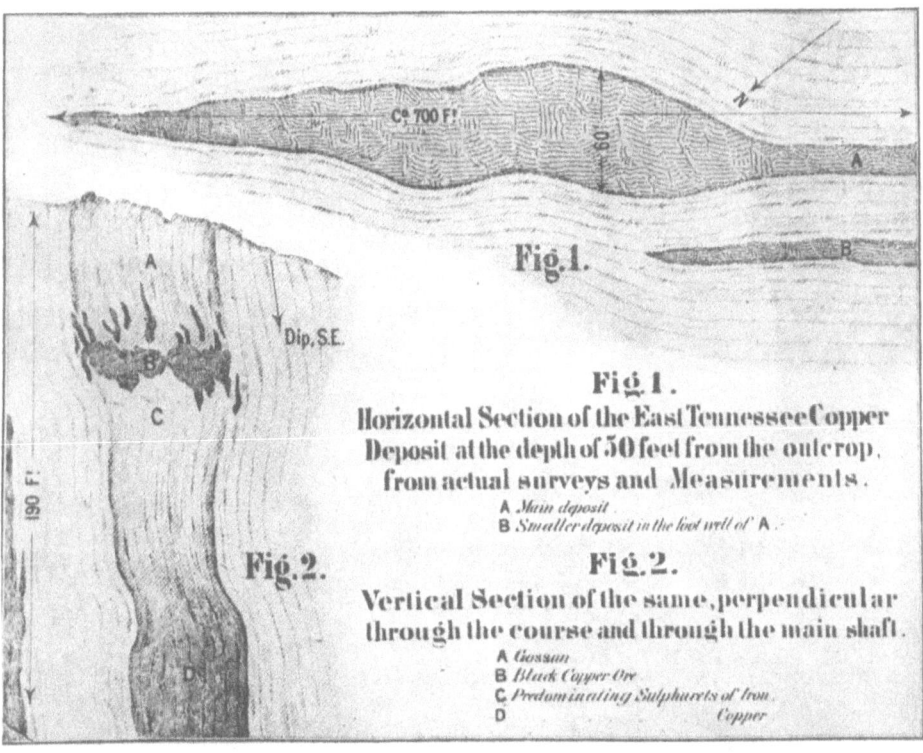

On this and the following page are diagrammatic representations of three original ore formations of the Ducktown district, upon which were located the East Tennessee, Isabella, Mary's, and Polk County mines. The plates answer Tuomey's question, "Now what is below the arsenical iron?"

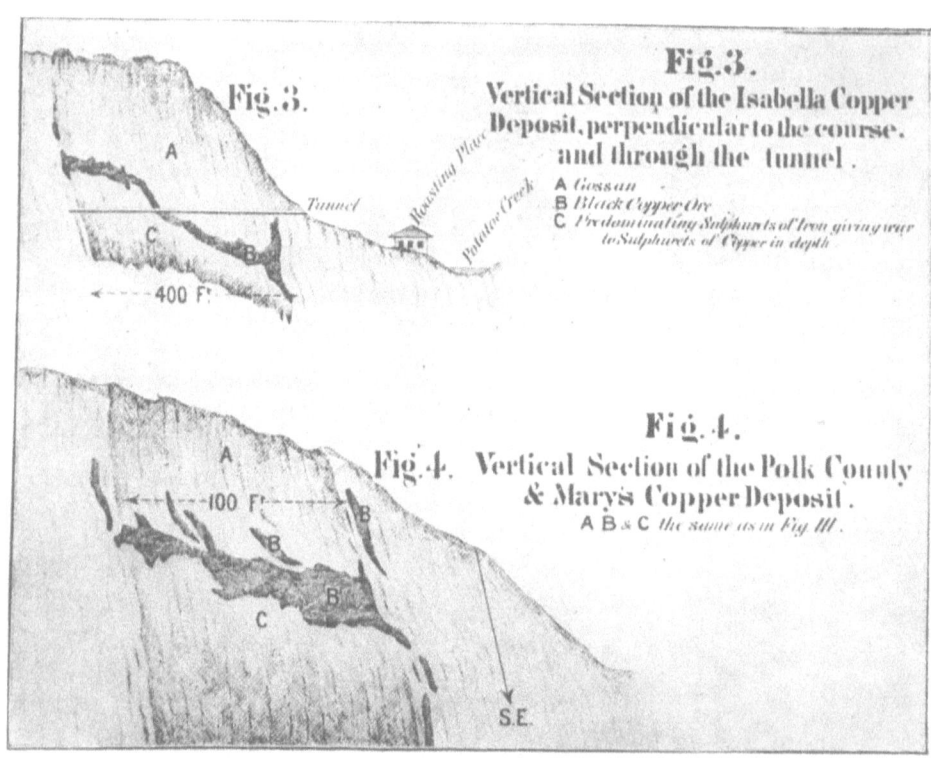

Diagrammatic representation of the ore formations upon which were located three of Ducktown's prominent mines, the Isabella, Mary's, and Polk County.

The Cherokee Mine, lying between the Tennessee Mine and the Ocoee River, was opened in December, 1852, by Samuel Congdon. It was probably the first mine examined by one of the many noted geologists who visited the district following the year 1852. The Cherokee Mining Company was incorporated on January 26, 1854, and was controlled by the Congdon interests. The production up to 1860 probably did not exceed 1,000 to 1,200 tons of copper ore and the black ore was almost exhausted. The mine was purchased by the Union Consolidated Mining Company in 1858. At the mine were ". . . 5 dwelling houses, 1 lumber house, 1 blacksmith shop, 1 ore shed, 1 sawmill, 2 horse whims, etc."

Located on Potato Creek about a mile and a half above the Tennessee Mine, the Eureka Mine was opened in April, 1853, by John M. Dow. To work the property a group of northern capitalists headed by Dow secured a charter under the title of the Eureka Mining Company on January 18, 1854. The mine was not fully acquired by the company until October, 1855, and then not before the United States Circuit Court at Knoxville had declared null and void a series of previous transactions involving the property between Dow and John Stanton and the mining company. The result of the lawsuit was the return to the omnipresent Thomas H. Callaway and Euclid Waterhouse of the ownership of the mine, after which the sale to the Eureka Mining Company was duly made. The litigation had interrupted the work of opening the mine, but as lawsuits seemed to be an accepted prerequisite of mining at Ducktown at the time, the interruption was of short duration.

Freed of legal restraint, the Eureka company promptly began preparations for mining in an orderly manner. It had an excellent organization. Josiah H. Macy was president of the company, T. J. Esterbrook was general agent, Captain Trenewith was in charge of the mines, and Alexander H. Tripple was superintendent of the smelting works. The Eureka was one of the better known of the Ducktown companies. Its stock was traded on the New York Stock Board and much of its production was sold in England.

Almost from the beginning the Eureka ore proved to be unusually low in copper. This led to the erection of smelting works, consisting of a furnace and a calciner, in the latter part of 1855. In April, 1856, another furnace was erected, and in the latter part of the year the works were enlarged again by the addition of two more furnaces and another calciner. The furnaces were of the Welsh, or Swansea, pattern, and embodied the new principle of "step grates" with the so-called "reserved combustion." The inimitable Tripple, co-author of the American Bureau of Mines Report in 1866, previously referred to, built the furnaces, and he had this to say about it: "You cannot conceive what an effort it is to erect a copper smelting establishment in a perfect wilderness, and to make all the fire brick, after having hunted up the materials in all directions, but at last I have succeeded in spite of all prejudices and opposition." Tripple failed to reveal the source of his opposition. However, as he was a frequent contributor to the pages of the mining press of his day, it could have been that he was merely giving his readers some spectacular news from a remote region.

Alexander H. Tripple resided at Ducktown from June, 1855, until 1861. In addition to the Eureka furnaces, he also erected the Polk County and Burra Burra smelting works prior to the war. After leaving Ducktown in 1861 he resided at Cleveland, Tennessee, where he was probably engaged at the copper rolling mill. He moved to Pennsylvania in 1863. Tripple was born in Switzerland in 1826, was reared there and in Germany, and came to the United States in 1848.

The Eureka company was beset by many difficulties. The price of copper suffered a sharp decline during the panic of 1857. The winter of 1857-58 was said to have been the wettest at Ducktown in fifteen years. The roads were impassable, and cordwood was scarce and too wet for effective furnace work. Wages were reduced as a measure of economy, but a strike promptly followed. Despite these obstacles the company continued to operate and to make necessary improvements at its works. Charcoal fuel began to be used at the Eureka furnaces in 1858. This relieved somewhat the wood problem with regard to both its scarcity and its dampness. Each furnace consumed three hundred bushels of charcoal daily, which was equal to eight cords of wood a day, only one-third of the amount of wood that had been used before changing to charcoal.

Besides the mines and furnaces, the Eureka property displayed many other improvements. There was a sawmill at the mines, operated by a large water wheel that developed a capacity of twelve horsepower. The main race to the large under-shot wheel was carried on a trestle six hundred feet long and twenty-six feet high. A tramtrack led from the sawmill to the smelters, situated on the west side of what is now Burra Burra Branch. There were also carpenter and blacksmith shops, roast sheds, sheds for materials and woods, and a large drying kiln. Tripple's brickyard was of surprising proportions. He reported the manufacture of five hundred thousand red bricks and fifty thousand fire bricks for the year ending March 31, 1857. A crusher and press had been installed which, Tripple said, would reduce the number of northern bricks required.

Operations were continued at the Eureka Mine until about 1860. The total ore produced there up to that time probably did not exceed four thousand tons. During the later years of operations the ore averaged but 7 per cent to 8 per cent copper. The production of fine copper in 1857 was 638,657 pounds. A dividend of $25,000, the only one declared by the Eureka Mining Company, was paid in 1857. The company finally became insolvent and in May, 1861, its affairs were turned over to three trustees, Josiah H. Macy, C. E. Lamson, and W. C. Sturges.

Opened in June, 1853, by John Tonkin, the East Tennessee Mine was presumably operated for several years by the East Tennessee Mining and Smelting Company. It is not known just how extensively the mine was worked during this period, but the production probably did not exceed three or four thousand tons. The East Tennessee property was included in the mines purchased by the Union Consolidated Mining Company in 1858. The improvements at the mine were meager, there being only "... 1 good house, 4 common houses, 1 horse whim, and shops, sheds, etc."

It was at the East Tennessee Mine that John Tonkin began his long period of service in the Ducktown district. Born in England in 1814, Tonkin began his mining career at the age of fourteen. Later he came to the United States and worked at mines in Pennsylvania and in the Lake Superior region before coming to Ducktown in 1853. When the Union Consolidated Mining Company took over the East Tennessee Mine in 1858, Tonkin was retained as mine captain. He remained at the mines during the years of the Civil War and protected as best he could the properties of the company. He later described this as being a very hazardous and dangerous undertaking.

The date of the opening of the Isabella Mine, as given by J. M. Safford, was July, 1853. On April 13, 1854, Francis Oram, the mine captain, wrote: "It will be just 8 months, the 22nd of this month, since the first pick was stuck in the ground on this mine, and within that time we have driven 285 feet of levels, 350 feet of open cut, have sunk 87 feet of shafts—No. 1, 57 feet and No. 2,

30 feet,—have built ore floors, dressing house 30' x 60', smith shop, boarding house, dwelling house, etc." This mine was opened by C. A. Proctor. Proctor was a civil engineer, and also served for a time as assayist for the state of Tennessee. His name appeared in the charters of incorporation of several of the Ducktown companies.

The Isabella Copper Company received its charter on January 26, 1854. But previous to this the company had been operating for some time under the name of the Potomac Copper Company. When the company was incorporated in Tennessee the stock of the Isabella company was transferred to holders of Potomac stock. Reference to the transfer of the stock was made in *The United States Mining Journal* of January 10, 1854: "The Tennessee mines are making headway. Captain Oram of the Potomac Mines, in Polk County, Tennessee, has just arrived in town [New York], and reports that the 'Isabella Mine,' whose stock goes to the holders of Potomac stock, is now opened, and that he can turn out at least 3,000 tons of ore from that mine during the next twelve months.... The Potomac company have also the Davis Mine, which joins the Isabella. The Directors of the mine express the belief that the Isabella will soon pay $5.00 to $7½ per share dividend every year." This belief was never realized; a dividend in any amount was never earned. The directors of the company in 1854 were L. W. Gilbert, president; Henry Adams, secretary-treasurer; and Isaac Otis, Alexander Hamilton, William Hickok, and John Stanton. The Davis Copper Company, controlled by the Isabella Copper Company, was incorporated on February 13, 1854.

The Isabella ore supply was abundant, but like the Eureka it early tended to decrease in copper content. Ovens and roast sheds for eliminating the sulphur from the ores were erected in 1854, and the company presumably utilized the Tennessee smelting works for the further reduction of its ores. The Isabella was referred to as the queen of the Polk County, Tennessee, mines in ore production. Much of the product of this mine was sold in England. The stock of the Isabella Copper Company was listed on the New York Stock Board. Its prevailing price ran about two. There were no complete records of ore mined at the Isabella up to the time of the Civil War, but the output was probably about ten thousand tons.

The Isabella property was taken over by the Union Consolidated Mining Company in 1858. The surface improvements included "28 dwelling houses, 2 stores, 1 office, 1 school house, 2 ore sheds, 1 blacksmith shop, 1 carpenter shop, 1 horse whim, barn, stables, sheds, 1 waterwheel, etc., etc."

A legend concerning the origin of the name of the Isabella Mine persists. It is told that one of the officials of the early Isabella company had a wife named Isabella. So completely did she dominate her cowering spouse that he never made a decision without first consulting his belligerent oracle. The official's constant refusal to decide definitely upon any question until he could "speak to Isabella about it" led to his associates naming the mine in her honor. It seems quite likely, however, that the story of the mine's being named after Isabella, the agreeable wife of Elias Davis, is the more acceptable one. Elias was a son of John Davis, one of the first settlers at Ducktown.

The 160 acres comprising what was later to be known as the London Mine was granted to William Hancock in 1842. For a time the property was referred to as the Hancock Mine, and the Hancock Mining Company presumably did some preliminary work on the premises immediately preceding the actual opening of the mine. Captain J. R. Pill opened the mine in September, 1853, and the next year the New York and London Mining Company was incorporated and secured possession of the property. Title to the mine passed from Hancock to John M. Dow in 1852. Dow transferred the title to George Wood, and in 1854 Warren Delano, Jr., acting as agent for the New York and London Mining Company, purchased the property from Wood for $85,000. The New York and London Mining Company was English-owned with George T. Braine of London as the principal owner.

Contrary to general belief, the English played but a small part in the early history of mining at Ducktown. The agent Warne who purchased the Hiwassee property in 1849 represented English capitalists, but the mine was soon afterward acquired by the Hiwassee Mining Company, an American-owned corporation. The only full-fledged attempt by the English during the first period of activity at Ducktown was at the London Mine. Unlike some of the other companies that operated at Ducktown prior to the Civil War, the New York and London Mining Company was not slow to realize that the Ducktown venture would be a costly one and that the longer the operations were continued the costlier it would become. Honest efforts, however, were made to work the London Mine. The company went to the expense of sending miners and mechanics from Cornwall to make sure of the mine's proper development.

It might be pertinent to state here that the Cornish miner enjoyed a monopolistic position in the mining industry at the time Ducktown was first becoming known. One reason for this was that it required mines in which to develop miners. Consequently when mines were opened in remote regions where but few of the natives knew the rudiments of the trade, it was necessary to secure, usually from Cornwall, experienced workers. There was not, however, a unanimous respect for the loyalty and efficiency of the Cornishmen. A contributor to the *Mining Magazine* of 1853 said: "An impression has taken deep root in the minds of the American people, that to secure success in a mining enterprise it is essential that a Cornish miner be hired to take charge of the mine, and all the rules and traditions be observed, connected with Cornwall and Cornish mines, thereby securing to the miner as much pay and as little labor as possible, and to the proprietors, or stockholders the smallest possible results; instead of employing Americans, or Irish laborers, and instructing them in the art of mining...."

Not only were men sent to Ducktown by the New York and London Mining Company, but in addition the company shipped a large Cornish engine to the London Mine from England. Like the Cornish miner, the Cornish stationary engine was supreme in its field. It was said that "a good Cornish engine, by the consumption of $1\frac{1}{2}$ pounds of coal, will perform as much labor as an able-bodied man working eight hours; five tons of coal, therefore, would evolve as much power as that of a man at work eight hours every day for twenty years. This is certainly a great triumph for science and mechanicism...." When the engine destined for the London Mine arrived at Cleveland, it proved to be too large to haul to Ducktown over the narrow river road. This was a fair example of the lack of information which the London officials seemed to possess of conditions at their mine in far-off Tennessee. The production of the New York and London Mining Company was 1,680 tons of ore after a year of discouraging operations.

In May, 1859, the Baltimore Copper Smelting Company took over the London Mine to satisfy a debt of $12,277.60 owed the company by George T. Braine. A judgment was secured against Braine, who was the equitable owner of the mine, and against Warren Delano, in whom the legal title was vested. The sale of the property took place at Benton in August, 1860, at which time the Baltimore Copper Smelting Company became the purchaser. Braine and Delano emerged from the sale with a certain equity of redemption in a portion of the property, the equity being valued at nearly eight thousand dollars. The equity was purchased by J. E. Raht, Samuel T. Waters, and James Giddings in August, 1861. The following November Raht purchased Waters' interest, and soon thereafter Giddings jeopardized his interest in the property by failing to comply with the agreement entered into by himself, Raht, and Waters. In the meantime other claimants, principally Martin Menko, Joseph Johnson, and S. G. Brown, had sued Braine, Delano, and others connected with the mine for lesser amounts, but these cases had evidently been settled by the time Giddings, Raht, and Waters entered the picture. The coming of the Civil War made the ownership of the London Mine a matter for the future to decide.

The Mary Mine, originally christened St. Mary's, was opened by C. A. Proctor in September, 1853. By this time the property had been acquired by Charles and Samuel Congdon and their associates, Lyman Gilbert and William Hickok, and on January 26, 1854, a charter was granted this group under the name of Mary's Copper Company. The mine adjoined the Polk County Mine on Copper Hill. Although this mine was busy more or less continuously until the time of the Civil War, no records were left of the ore produced. J. E. Raht was mine captain at Mary Mine in 1857 and 1858. He was succeeded by James Jory, who served until the mines closed in 1863. The Mary Mine was taken over by the Union Consolidated Mining Company. There were "6 dwelling houses, 1 ore shed, two horse whims, shops, sheds, etc. etc." at the mine.

The last mine to be opened in the district which produced ore in any appreciable quantity during the pre-Civil War days was the Callaway Mine, opened by C. A. Proctor in November, 1853. The preceding January, Thomas H. Callaway and Euclid Waterhouse had sold the Callaway Mine to John M. Dow, and in March, 1854, Dow sold the property to the Cocheco Mining Company. While it may be assumed that the Callaway Mining Company, incorporated on January 18, 1854, had some connection with the mine, yet by whom or to what extent it was worked is not definitely known. Some ore was taken out of the mine after it was purchased by the Union Consolidated Mining Company in 1858. The Callaway was opened northeast of the Mary's and Polk County mines on the same ore body. At the mine were "6 dwelling houses, 1 ore shed, 1 blacksmith shop, cribs, etc. etc."

The opening of the Culchote, United States, and Biggs mines

in the year 1854 brought to a close the era of ushering in new mines at Ducktown. The only thing known definitely about these mines is that James Jory, who came to Ducktown from England in August, 1854, first worked sixteen months at Culchote, where William Bunter was agent. Here, as at the Biggs Mine, mining was confined to the black ores near the surface. Mention was rarely made of the Culchote, United States, and Biggs mines in accounts of mining at Ducktown before the Civil War, and none of them was included in the consolidations that took place in the late fifties.

The Ocoee Mine seems to be the "lost mine" of Ducktown, for there is no record of a mine by this name having been opened during the 1850's. However, the Ocoee Mining Company was operating in 1853 and had a crew of about sixty men. The company owned two tracts of land adjoining the Tennessee and Cherokee properties on the west, but whether work was done on these tracts or at some other place in the district is not known. The Ocoee Mining Company was evidently active for only a short time, as the Union Consolidated Mining Company acquired the Ocoee properties by sheriff's execution in May, 1859.

Although no copper mines of value were discovered in the state of Georgia, it seemed for awhile that Fannin County would prove to be the exception because of the county's proximity to the copper deposits just across the state line in Polk County, Tennessee. Three out-croppings of gossan were discovered south of the Ocoee River in Fannin County soon after the principal bodies of ore were found at Ducktown. There was every reason to believe that the masses of copper ores lying north of the river extended to the southwest. This was in line with the general strike of the ore bodies in the district, and the optimism that prevailed in Fannin County seemed to be well founded. By the latter part of 1854 the mineral wealth of the county was being proclaimed by the press of Georgia. Said the *Crossville Standard,* as quoted by the *Mining Magazine:* "There is no county in the state so rich in minerals as Fannin ... a large number of persons are testing for copper in various portions of the county, with fair prospects of success...."

The same activities that prevailed at the nearby Tennessee mines—prospecting, opening shafts, and speculating in mining properties—were present in Fannin County. While there seems to have been no detailed geological reports on these mines like

FIRST DECADE OF MINING 75

those made on the geology of the Tennessee district, yet fabulous sums were spoken of in regard to values of certain land lots in Fannin County. Several companies were organized to exploit the copper resources south of the Ocoee River. The Georgia companies, all incorporated by the Georgia General Assembly on February 17, 1854, were Spring Place Mining Company, Blue Ridge Mining Company, Tocoah Mining Company, Conasauga Mining Company, and Cohutta Mining Company. The acts granting charters to the five companies stated that each "... shall keep an office in Fannin County." With the exception of the Spring Place Mining Company it is doubtful that any of the other companies found it necessary to open an office. The Spring Place company apparently operated the Mobile Mine.

Mines were opened on the three out-croppings of gossan across the river from Ducktown. They were given the names of Sally Jane, Number 20, and Mobile. Prospecting to some extent was also done at what is known as Mt. Pisgah, near Higdon's Store. The Mt. Pisgah deposit does not belong to the Ducktown type and it is to be doubted that ore of commercial value was ever mined there.

The Sally Jane Mine, located about two miles southwest of Copperhill, was opened in the latter part of 1854. It was owned and operated by Smith and Summerour. William G. Smith, of Morgan County, Georgia, and his associate were experienced miners, for they had been engaged in mining in California before coming to Fannin County. Two shafts were opened at the Sally Jane, only one of which was reported to have produced ore. The output, which probably amounted to only a few hundred tons, was shipped to Baltimore, Maryland. The Sally Jane was the first mine in the state of Georgia from which copper ore was shipped. Lack of ore, however, soon forced the owners to cease operations and the mine was never again worked on a commercial scale.

The Number 20 Mine, named after land lot number 20 on which it is located in the second section of the ninth district of Fannin County, is about one mile southwest of the old Sally Jane Mine and is three miles from Copperhill. Number 20 was opened in 1856, presumably by R. H. Moore, who was first reported as exploring for copper in Fannin County in 1854. Professor Julian Deby examined the mine in 1856 and said that the ore body was a prolongation of the Ducktown deposit and that prospects of a prosperous mine were good. At that time shafts and trenches were being dug, and the stage of actual mining was reached. However, the mine was closed after about a year and remained idle for some two or three years. About 1860 work was resumed by three Cornishmen, James Phillips, Harvey Falls, and Thomas Pill. Operations were continued this time for about two years, until the mine was forced to close on account of the war. The ore was sold to the Union Consolidated Mining Company at Ducktown.

Opened about 1854, the Mobile Mine, located at Pierceville about one mile southwest of Number 20 Mine, was the most extensively worked of any of the Fannin County mines of the period. For several years operations at the mine were on a scale comparable to those at some of the larger mines across the river in Tennessee. Developments consisted of two shafts, one 170 feet and the other 155 feet deep. Drifts from the shafts were driven along the strike of the lode for about three hundred feet. Smelting works were also erected. Stamps operated by water power were used to crush the ore and the heap-roasting method was used to eliminate its sulphur content. Three furnaces, one calciner, and a stack 150 feet high were erected. A steam engine furnished blast for the furnaces. The steam boiler, on wheels, was hauled to the mine from Cleveland, Tennessee, by Samuel Waters. Eight mules and eight oxen, working in relays, were required to move the boiler to its destination.

Probably the first fatal accident in connection with the mining industry at Ducktown occurred at the Mobile Mine. After the new steam boiler had arrived at the mine and had been fired, a group of girls gathered at a safe distance to view the pulsating monster. The engineer, noticing the rustic curiosity of the girls, suddenly pulled the whistle cord and the unearthly scream that poured forth was terrifying. The girls were so badly frightened that one of them, named Blalock, who was holding a large one-cent piece in her mouth gulped so violently that she swallowed the coin and choked to death.

A village of several hundred population sprang up around the mine. About two hundred men were employed at the mine, besides several wood and charcoal contractors. The company erected several dwellings, maintained a commissary and a boarding house, and also kept a physician named Powell at the mine.

It seems that the ore supply at Mobile was virtually exhausted by 1860. Further misfortune overtook the company when a fire destroyed the smelting works at about the same time.

CHAPTER 10

CONSOLIDATIONS

Turning back now to the Tennessee side of the Ducktown district, we find the mining industry in Polk County in the process of disintegration. Of the fourteen mines that had been opened at Ducktown by 1854, only five of them, the Tennessee, Mary's, Isabella, Eureka, and Hiwassee, were being worked with any degree of regularity in 1857. The breaking-up of the industry was due to economic and not to geological reasons. There were millions of tons of good copper ore here and only the means and equipment to mine them were needed. Indeed, it can be truthfully said that the amazing amount of ore that was in evidence contributed in no small degree to the disaster facing the poorly equipped companies. So glowing were the prospects of huge dividends that in almost every case the companies squanered their original capital on mining properties and other real estate and depended for working capital on current operations. When expenditures for enlarged furnace capacities and for deep mining became necessary, current incomes were wholly inadequate to meet them.

Even as early as the latter part of 1855 many of the companies were in need of additional capital. It will be remembered that in most instances each mine represented a duly chartered enterprise. While certain individuals of means controlled several of the companies, still each was a distinct corporation dependent for its welfare upon the proceeds from its own mine. And almost without exception each had made the common mistake of investing too heavily in lands and had made no provision for operating deficits. These factors, plus the inability of any of the companies to pay even moderate returns on the capital invested, made it difficult to secure additional funds when needed. It was only by the formation of consolidated companies at this time that the mining industry at Ducktown was continued.

Some thought had been given abroad to purchasing and consolidating under one ownership several of the Ducktown mines as early as the year 1854. Much of the ore mined up to that time had been sold in England and had established a good reputation there for the Ducktown industry. When the mining engineer Bray visited Ducktown in 1854 he had made preliminary arrangements for purchasing for his English principals the Mary's, East Tennessee, and Callaway mines, as well as several other mines. The name of the proposed company was to be the Great Consolidated Company of Tennessee. In the following year Lyman W. Gilbert of the Isabella Mining Company, with a representative of the Eureka Mining Company, went to England to further the negotiations but nothing came of the plans. However, passage by the British Parliament of the Joint Stock Companies Act in July, 1856, gave English capitalists a freer disposition to form joint enenterprises, and within a short time plans were once more being made to return to Ducktown.

There was little improvement in the financial conditions at Ducktown in 1856. The *Mining Magazine* of April, 1856, reported that "the Tennessee mines are not doing much at present. One or two are being worked favorably, but the greater number are lying fallow, and all are still being offered for sale in Europe. The mines have an undisputed reputation for riches."

Hope was engendered that British interests would again invest in the district on a large scale when it was learned in 1857 that another company, the Tennessee Consolidated Copper Mining Company, Ltd., had been organized in London. This company contemplated the purchase of the same mines as those which the Great Consolidated Company of Tennessee had considered buying in the previous year. For the benefit of prospective investors the Tennessee Consolidated Copper Mining Company issued a folder containing an abstract of Ansted's report on several mines in the district which he had visited in the winter of 1854-55. This report was an able presentation of the geology of the Ducktown district and predicted profitable results if operations were properly begun and carried on under competent management.

To merchants and others at Ducktown who depended upon the mines for a livelihood the information that a new English company was interested in the mines was extremely good news. To the natives scattered throughout the district, however, the news probably meant but little. The original settlers had by no means become industrialized and they would go on living their lives as they always had whether the mines operated or not.

Therefore, to those who depended upon markets and payrolls for food and clothing was left the burden of worrying over what might happen to the mines. For this latter group the knowledge that English representatives would not investigate the district because of failure of negotiations to purchase the properties was sad indeed.

Hard upon the heels of the failure of the struggling copper industry at Ducktown to secure foreign assistance came the panic of 1857. The *Mining Magazine* of October of that year stated: "A cloud of the blackest kind has come over all kinds of securities. The market has been dull for every kind.... No sales have been made for many days at the new Stock or Mining Board. The state of the money market has been more stringent than at any time for the last five or ten years. It has been at last found impossible to carry floating debts by any company."

With the financial market depleted and pessimism knee deep, the outlook for Ducktown was gloomy indeed. Although many of the mines were idle and the others were sorely in need of financial assistance, it must be remembered that the Ducktown and Lake Superior districts were at that time the two principal centers of copper production in the United States. Samuel F. Tracy said that if the East Tennessee copper mines had railroad facilities they could produce one-eighth as much copper as could be produced in the world. It was unlikely that Ducktown, possessing such resources, could not be made to produce copper continuously and in appreciable quantities. These facts make it a little less surprising that in 1857, with the panic at its worst, American capitalists began making preparations themselves to reorganize the mining industry. The fault at Ducktown had been in management and not in the ore supply. To remedy this condition consolidations such as those that had been contemplated by the British had to be effected. Different groups, among whose members were many southerners, visited the district in 1857. Out of these visits came new and bigger companies at Ducktown.

The groundwork for a contemplated consolidation had been laid when a charter was granted the Union Consolidated Mining Company of Tennessee by the Tennessee Legislature on March 1, 1854. This company had, however, remained inactive and had neither owned, leased, nor worked any of the properties at Ducktown. In the latter part of 1857 a group of New York, Charleston, and Savannah capitalists assumed the charter rights of the company and on January 20, 1858, formally organized it into an active concern. The company was capitalized at $2,200,000 represented by 220,000 shares at $10 each. The home office was in New York.

The company was "... formed for the purpose of consolidating and working under one simple and efficient management, the several valuable copper mines and mining properties in Polk County, Tennessee...." These mines were the East Tennessee (480 acres), Mary's (160 acres), Callaway (320 acres), Maria (80 acres), Isabella (240 acres), McCoy (140 acres), Buena Vista (240 acres), Johnson (315 acres), Beaver (40 acres), Cherokee (320 acres),

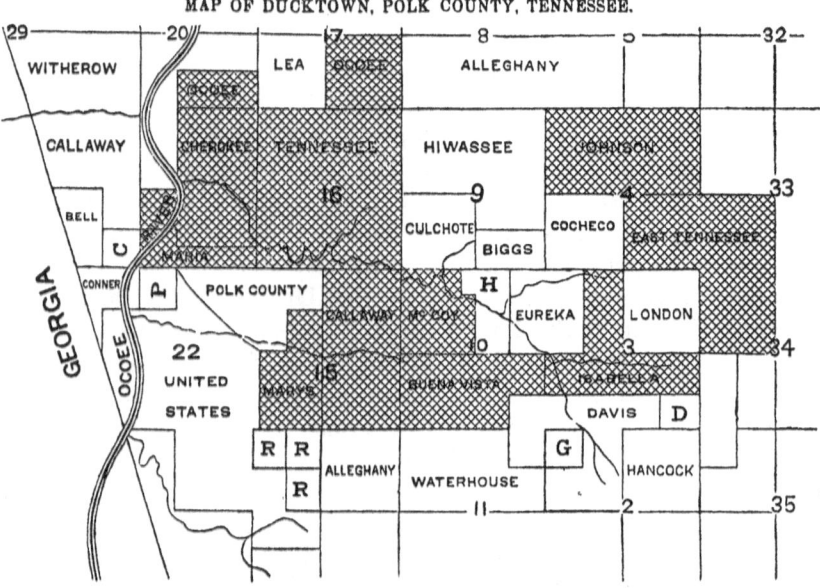

MAP OF DUCKTOWN, POLK COUNTY, TENNESSEE.

A map showing the mining properties to be purchased by the Union Consolidated Mining Company in 1857. Some of the unrelated numbers appearing on the map represent sections of the township division.

and Ocoee (240 acres). The mines and properties were purchased for $2,050,000, "payable mostly in the shares of the Company." Officers of the company were Charles B. Tatham, president and treasurer; Walter Congdon, secretary; and Samuel Congdon, managing director. The directors were Charles B. Tatham, William Oothout, Charles Congdon, William Hickok, James A. Alexander, Edmund Perkins, and Samuel Congdon, all of New York; George S. Cameron and Robert Caldwell, both of Charleston; and Edward Padelford and Andrew Low, both of Savannah, Georgia.

CONSOLIDATIONS 81

Immediately following the organization of the company, Samuel Congdon, who had resided at Ducktown since 1853, returned to New York. Upon his recommendation, J. E. Raht, a young German who had served for several years as foreman and mine captain at both the Polk County and Mary's Mines, was employed as superintendent of the Union Consolidated Mining Company. Congdon sold to Raht at this time his commissary at the Tennessee Mine and granted to Raht the privilege of selling goods to employees and collecting for them through the payrolls.

The second step in the revitalization of the distressed mining industry at Ducktown was effected when the old Polk County Copper Company was reorganized on August 23, 1859. When John Caldwell, A. H. Keith, and the heirs of Thomas W. Mastin had sold the Polk County Mine to the original Polk County Copper Company in 1854, a law suit followed to prevent the sale by the Mastin heirs of their equity in the property. The case finally reached the Supreme Court of the United States where a decision in favor of the right of the Mastin heirs to dispose of their property was handed down. In the meantime an appraisal of the mine had been made by financiers of New Orleans, and, following the favorable court decision, the company underwent a complete reorganization.

On November 21, 1859, L. W. Gilbert, president, and Samuel Congdon, T. H. Callaway, and A. H. Keith, directors of the old Polk County Copper Company, transferred all their interests as directors in the old company to the newly organized company of the same name. The new company, with principal offices in New Orleans, was capitalized at $1,000,000, represented by ten thousand shares at $100 each. The new officials were John G. Gaines, president; George O. Sweet, secretary; and John G. Gaines, William H. Peet, James D. Denegre, Gabriel W. Couves, and John Thomas, directors. J. E. Raht was hired as the company's mine superintendent.

The third and final consolidation of mining interests at Ducktown took place in 1860 when the Hiwassee Mining Company and the Cocheco Mining Company properties were acquired by the newly organized Burra Burra Copper Company of Tennessee. The new company assumed the charter rights of the inactive Toccoee Mining Company. The Burra Burra company was formally organized on April 10, 1860, with principal offices in New Orleans. The capital stock of the company was fixed at $1,500,000, and the officers elected were William H. Peet, president; George

O. Sweet, secretary; and William H. Peet, John G. Gaines, Gabriel W. Couves, John Thomas, E. MacPherson, and Lyman W. Gilbert, directors. John Thomas later served for several years as president of the Union Consolidated Mining Company, and E. MacPherson was later president of both the Burra Burra Copper Company and Polk County Copper Company.

Titles to the Hiwassee and Cocheco properties passed to Lyman W. Gilbert on March 1, 1860, and on the tenth day of the following month he transferred the titles to the Burra Burra Copper Company. Gilbert also sold several other tracts of land to the new company. In exchange for his mining and other properties he received $1,450,000 in shares and $400,000 in bonds of the company. This company owned over five thousand acres of land, the greater part of which was situated in the Turtletown district.

At the first meeting of the board of directors of the Burra Burra Copper Company, held on April 10, 1860, it was "Resolved; That Capt. J. E. Raht, of Ducktown, Tennessee, be employed to take the superintendency of the Company's operations in Polk County, Tennessee, for the term of one, two or three years; and that he be requested to name the terms on which he will take the management." Satisfactory terms were reached and Raht took charge of the company's business at Ducktown.

The Burra Burra Copper Company began at once preparations for mining and smelting on a scale much larger than had been undertaken by its predecessor. In fact, so bright were the prospects that in searching for a name befitting both the size and aspirations of the company the name Burra Burra, after a famous Australian mine of the day, was chosen. And it was predicted by Professor Charles Upham Shepard that the value of the Burra Burra Mine at Ducktown would make it well worthy of its Australian namesake.

The year or so just preceding the outbreak of the Civil War were glorious days at Ducktown. The copper industry which had been limping under the weight of a dozen feeble companies had been reorganized under three ambitious companies headed by men wise in the ways of finance and management. Hiwassee was a busy little village; the ore supply seemed unlimited; and persistent efforts were being made to build a railroad into the district. Thus, while the country was moving slowly toward the cataclysmic upheaval of a civil war, the South's little copper empire was unheedingly making preparations for a long period of prosperous times. With these conditions in mind, it will be well to review briefly the manner by which the new companies undertook the rehabilitation of the run-down district.

In May, 1860, a comittee composed of William Hickok, Edward Perkins, and George S. Cameron, visited the Ducktown mines for the purpose of reporting on the condition of the properties of the Union Consolidated Mining Company of Tennessee. The report as submitted contained minute details of every phase of work being done at Ducktown. Only three mines owned by this company were being worked, the East Tennessee, Isabella, and Mary's. No figures on ore production were given, but it was stated that the tonnage of ore mined was limited to the capacity of the furnaces. The smelting works at the Tennessee Mine were being used, but similar works of the company's own were being erected at Isabella. There were four furnaces at the Tennessee plant, only two of which were operated at the same time. Each furnace had a capacity of twenty tons of ore a day, and produced about six tons of matte. About three hundred men were employed at the mines and furnaces.

About thirteen thousand pounds of 85 per cent copper was being recovered each month from the Isabella mine water. The committee described this process as follows: "The water pumped out of the mine is discharged into a trough, and conducted through a series of them about 1400 feet in length; the bottoms of these troughs are covered with old iron, and as the water passes through, the copper held in solution is precipitated upon the iron; this precipitation is removed by the use of brooms, three or four times a week." This simple process of recovering copper from mine waters was employed also at the Eureka and Hiwassee and possibly at other mines in the district.

A 5 per cent dividend declared in June, 1860, proved to be sadly premature. Within six months the company was running short of working capital. It was the same old story of overanxiousness on the part of early companies at Ducktown to provide money for land and dividends at the expense of sufficient funds for operating purposes. By January, 1861, the company's financial condition was so strained that their superintendent, J. E. Raht, was induced to endorse drafts of the treasurer in order to secure funds needed at the mines. Raht was given a lien on the company's personal property as security.

It is probable that more development work had been done at the Polk County Mine, in the way of shafts and adits, than at any other mine in the district up to 1860. When work was resumed there under the direction of the new Polk County Copper Company in the early part of the year, it was found that nine shafts had been sunk, and six adits driven. Construction of smelting works was begun at once. This plant, though not completed until after the beginning of the war, boasted a forty-horsepower steam engine, four blast furnaces, two reverberatory furnaces, a calciner, and a battery of stamps. The steam engine was built and installed by Thomas Webster of Chattanooga in 1859. J. E. Raht wrote to Webster in 1866 and told him that the engine was still running in perfect order.

Auxiliary buildings, in addition to twenty tenements for laborers, included a laboratory, an office, and blacksmith and carpenter shops. A mine captain, a metallurgist, and about ninety mechanics and laborers, of whom fifty-three were miners, were employed by the Polk County Copper Company in 1860.

Immediately after taking charge of the affairs of the Burra Burra Copper Company in 1860, J. E. Raht abandoned both the Hiwassee shaft and the Hiwassee smelting works on Potato Creek. Shafts were opened farther to the east, on the Cocheco ore body on the hill between the present Burra Burra and McPherson shafts. Work of erecting a new smelting plant was also begun at the foot of the hill, just east of the new shafts. For this change in the scenes of operations, Captain Raht was severely criticized by Eugene Gaussoin. (Raht, it should be stated, had succeeded Gaussoin as superintendent when the Hiwassee and Cocheco properties were taken over by the Burra Burra Copper Company.) From the Hiwassee Mine it had been necessary to haul the ore by wagon a distance of half a mile to the furnaces on Potato Creek. Under Raht's arrangement, however, the shafts were situated on the hill above the furnaces and this permitted the ore to be delivered to the furnaces by means of adits and chutes.

The smelting process in vogue at Ducktown, as it had been developed by the year 1860, was probably the result of many home-made innovations which were put into practice in the attempts to treat successfully the ores, which possessed some unusual characteristics, in the small, crude furnaces. The first furnaces erected in Ducktown turned out a matte, or regulus, averaging 30 per cent to 50 per cent copper. Improvements, principally in furnace construction, resulted in refined copper being produced by the time of the Civil War. One improvement was in furnaces embodying the Welsh principles of "step grates" and "reserved combustion." Another was in the use of steatite, or soapstone

CONSOLIDATIONS

(known locally as "cotton rock"), as a furnace lining. This material added greatly to the life and efficiency of the furnaces through its ability to withstand heat without quick deterioration. A third improvement came about by the use of steam engines in the place of water wheels for producing blast.

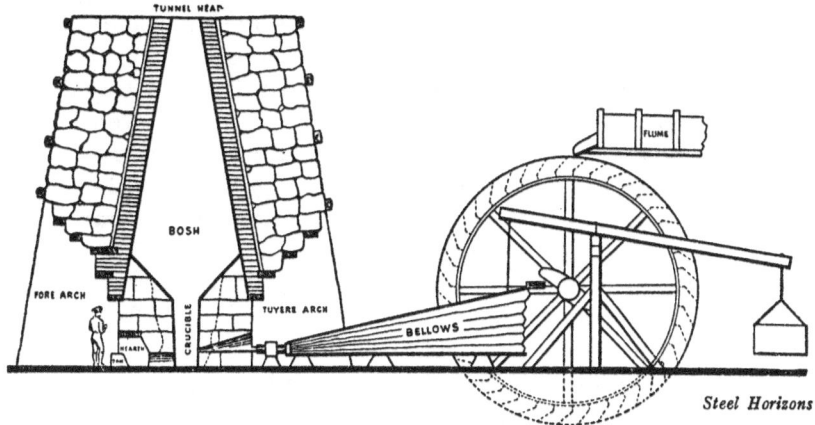

An old-fashioned water wheel. Bellows operated by waterpower were used to produce blast for the smelting furnaces at Ducktown until the wheels were replaced by steam engines.

The furnaces were small, measuring about six to eight feet square. Ordinary baskets were used in regulating the amount of charcoal to be used in the charge. Despite improvements that were made, it required four months to produce metallic copper from the time the ore was first placed on the roast piles. During this process the material was passed back and forth through the different smelting arrangements several times.

Seven different smelting works had been erected, or were in process of erection, in the Ducktown district by the year 1860—the Tennessee, Eureka, Hiwassee, Polk County, Isabella, Burra Burra, and the smelters at the Mobile Mine. It was about this time that the smelting process reached the stage where refined copper, or ingots, could be produced. As a measure of convenience and economy one such refinery was provided by the three companies. The plant, located at Polk County Mine, was operated as the United Refining Works and handled the impure copper from the furnaces of the three companies. The cost of operating the refining works was borne in proportion to the amount of work done for each company.

Nearly five hundred employees, including both men and boys, were engaged in the copper industry at Ducktown in 1860. Perhaps two hundred more were employed at the Mobile and Number 20 mines in Georgia. Adding to these the number of workers engaged in hauling copper to Cleveland and in furnishing rock, charcoal, and cordwood for the furnaces, gives a total of approximately one thousand employees who were deriving a livelihood from the industry as the Civil War approached.

The thunderheads of impending disaster that had for months been hanging over the nation's horizon were gathered into a cloud of dark reality when the state of South Carolina formally withdrew from the Union on December 20, 1860. Within a few months the country was irrevocably committed to the ravages of war, and every plan that had been so hopefully and so expensively formulated for profitable operations at Ducktown was frustrated. Organization of the Union Consolidated Mining Company, Polk County Copper Company, and Burra Burra Copper Company had been completed. The companies were adequately financed, for the time being at least. The Polk County, Isabella, and Burra Burra smelting works were almost completed and the mines were producing all the ores that could be treated. The average price of copper in 1860 was 22.88 cents a pound. Under normal conditions this price would have meant a profit for Ducktown copper. But normal conditions were rent asunder by the shock of war in 1861 and the price of copper for several years thereafter meant but little to this unfortunate district.

CHAPTER 11

DUCKTOWN DURING THE CIVIL WAR

Conditions at Ducktown during the Civil War can best be described by dividing the years of the war into two periods. During the first period, from the time war was declared until the latter part of 1863, the mines continued operating under sponsorship of the Confederacy after their ownership had been wrested from nothern capitalists and placed with southern sympathizers. During the second period, from the latter part of 1863, when the railway through Cleveland fell to the Union Army, until the end of the war, the mines were closed, all business was suspended, and the district was overrun by bands of guerrillas. The war came just as the industry at Ducktown was experiencing its first flush of renewed energy following the period of consolidations. The mines were producing all the ores that could be treated. New and enlarged smelting works were being erected at the Polk County, Isabella, and Burra Burra mines. Stockholders, employees, and businessmen throughout the district were looking forward to prosperous times. But Ducktown received a terrific shock from events that were transpiring in political circles far removed from the district. So great, and yet so minutely penetrating, were the ramifications of southern secession that they affected even the placid lives of the charcoal burners at their stations overlooking the Ocoee. Charcoal pits soon found their counterparts in graves, sulphur smoke was blown away by powder smoke, stockholders' interests were confiscated, employees became soldiers, and inhabitants turned to, or fled from, guerrilla warfare before peace and sanity again returned to Ducktown.

It is doubtful that there was in the South a purely industrial interprise so immediately and so disastrously affected by the outbreak of the Civil War as was the Ducktown copper industry, the entire output of which was being sold to northern refineries. With the peaceful flow of traffic between North and South disrupted, markets for Tennessee copper were closed. Also the Ducktown works were largely financed by northern capital. Such a state of affairs could result in nothing short of a complete shut-down of the industry unless new and available markets for the only product of the district could be found. Payrolls could not be met without buyers of the copper.

Manufacturing plants for converting Tennessee ingots into finished copper products had not been established in the South up to the time of the Civil War. This weakness in the Ducktown industrial structure, however, was beginning to be overcome at the time the war began. The Tennessee Rolling Works Company, headed principally by William H. Peet, John Thomas, and George S. Cameron, had begun, just before the outbreak of the war, the erection of a copper rolling mill at Cleveland, Tennessee. Copper products such as sheets, bars, bolts, and rivets were to be manufactured from Ducktown copper. The operation of a rolling mill so near the source of ingot copper was expected to add greatly to the scope and stability of the copper industry as a whole in Tennessee.

After the war became a reality the first move by J. E. Raht, mine superintendent of the Ducktown companies, was to curtail operations at the mines and continue the furnaces in operation largely on ores then in process. He began storing the ingots of copper against the day when they would be in demand from sources not then determinable.

While Ducktown was experiencing its period of uncertainty, the newly created Confederate government was thumbing the records of Dixie enterprises, discovering who owned them and how the owners felt about the war. Enemies of this great venture in behalf of states' rights were not to be allowed to line their coffers with southern profits. By late summer of 1861 the courts of the Confederate government, pursuant to the Sequestration Act of August 30, 1861, were preparing to investigate ownership of the mines at Ducktown. One of the first moves in this direction was the serving upon J. E. Raht of a questionnaire, "Interrogatories of the Receiver," by the receiver for the Eastern District of Tennessee, on November 7, 1861.

After receiving Raht's answers to the interrogatory, the receiver, Landon C. Haynes, later to represent Tennessee in the Confederate Senate, made the following report on the properties of the Burra Burra Copper Company to the District Court of the Confederate States for the Eastern Division of the District of Tennessee, held at Knoxville on November 27, 1861:

To the Honorable West H. Humphreys, Judge of the District Court of the Confederate States in and for the District of Tennessee, holding the Court at Knoxville:

The petition of the Confederate States of America, by Landon C. Haynes, Receiver for the Eastern District of Tennessee, respectfully showeth that there is within the jurisdiction of the said Court, and which has been sequestered by the Act of the Provisional Congress of the said Confederate States, entitled "An Act for the Sequestration of the Estates, Property and Effects of Alien Enemies, and for the indemnity of Citizens of the Confederate States, and persons aiding the same in the existing war with the United States," approved August 30th, 1861, the following property, namely; a copper mine called the Burra Burra in the County of Polk and State of Tennessee. Said mine and the lands connected with it, belong to an incorporated Company by the name and style of the "Burra Burra Copper Company" as said States have been informed and believe. Said lands and mine was assessed at the last assessment at the sum of three hundred and fifty seven thousand dollars. Said States do not know the amount of the capital stock, the quantity of land, the issues of the said mine, or the present or future value thereof, nor the Directors, or Treasurer or agent controlling and managing the same, all of which and whom are known to the President thereof, Wm. H. Peet. Said States represent that there are fifteen hundred shares in said Company of $100. each, one thousand shares of which are guaranteed to be worth $100. each within three years from the first of March 1860 by L. W. Gilbert, John Thomas, and William H. Peet, the former of New York and the latter of New Orleans. Said States have not the said instrument of guarantee and the said Peet is called upon to furnish and file the same with his answer as it is under his control. Said fifteen hundred shares are worth, as said States believe, about $150,000. and are held, owned, possessed and enjoyed for the following Alien Enemies, to wit: Lyman W. Gilbert, who has his domicile within the State of New York. That the person holding, exercising supervision over, in possession of, or controlling the said lands, mines and property and shares of the said Company as the only person known to said States is the following, namely; William H. Peet of New Orleans, who is called upon to answer on oath all the allegations of this petition and set forth the capital stock, the shares issued, the directors and stock holders of said Company. Your petitioner prays that the said Company be made a party to this petition, that a copy and notice be issued according to law, that the said Peet be made a party and that the said shares, property and effects of the said Alien Enemy and all and every right and interest therein held, owned, possessed or enjoyed by or for the said alien enemy, shall be declared sequestered and be seized, held, controlled and disposed of as provided for in the act aforesaid; and that all such other and further proceedings may be had herein as shall be right and proper, and may be deemed necessary or requisite by the Court.

(Signed) LANDON C. HAYNES, *Receiver.*

A true copy:
(Signed) WM. G. MCADOO, *Clerk.*

Acting upon the petition as prayed for by the receiver, the court issued the following decree at the November, 1862, term:

Confederate States District Court November Term 1862
  Eastern District of Tennessee December 13, 1862
    Present, The Hon. West H. Humphreys, Judge, etc.
  Confederate States of America
            vs
  The Burra-Burra Copper Company
Decree

This day the Receiver on behalf of the Confederate States of America came, and presented a Petition to the Court, for the sequestration of the stock owned by the persons alleged to be alien enemies therein, to wit: Lyman W. Gilbert or his assigns, and the owners of fifteen hundred shares in said Company, of the nominal value of one hundred dollars each, which Company is chartered by the Legislature of Tennessee, and having an office and doing business in Polk County, Tennessee: It is ordered by the Court that a jury come to find whether the said Gilbert, who is alleged to be the owner, is an alien enemy, and the said jury, to wit: John Shumake, D. C. Hammell, G. P. Nance, L. F. Ragsdale, Isaac Lewis, T. C. Champe, S. B. Ault, I. Harmon, Jacob S. Stuart, W. B. McNutt, John L. Lonas, and S. B. Boyd, being duly and lawfully sworn, to ascertain, find and declare, do find and declare upon the proofs exhibited, that Lyman W. Gilbert is a citizen of the United States and an alien enemy, and that he or his assigns own fifteen hundred shares of stock in said corporation.

It is therefore found, ascertained and declared by the Court, that said Gilbert or his assigns is or are citizens of the United States and alien enemies; that he or they own the number of fifteen hundred shares in said Company, and the verdict of the jury being approved by the Court, it is ordered that said shares of stock be hereby sequestrated according to law, and the Receiver is ordered to assume the ownership of the said stock, and control the same according to law, and the charter of said company; and on motion of the Receiver, and on the application of part of the Confederate Stockholders, it is ordered that said shares of stock be sold by the Receiver on such terms as he may deem proper, the Court being of the opinion that it is necessary and proper to sell said stock to secure the same from waste, loss or destruction; but it is hereby ordered that such sale shall first receive the approbation of the Secretary of the Treasury of the Confederate States, if he shall deem it proper to act in the premises, and in that event the Receiver shall act under his instructions.

I, Henry Elliott, Clerk of the Confederate States District Court for the Eastern District of Tennessee, do hereby certify that the foregoing is a true and perfect copy of the Decree had in this case on the 13th day of December 1862.
Given under my hand, and private seal, (there being no seal of Office) at Office, in Knoxville, this 28th day of July 1863.
(Signed) HENRY ELLIOTT, *Clerk*
C. S. Dist. Court, E.D.T.

The Court having determined to its satisfaction that Lyman W. Gilbert was the principal alien enemy stockholder of the Burra Burra Copper Company, the fifteen hundred shares of stock owned by him was sequestered and sold at public sale on June 30, 1863. The stock was purchased for $7,500 by William H. Peet.

The stock of the Union Consolidated Mining Company, also held by alien enemies, was sequestered and disposed of at the same time and in the same manner as the stock of the Burra Burra Copper Company. One hundred and ten thousand shares of Union Consolidated stock were owned by C. B. Tatham, Samuel and Charles Congdon, William Hickok, Lyman Denison, James A. Alexander, Edward Perkins, B. Cutting, W. Cutting, Lyman W. Gilbert, Charles Clark, and Benjamin Tatham. It being adjudged that these stockholders were enemies of the Confederate States, the entire lot of 110,000 shares was also sold to William H. Peet for $27,500. While no records were available giving the allegiance of the stockholders of the Polk County Copper Company, it is to be assumed that any stock of that company held by enemies of the Confederacy was sequestered and sold as was the stock of the other two companies.

Following the service of the first paper upon Captain Raht by an agent of the Confederate government on November 7, 1861, which was the beginning of what amounted to the confiscation of all Ducktown properties owned by Union sympathizers, ownership of the mines here was purely mythical until the end of the war.

A rare document of the early war years is a report, "Abstract of Information," which William H. Peet and his associate John Thomas made to the Confederate authorities on the amount of copper that could, under favorable circumstances, be produced at Ducktown. Peet was at the time president of the Burra Burra

Copper Company and a director in the Polk County Copper Company, and John Thomas was a director in both companies. The report, made in either the year 1862 or 1863, throws much light on conditions at the mines after the beginning of the war. Extracts from the report follow:

> Present condition (of works): Good working order.
> Kind of Power: Water and steam.
> Yield of ore per month: 300 tons.
> Number of hands employed: About 300.
> Head of stock employed: About 180.
> Furnaces: In blast, 3; out of blast, 9.
> Capacity per month: 300,000 to 400,000 pounds fine copper.
> Maximum capacity per year: 2,000,000 pounds fine copper.
> Contract price: 25¢.
> Increase in price due to rise in provisions, etc.: 25¢.

It will be noted that only about 300 men were employed at Ducktown at that time.

Regarding sheet and bolt copper that could be produced by the Tennessee Rolling Works Company, at Cleveland, of which Peet was president, the abstract shows:

> Present condition: Nearly completed; about ready for active operation.
> Kind of power: Steam.
> Prospect of source of supply: Depending upon the Refining Works (at Ducktown).
> Yield per day: 5,000 pounds.
> Number of hands employed: 40 to 50.
> Contract price: 37½¢.
> Increase due to rise in provisions, etc.: 37½¢.

The rolling mill was completed and a quantity of finished products turned out before Federal forces occupied Cleveland in the fall of 1863.

In the "Remarks" column of the abstract is a vivid description of the handicaps under which the mines at Ducktown were laboring. Provisions and mine supplies were scarce. The operating crews had been greatly depleted, and there was little enthusiasm for possession of Confederate currency. The "Remarks" are reproduced here in full:

The mines which are furnishing the ores for the production of ingot copper as per the accompanying abstract are supposed to be inexhaustable, and were, at the commencement of the war, delivering a thousand tons of copper ore per month to the Smelting Works. Since then the operations have decreased gradually but steadily on account of the price and scarcity of all mining materials, especially blasting powder, steel, iron, etc. Also the want of subsistence. The latter is now the great hindrance to working successfully, and the mines may stop on account of a want of supplies for the employees and working stock, unless the Government will furnish the most necessary munitions, which the farming population of East Tennessee are unwilling to spare or dispose of for Confederate Treasury Notes, if not *compelled* to do so by military authority. These supplies being obtained, we can furnish copper, ingot, sheet and bolt at the prices mentioned, which is only about double the peace price of copper, while all other metals are *five* to *ten* times their peace prices. The "Rolling Mill" for making sheet, bar and bolt copper, nails, rivets and wire is just about going into operation. We have been unable as yet to procure all the machinery necessary. The Company has had many difficulties to contend with in procuring mechanical skill, machinery and transportation, owing to their absorption by the Government and they would ask for facilities in obtaining them.

It was common knowledge that to wage a war of duration the South would be forced to find within her own borders many articles that had hitherto been secured from the North and from abroad. The raw materials from which many of the more sorely needed implements were manufactured were to be found in the South, but they were, to a great extent, undeveloped. In commenting on the undeveloped resources of the South, and on the progress that was being made to overcome these handicaps, the New Orleans *Daily Crescent* of January 13, 1862, had this to say in regard to the source of supply of copper:

SUCCESSFUL SOUTHERN ENTERPRISES

Since the North commenced waging an unholy war of subjugation upon the South, the exhibition of Southern enterprise, thrift, industry and inventive faculty has been in the highest degree gratifying, and has demonstrated the absolute verity of what we have said on numerous occasions, in months and years past, that the Southern people, once compelled to rely upon their own resources, would speedily become, within themselves, the most independent nation on the surface of the globe. We have never known what we were actually worth, or all that we are really good for or at until the Abolition war and blockade compelled us to rely upon ourselves. This brought us out magnificently; and the lesson we have learned in the stern school of necessity will never be forgotten, and were the war to terminate finally tomorrow, that lesson would, in the future, be worth to us many scores of millions more than the expenses of the war up to this time.

We are now making cannon, muskets, bayonets, swords, rifles, powder, shot and shell, in quantities ample to support our immense armies in the field. Had any one asserted that this could be done twelve months ago, a vast majority of our people would have deemed him a fit subject for a lunatic asylum. Yet we have the indisputable fact staring us in the face. There it stands; let all doubters look at it, and be encouraged as to the future. Whenever a necessity arises, a resource is always found.

The article of copper is indispensable in war times. We have heard doubting Thomasses express apprehensions on that score. Yet all difficulties have vanished before a pressing need. The mines of the Ducktown (Tenn.) company will alone furnish an adequate supply to the Government, and soon a rolling mill will be established, but the time is not very far back when people held to the belief that manufactures of copper must come from the North or foreign countries. The war has proved this not to be the case.

The article continued at great length enumerating the many ways in which Southern ingenuity and resourcefulness were meeting both the war and civilian needs of an inspired people.

Contracts were, of course, entered into between Confederate authorities and southern representatives of the copper companies for all copper produced at Ducktown. The price ranged from forty-five to seventy-five cents a pound. During the early days of the war much of the Ducktown copper was consigned to A. L. Lee, at Richmond, Virginia. It was necessary, as Raht said, that all copper produced here be delivered to the Confederates, as any of the metal found not properly accounted for would be promptly confiscated.

In addition to copper, however, considerable quantities of copperas and bluestone were produced at Ducktown during the war. These products were disposed of at Atlanta, to which place they were transported by wagon. This phase of the business proved to be, as Raht later reported, highly profitable.

In the meantime, while court action was proceeding that would place in possession of southern sympathizers all copper works at Ducktown, the mines and smelters were being operated on a much reduced scale. Raht remained in charge of all operations. He was able until late in 1863 to keep in contact with the head offices of the Polk County Copper Company and the Burra Burra Copper Company at New Orleans. Communication with the office of the

Union Consolidated Mining Company at New York, however, was more difficult. It therefore devolved upon him to conduct as he saw fit the operations of the largest company at Ducktown. In financial matters he was assisted by George S. Cameron of Charleston, South Carolina. Cameron was a director of the company and made his residence at Cleveland during this period. Despite the uncertainty existing with respect to ownership, or to when order would be restored, a record was kept by Raht of the amount of copper sold direct and the amount sent to Peet's rolling mill from the works of each of the three operating companies. The Captain was one who believed in a "hereafter" for all things, and in this instance he prepared himself to be able to account for all copper produced by him should the information ever be necessary.

The purchase by Peet of the 1,500 shares of stock owned by Lyman W. Gilbert in the Burra Burra Copper Company had little effect upon the management of the company. However, his purchase of the 110,000 shares of stock of the Union Consolidated Mining Company, as well as of George S. Cameron's interests in the Union Consolidated Mining Company sometime later, placed the control of this company in his hands. While the ownership was of short duration, because of the changing fortunes of the war, Peet, nevertheless, was placed in temporary control of the entire copper industry in East Tennessee. For a few months in 1863 he owned controlling interest in the Union Consolidated Mining Company, was a director in the Polk County Copper Company, and was president of both the Burra Burra Copper Company and the Tennessee Rolling Works Company. Even before he had acquired controlling interest in the Union Consolidated Mining Company, he had, on January 1, 1863, been appointed acting sales agent of the company by George S. Cameron, the southern member of the board of directors of the Union Consolidated company. Loyal to the South's cause though he was, Peet was first a loyal associate of those engaged with him in mining at Ducktown.

Soon after Cleveland was occupied by Federal troops in the latter part of 1863, inquisitive soldiers found 57,900 pounds of ingot, sheet, and slab copper hidden in a cellar near the rolling mill. The copper was taken to Chattanooga and was later transferred to Cincinnati, where it was ultimately sold; but only after Captain Raht and officials of the Union Consolidated Mining Company at New York had exhausted their every means to secure possession of it. Peet, who fled deeper into the South at the approach of the Federal forces, reported that thirty thousand pounds of the metal belonged to the Union Consolidated Mining Company and that the remainder was his personal property.

With a portion of his copper properties destroyed and the other beyond his reach, Peet, in company with William Bartlett, began running the Federal blockade with cotton which was shipped to Nassau in the Bahama Islands. This activity was short-lived, as Peet died at Wilmington, North Carolina, on May 8, 1864. The complications following Peet's death, insofar as they affected those with whom he was associated in business, will be discussed later.

The occupation of Cleveland by Federal forces spelled the doom of the struggling copper industry at Ducktown. The rolling mill at Cleveland was destroyed by Federal troops, operations at the mines came to a close, and Ducktown copper ceased to be an asset, so sorely needed, to the faltering Confederacy. The closing of the mines marked a general exodus from Ducktown of many of the inhabitants who had remained in the isolated district since the beginning of the war. With the disappearance of Confederate interest in the mines, and with no effective military or civil authority to restrain them, guerrillas at once became active throughout this mountainous region. Union sympathizers and others seeking protection began moving to places of safety behind the Union lines.

We have seen how the closing of northern markets to Tennessee copper at the beginning of the war forced a prompt curtailment of work at the Ducktown mines. This partial stagnation of the copper industry was accompanied by the disappearance of many of the young, able-bodied men into the military ranks. Of the five complete infantry companies organized in Polk County for service in the Confederate Army two were recruited at Ducktown. The first company to be made up in this district was organized in the summer of 1861 and its members elected J. H. Hannah as captain; P. C. Gaston, first lieutenant; Dr. Holmes, second lieutenant; and J. M. Sims, third lieutenant. The other Ducktown company, organized in the fall of 1861, chose as officers Dr. John Goodman, captain; W. H. Wimberly, first lieutenant; John Tonkin, Jr., second lieutenant; and Charles Taliaferro, third lieutenant. These companies saw much hard service throughout the four years of war. Soldiers from Ducktown served in other Confederate units, and several from the district enlisted in the Federal Army. The company commanded by Hannah became a part of the

Nineteenth Tennessee Regiment. Among the important battles in which this regiment was engaged were Shiloh, Murfreesboro, Chickamauga, Atlanta, and Nashville. Goodman's company, of which John Tonkin, Jr., was later made captain, was organized into the Forty-third Tennessee Infantry. This regiment was in the siege of Vicksburg, and later formed a part of Longstreet's command at Knoxville.

Other than to be visited by scouting parties of both armies late in the war, the Ducktown district was singularly free from the ravages of contending armies during the entire period of the Civil War. The nearest approach to armed conflict in the district was the meeting of scouting parties of both Confederate and Federal forces at Hiwassee on December 17, 1864. Two men, Donaldson and Luttrell, were killed in this encounter. But if Ducktown and the surrounding countryside were fortunate in escaping the horrors of actual warfare, they paid dearly for their isolation by being easy prey to roving mobs of plunderers.

The slowing down of operations at the mines in 1861 was the beginning of a distracting period for the thriving village of Hiwassee. Removed though it was from the beaten pathways of social and industrial intercourse, the Ducktown district was as completely and as promptly throttled in an economic way as if it had been besieged by both armies. Since they were wholly dependent upon the payrolls of the mines, all sources of income vanished with the gradual cessation of paydays. The population of the district decreased sharply, and merchants found themselves with stocks of "store-bought" goods on hand for which there were but few customers. Hiwassee had become a busy trading center, but with its chief industrial support gone, the little village became strangely quiet and uninviting.

Business conditions improved somewhat after the Confederate government became the purchaser of Ducktown copper. The improvement, however, was of meager proportions. Confederate green-backs, too, became the medium of exchange. This currency, especially the paper bills in denominations of less than one dollar, dubbed "shin plasters," was considered a poor substitute for money. The closing of the mines and the departure of a large number of its citizens to more peaceful places of habitation, reduced Hiwassee to a lonely mountain outpost whose memories of the past magnified the uncertainties of the future.

There was much stirring about at Ducktown when it was learned in the summer of 1863 that the Federals were gaining control of East Tennessee. Weary of the suspense under which they had been living for two years, during which time social and economic conditions had grown steadily more serious, many citizens began to consider escaping from the district. Accordingly, a group decided to try to reach the Federal lines which at that time rested west of the Tennessee River. Forming a convoy of six teams of mules and six teams of oxen, the party quietly moved out of Hiwassee. When nearing Cleveland they were captured by a detachment of Confederate cavalry stationed there and escorted into the town for questioning by the military authorities. After some delay the refugees in the mule-drawn wagons, most of whom were British and German subjects, were permitted to proceed. Those in the ox-drawn wagons were returned to Ducktown in wagons of copper haulers. Their oxen were confiscated for food while their wagons were stored at the copper rolling mill where they were later destroyed when the mill was burned.

A short time after the first party of refugees left Ducktown the Federals gained control of the railroad through Cleveland, and the mines at Ducktown were closed. Practically all business at Hiwassee was suspended, and fear and anxiety gripped the whole district. The Union Army was intent solely upon breaking the Confederate grip on East Tennessee; there was little time or inclination on their part to police the adjacent mountainous regions. The result was that guerrilla activities immediately increased.

Safety from these outlaws lay only in flight. Thus it was that the late summer of 1863 witnessed a general exodus of Ducktown citizens seeking shelter within the Union lines. Wagons rumbled down the old copper road, loaded not with wage-paying copper but with disconsolate families and their bed clothes and cooking utensils. Furniture, live stock, and other cumbersome possessions were left behind, because, as Captain Raht said, "What, after all, does property amount to..." when personal safety is at stake. James Nankivell, who was returned to Ducktown with the first party detained at Cleveland, this time made his escape and went, as did William Pill, to Indiana. Others, including the Spargo, Jory, and Quintrell families, made their way to the Michigan copper mines. John and Samuel Davidson returned to North Carolina. The family of Joe Chancey, who was serving in the Federal Army at Nashville, was given passage to that city. Captain Raht joined the ranks of the refugees when he sought safety in flight in January, 1864. He made his residence at Cincinnati, where he remained until the war ended. John Tonkin, faithful mine captain, was left in charge of all mining properties. The movement from Ducktown continued until the summer of 1864, when practically all who desired to do so had left the copper district.

In March of 1864 the Union sympathies of Dr. Augustin Gattinger, who had been resident mine physician since 1858, became increasingly repugnant to his associates. Since the outbreak of the war Dr. Gattinger had been embroiled in difficulties at Ducktown because of his opposition to the rebellion. As he said: "Opposed to the disruption of the Union, knowing from experience the misery of a great nation split into petty principalities (as was the case with Germany for centuries), seeing in the growing greatness of this Government the future liberation of all nationalities through its physical power and moral influence, I advocated the cause of the Union, and created such displeasure to my former friends that I found it advisable to leave my domicile and part with my family. On a cold, starry March night, afoot, no money, with a small satchel as traveling outfit, I wound my way through the Ocoee gorge and reached the town of Cleveland, forty miles distant, without an accident."

From Cleveland the Federal authorities sent Gattinger to Nashville where he served as an assistant surgeon in the Union Army. He next held the position of state librarian until 1869. From that time until his death on July 18, 1903, much of Dr. Gattinger's time was spent in the scientific study of botany. The results of his many years of research in this field are embodied in his *The Flora of Tennessee,* from which the foregoing quotation was taken.

Augustin Gattinger was involved in a rather peculiar incident while he was residing at Ducktown. In an altercation at Hiwassee one day a Williams boy was stabbed by a lad named Harris. The injured youth was taken to the home of Dr. Gattinger for treatment. After examining the wound the doctor took a pair of scissors, snipped off the spongy fat that was oozing from the wound, and told the boy to go home. He did, and died a few days later.

From the time of the occupation of lower East Tennessee by the Federal troops until the end of the war was the most tragic period in the history of Ducktown. Guerrilla bands infested this mountainous section without fear of opposition or punishment. Homes occupied only by women and children were often ransacked, and every article of food or clothing that could be found was taken or destroyed. Horses and other live stock that had not been hurried away before the arrival of the outlaws were taken without question.

In a letter to Samuel Congdon in April, 1864, Captain Raht, writing from his residence at Cincinnati, said that the guerrillas were in complete control at the mines. A squad of Confederate cavalry, fifty in number, had visited Ducktown but had done no damage. The guerrillas, however, had stolen two of the company's mules, the harness, a wagon, and a quantity of corn. They had also stopped Captain Tonkin and robbed him of his horse, watch, and money.

The guerrilla ranks were made up principally of the baser element of backwoodsmen. The result was that many murders were committed to satisfy old grudges or to avenge real or fancied wrongs. Elam Stewart and Solomon Stansbury were murdered on Sugar Creek, in Fannin County. Sydney McLeod was taken from his home on Grassy Creek and killed on John Waters' farm at Epworth. McLeod left a wife and six children. Clayton Fain attempted to escape from his captors by leaping from Edwards' ferry and fleeing down the river. He concealed himself under a bridge near the present Louisville and Nashville Railroad Company passenger station at Copperhill, but was found and shot to death.

Two of the most notorious leaders of guerrillas operating in this region were William (Bill) Slate and Captain Gatewood. The latter was described as being a "long-haired, red-headed beast from Georgia," whose pleasure and pastime was to take human life. He made several raids into East Tennessee, but his last, late in 1864, was the bloodiest. At Benton he murdered William Kinser, a Confederate Soldier, because Kinser was not at the front. He crossed into McMinn County, where his depredations were continued, and from there advanced on Ducktown, by way of the copper road. Near the Halfway House at Greasy Creek, the band of raiders met a young man, Alonzo Jones, aged about nineteen, who was driving an ox wagon. Gatewood stood the boy up against a large rock and shot him. The blood stains remained on the rock for several years, and it was long affirmed in all candor by citizens living in the vicinity that Jones's ghost could be seen at night sitting on the rock where he was murdered. Two other young men, Jack and Simon Orr, former copper haulers, were hanged at Greasy Creek.

Farther up the river Gatewood met eight Union soldiers on their way to their army. The men fled up the mountain, but upon being assured that Gatewood's band was friendly, they returned to the road where seven of them were murdered. The lone survivor succeeded in escaping across the river. Nearer Ducktown, the outlaws shot George Barnes through the head and left him, thinking him dead. Barnes recovered, but was permanently blinded in one eye. He afterwards gained renown as the "fiddle playin' " copper hauler. On this raid twenty-four murders were committed, Gatewood himself taking credit for having killed twenty-two. Following the close of the war Gatewood sought safety in Texas, where he was reported as having been slain in an affray at Waco in March, 1871.

The end of the Civil War found the once proud little village of Hiwassee bedraggled, despondent, and almost deserted. Throughout the Ducktown district there was an air of utter abandonment. Houses and shacks around the different mines stood vacant and dilapidated, whims and windlasses were bowing under the weight of disuse, and rust was thick upon the comparatively new machinery at the mines and smelters. Water had again sought its level in the mines. Ore buckets, half-dumped, lay where they had been abandoned, and the ambitious little furnaces were solidly chilled. Trees and undergrowth that had been in the last throes of death from sulphur fumes when the roast-yard fires died out two years or more before, were once again putting on new coats of green. The old copper road was washed away at many places, and trails that led to the mines had grown up in weeds. The entire district, even when under the watchcare of fabled old Duck, had never been more somber and forbidding.

CHAPTER 12

SOCIAL DEVELOPMENTS, 1865-1890

THE WORDS OF PEACE THAT WERE SPOKEN AT APPOMATTOX Court House in distant Virginia in April of 1865 echoed immediately through the gloom and despondency that enshrouded Ducktown. Word soon came that Captain Raht was returning to reopen the mines. Merchants began at once preparations to replenish their depleted stocks, boarding-house mistresses busied themselves by fluffing up lifeless straw mattresses, farmers turned to clearing new ground on hillsides and appraising their stands of timber suitable for charcoal and cordwood, and blacksmith shops and grist mills were put in readiness for renewed activity.

Former residents who had fled the district some two years previously began making their way back over the forlorn old copper road to Ducktown. This, the second trek to Ducktown within less than two decades, was vastly different from the influx of fortune seekers in the early 1850's. Now families were returning to homes that had been hastily deserted, and men were seeking old places of employment. There was no gold to be panned in the streams and no fortunes were to be made in land speculation. This time the lure was familiar haunts, reunited families, places of business, blazing furnaces, and regular paydays. After all these things were assured by preparations that were going forward to resume mining operations, the returning refugees began the task of reestablishing old routines. Truly the little village of Hiwassee began taking on new life and preening itself for busy days ahead.

If Ducktown was quick to feel the paralyzing effects of the Civil War, it was equally quick to experience a return to normal conditions following its close. In weighing its advantages and disadvantages as compared with other localities throughout the stricken southland, Ducktown could claim two paramount advantages. One was in being possessed of a product that was in constant demand, and the other was in a citizenship that evinced little desire to perpetuate the animosities created by the conflict. The spirit to forgive and forget the tragedies of the war was expressed by George Barnes, who had been permanently injured by Gatewood's raiders. In response to a query by a visitor to Ducktown soon after the war as to how Gatewood would be treated should he again come into the district, Barnes replied by saying that he would probably not be molested as everyone realized that the unfortunate occurrences during those trying years were merely the result of "war times." Reconstruction at Ducktown was, therefore, hampered by neither economic displacement nor galled sensibilities.

Notwithstanding the fact that the citizens of this region had accepted the war's outcome as marking the end of strife and dissension and were busily engaged in rebuilding the social and industrial fabrics of old, yet subversive forces beyond their control continued for some time to present problems that could well have led to further difficulties. The principal obstacle to continued harmony was the influence exerted through political channels by the Radical party. This party, composed of anti-Southern elements within the state and headed by Governor William G. ("Parson") Brownlow, began in 1865 a period of political persecution of all southern sympathizers in Tennessee that lasted until the overthrow of the Radicals four years later. The right of franchise was denied all who had in any way displayed loyalty to the Confederacy. How this affected the voting strength in the once proud little "Rebel" county of Polk can be seen when it is understood that in the year 1866 only 172 citizens of this county were qualified to vote. And of this number, thirty-six were residents of the Ducktown area.

The disqualified voters included all who had in any way shown sympathy for the Confederate cause. This included practically all Democrats, of course, as well as a great many Republicans who realized that "Parson" Brownlow was pursuing a policy of personal revenge, which would come to no good end. The meager list of qualified voters at Ducktown in 1866 was eloquent testimony to the "forgive and forget" spirit of the district. The preoccupation of the citizens here mitigated to a large extent the bitterness that resulted from the great mass of disqualified voters in their midst. The friction from this source was effectively removed, however, when the Radicals lost their power in 1869. Thereafter party affiliations became the sole line of cleavage at Ducktown in matters pertaining to government.

One of the first objectives of the citizens of Hiwassee following the return to Ducktown in 1865 was that of better school facilities. For the first two or three years subscription schools were continued in the Southern Methodist Church building. One of the teachers who held school in the church building was J. F. Kincheloe, who later served as superintendent of the Polk County schools. The enlarged educational program got under way in 1868. The first fruits of this movement appeared in an advertisement in the Cleveland (Tennessee) *Banner* of July 9 of that year, as follows: "Wanted, at Mine City University, Ducktown, a principal who must be a graduate of a reputable institution, and a man of unblemished character. Must be willing to take not exceeding 85% of the fees in lieu of a fixed salary." The advertisement was signed by A. A. Campbell, president of the Board of Trustees, and by Henry Jory, secretary and treasurer.

It was not at all fitting that the "University" should be housed in a church building. Therefore, plans were immediately launched which resulted in the erection of a school building at Hiwassee in 1869. The school failed to attain the rating of a university but came to be known as the Mine City Institute. It later was known simply as the Academy. The first faculty was composed of a principal, A. M. Dawson, and an assistant, Miss Matthews. They were succeeded about the year 1873 by John M. Biggs and his wife.

The Academy was not a closely graded school, but the more advanced subjects taught were comparable to those taught in the high schools of that period. The school at Hiwassee was favorably known, although its students were required to take entrance examinations before entering college.

Throughout the decade of the eighties, during which time the mines at Ducktown were idle, the Academy continued to operate at a high degree of efficiency. Some financial assistance was rendered the Academy through the Peabody Fund. Two principals of the school during this time were Professors Henshaw and Blakely. The era of the shut-down of the mines witnessed the transformation of Hiwassee into a quiet, dignified little village, and this fact, plus the reputation of the school, drew many students to Hiwassee from both Fannin and Cherokee counties.

At least five Ducktown youths who attended the school at Hiwassee between 1865 and 1890 later entered the medical profession. The first of these was J. N. Ketcherside, son of J. D. Ketcherside, pioneer physician of Ducktown. The younger Ketcherside graduated in medicine at New York University about 1872.

James R. Nankivell and H. A. Rogers graduated in medicine at the same university in 1878. Ten years later, in 1888, Lucius E. Kimsey completed the medical course at Vanderbilt University, as did his brother, Fred M. Kimsey, in 1890. With the exception of Nankivell, all of these youths returned to Ducktown where they served as practicing physicians. The quality of many of the graduates of the Academy was indeed a splendid commentary on the discipline and curriculum of the institution.

Other than at Hiwassee, school facilities in the copper-mining district for several years following the war were but little improved over those of the pre-war years. Public funds for schools were scarce in both Polk and Fannin counties, and not a great deal of interest was shown in education. Subscription schools were conducted at the East Tennessee Mine and at Isabella much of the time between 1865 and 1878. Elsewhere throughout the district schools were conducted at intervals during this period. With but few exceptions they were conducted in church buildings, which were unfit for occupancy in winter weather, and rough church pews served as desks. For the youth of this district there was little in the schools to induce serious and prolonged study.

Across the Ocoee River, in Georgia, school facilities also were given little attention. It was not until about 1877 that the first public school, of a few weeks' duration each year, was opened at the Camp Ground, or Epworth. Hugh Boyd, later a prominent Methodist Episcopal minister, said in a letter to R. H. Robb on June 25, 1935, "I think you will find I taught the first school at Epworth." Two other early teachers there were William Stone and John Marshall. This school was continued until the founding of the Epworth Seminary several years later.

The one unchanging element of life in the mountainous district of Ducktown was that of religion. As the disturbed conditions attendant upon the war gave way to peaceful routine, religious services were resumed at the many sites that had already been established in the environs of Ducktown. All were Baptist churches except one of the churches at Hiwassee, and the Flint Hill and Hopewell churches, which were Methodist. However, Methodist churches later became more numerous. Organized as they were along political lines, the northern branch became the preponderant body of Methodism at Ducktown.

It was not until about 1869 that the Baptists at Hiwassee secured their own place of worship. In this connection, two letters of J. E. Raht addressed to E. MacPherson, president of the Burra

Burra Copper Company, are illuminating. In the first letter, dated December 22, 1868, Raht said: "Some of our employees, who are members of the Baptist Church are desirous of having a meeting house of their own, and desire me to request you to donate for that purpose an acre of ground to them. I can only recommend this, and have drawn up a deed, which please fine enclosed. If you approve it, please execute and return it to me at your convenience." The deed was returned to Raht for correction as, in the second letter, dated February 22, 1869, he said: "Enclosed I beg to hand you another deed for the Baptists which, I trust, will answer. They have been preaching in the Methodist meeting house the last few years, and are all very tolerant. I inserted the condition of the free use of the graveyard but omitted the use of the meeting house, as this cannot well be expected unless persons contribute to the building of the same." The building was soon erected, and came to be known as the Mine City Baptist Church.

There seems to have been no serious breach in the ranks of Wesley's followers at Hiwassee prior to the war. All Methodists, many of whom had but recently come from England, attended the Southern Methodist church. Following the war, however, inevitable disunion occurred and a Northern Methodist church was organized. But for several years following, both branches of Methodists as well as the Baptists came together in one consolidated Sunday school, which was held in the Southern Methodist building. The Sunday school was presided over at first by James Nankivell and later by I. J. Stamper.

In Methodist realignments beginning in this region in 1865, Northern Methodist disciples also proved to be much in the majority in the Fightingtown district. This resulted in the Flint Hill church being reorganized into a Northern Methodist church on June 25, 1865, as, according to Dr. R. H. Robb in his history of Epworth, the first church of this denomination to be established in the state of Georgia. It was the vigor and resourcefulness of this organization, founded by the Reverend Alexander Haren, that later secured the removal of the Ellijay Seminary to Epworth.

Hopewell Church, serving the sparsely settled region between the Camp Ground and Edwards' Ferry at what is now Copperhill, was disorganized and abandoned during the war. Several years later the church was reorganized as a Northern Methodist church, and a newly erected building was dedicated in September, 1872. Another Northern Methodist church, Hipp's Chapel, was organized soon after the war. Mountville Hipp, a Northern Methodist circuit rider who lived at Ellijay, came over the divide and preached and held revival meetings in the region of upper Fightingtown Creek. The permanent church established there was named after Hipp, as were two others—in Mountaintown, near Ellijay, and in Murray County, Georgia.

The Southern Methodists found strength sufficient to organize and establish a church in the Turtletown district. This church, Croft's Chapel, was named after W. M. Croft, one of the leaders and principal members of the denomination in that district. The first building, of log construction, was erected about 1874. Some seven or eight years later the log building was supplanted by a more modern frame building.

Other than the churches at Hiwassee, none of the churches throughout the district were able to maintain permanent pastors. And it was only through donations made by J. E. Raht up until 1878 that the pastors at Hiwassee received sufficient remuneration for their material needs. Raht recognized the influence of the local churches upon moral conditions at the mines, and was liberal in his support of them. He erected the Union church house on a hill east of the Isabella store. It was in this building that school was taught for several years.

Preaching services and protracted meetings at outlying churches in the district were conducted by circuit riders, and by ministers ordained by local church bodies. Services were held at these churches at least once or twice a month, and at each there was usually one big revival during the year which lasted from two to three weeks in the summer or fall.

Each summer for a quarter of a century following the Civil War the devout forces of Ducktown and its environs would display for Satan's benefit two convincing demonstrations of the might of right. One of these was the Sunday school picnic at Hiwassee, and the other was the camp meeting at Fightingtown Camp Ground. These memorable occasions, veritable outgrowths of inherent and unashamed faith, are fast being forgotten in the face of more tightly drawn denominational lines and modern streamlined rituals of graded religion. While differing somewhat in their immediate objectives, the picnic and the camp meetings were both products of devout endeavor. Not only was the big annual picnic a demonstration of religious amity and co-operation among all denominations, but it was the big social event of the year as well. It was looked forward to for months, and discussed for as long afterwards. By 1871 the picnics were being discussed in news items and in special articles from Ducktown. The art of picnicking was indeed developed to a high degree here. There were band music, refreshments, dinner on the ground, races, climbing the greased pole, catching—or more often chasing—the greased pig, inevitable volumes of oratory, courting, and, sometimes, a wedding. And so well in hand did the officials have the outings that moonlight picnics were being held by 1882.

To a Morganton, Georgia, correspondent we are indebted for a description of one of these picnics. A letter, signed L. H. T., was published in the Ellijay *Courier* of June 16, 1877, and is reproduced here in full:

THE DUCKTOWN PICNIC—A GRAND SUCCESS

I beg leave to speak a word through the columns of your valuable paper in regard to the Ducktown picnic, which was held on Saturday, May 26, 1877. It was a union picnic, composed of eleven Sunday Schools, each school averaging about one hundred scholars, making something over one thousand Sunday-School Scholars in all. It seemed to stimulate everyone to action when the loud and long ringing of the different church bells began, which was the signal for the different schools to march and meet at the place appointed, viz: the lower end of Main Street, where they all joined in one long procession, marching through the street and back again, headed by the brass band, Dr. J. N. Ketcherside being their leader.

I seated myself where I could command a view of three of the schools, and it was really interesting to see the little soldiers—some so small they had to be led by the larger ones—each wearing their badges, passing in different directions to their respective schools. Everything seemed to be carried on in perfect harmony, all hearts seemed to be glad that after so long a time the people of Ducktown had laid aside all contention, had ceased to pull against each other and come together as one to enjoy themselves in a union Sunday-school picnic.

The picnic grounds, about one mile from Hiwassee, are a lovely spot—well covered with young trees, forming beautiful shades, which were very acceptable to the weary soldiers.

Once on the march I could see far out in the distance the thick clouds of dust rising, and here and there squads of countrymen almost wild with excitement hurrying onward to the ground and the music dying away in the distance as the happy throng passed on, each school bearing their different colors.

On the grounds we listened to several speeches delivered by very prominent men, among whom were: Revs. J. K. P. Marshall, T. Higdon and M. Higdon.

Situated on the ground was a store containing candy, crackers, cigars, oysters, oranges, figs, nuts, canned peaches, lemonade and many more such things, which were sold for the benefit of the Sunday Schools.

There were more beautiful young ladies present than I ever saw on one occasion before, all dressed in white, which, of course, was sweetning in the coffee. All passed off peaceable and quietly during the day, and as night approached one might see couples going in different directions, heads bent towards each other, no doubt, asking how did you enjoy yourself today, and now and then speaking a sweet word for themselves.

The era of camp meetings at Fightingtown Camp Ground began prior to the Civil War. Discontinued during the war, they were revived some few years later and were held each summer until near the close of the century. Though revival meetings were by no means peculiar to this region, it is to be doubted that many such meetings held elsewhere exceeded those at the Camp Ground in organization, attendance, and religious enthusiasm.

Conducted by the Methodists, the camp meetings were organized on schedules of full-time religious activity. Services were held four times daily, at eight and eleven o'clock in the mornings, and at three o'clock in the afternoons and at night. Visiting preachers and other church dignitaries, of whom there were many, alternated in exhorting the sweltering congregations.

An immense brush arbor served as the place of worship. Rough planks served as seats, while an improvised platform supported the speaker, his fellow exhorters, and an organ. Near the platform hung a large clock, and oil lamps and lanterns, carefully arranged to avoid igniting the leaves and boughs of the arbor, funished dim illumination at night services. A headlight from an old Union Consolidated Mining Company locomotive was secured for use at the arbor after the mines closed in 1878.

The area around the flimsy tabernacle presented a carnival appearance. The meetings would last from two to three weeks. During this time the Camp Ground was the mecca of the surrounding countryside. Whole families attended. Some lived in tents, some erected permanent huts which they occupied year after year, many camped in and under their wagons, while others swooped down upon the homes of friends or relatives who lived in the vicinity. Those who lived in tents and in huts brought with them their cook stoves, cooking utensils, and bed clothes. Those who lived in wagons prepared their meals over camp fires. It was not uncommon for the more seasoned campers to bring along their milch cows. A large spring on the grounds afforded a plentiful supply of clear, cool water.

There was a constant shift in attendance at the meetings after the first few days. Wagons were moving briskly away each day while others were rumbling in slowly behind painting, dust-covered mules, horses, or oxen. But capacity crowds filled the arbor at every service. Children played happily about the grounds, while ardent swains and coyly designing maidens strolled through shaded nooks near by. Many a successful romance budded in secluded retreats while faint echoes of evangelistic appeal passed unheeded overhead.

Out of the camp meetings each year came great numbers of new converts to be added to church rolls throughout the region. Sponsored and conducted though they were by Methodists, those of the Baptist faith were enthusiastic attendants and workers at the meetings.

Paradoxical though it may seem, it was the very excitement and strain of these camp meetings that finally led to their abandonment. Especially was this true insofar as the women were concerned. The day's activities began at the sound of a bugle at six o'clock in the morning. From that time until far into the night there was no period of quiet or repose for the faithful mothers. They cooked, milked the cows, washed and mended clothes, cared for the children, sat for hours in hot, crowded arbors, and aided no little in the general daily programs. Whereas the camp meeting period each year served in a way as vacations for the men and younger members of the families, it was a different matter for the wives and mothers. For the women it proved to be the most gruelling period of the year and as a result of the uneven, unbearable burden, many of them came to the close of each year's meeting in a state of physical exhaustion. When the meetings came to be anticipated with dread and misgivings by the women, camp meetings in this region came to a close.

It will be remembered that prior to the Civil War a mail route between Ellijay, Georgia, and Turtletown, North Carolina, served the Pierceville, Ducktown, and Kimsey's Store post offices. A second route between Dahlonega and Benton served the Morganton and Ducktown post offices, while a third route was operated between Ducktown and Murphy. While it was not determined exactly when direct mail service between Cleveland and Ducktown was established, it can be assumed that this came about not long after the wagon road was opened down the Ocoee River in 1853. At any rate, mail service between Cleveland and Ducktown was disrupted during the Civil War and was not re-established until August, 1866. Until regular service was restored, the copper companies' mail between these two points was carried by copper haulers and special messengers. The mines at Ducktown had been back in operation for a year before this mail route was again taken over by the Post Office Department.

Restoration of United States mail service in the South following the close of the Civil War was on a staggered basis. From May 31, 1861, until the war's end the Confederate government had maintained its own postal system. Following the collapse of the Confederacy, the federal government turned its attention to restoring mail service in Dixie. Some light is thrown on this subject by the following extract taken from the annual report of the Postmaster General for the year 1865:

> In July, 1861, in pursuance of an act of Congress, he [the President of the United States] issued his proclamation declaring the following named States to be in rebellion, to wit: South Carolina, Florida, Georgia, Alabama, Louisiana, Texas, Mississippi, Arkansas, Tennessee, North Carolina and Virginia, with the exception of certain counties now constituting the State of West Virginia.
>
> On the 27th of May, 1861, the mails, post offices, postage stamps, and other property of the Post Office Department, situated or found in the rebellious States, having been seized by the insurgents, the Postmaster General issued an order that all postal service should be suspended in those States from and after the 31st of May, 1861....
>
> The mail service on most of the mail routes in the States designated had practically ceased before the issuing of this order. The so-called confederate authorities had seized and appropriated to the service of the insurgents the post offices, mail bags, and all the material by which the United States mail had been served in the rebel States. Many of the postmasters, contractors, and other officers and employees of the Post Office Department, voluntarily or by coercion, entered into the mail service of the rebels. With some few and most honorable exceptions, they retained themselves or delivered to the confederate authorities the money, postage stamps, stamped envelopes, and other property of the United States....
>
> ... The closing of the war brought with it the necessity of restoring the postal service in the southern States. No time was lost in offering to the citizens of those States all the facilities which they were in condition to accept. Special agents were appointed to assist in the work of restoration.

Mail schedules into Ducktown were adherred to rather faithfully so long as the mines were in operation. But following their close in 1878, Ducktown's importance suffered such a decline that even mail contractors shirked their duties to the district with impunity. Ducktown news correspondents during that period often complained of poor mail service. In the Ellijay *Courier* of April 13, 1882, "Theseus," a Ducktown scribe, lamented the irregularity of mail from Cleveland. The writer said that the contractor, who lived in Kentucky, had bid in the route at $1,300 a year, but later took his horses off the route because of the low pay. "Theseus" demanded that a local man be given the route and paid enough to carry the mail without interruption. Only one mail trip a week was scheduled between Ducktown and Ellijay up to 1879. The schedule was later increased to three round trips a week, and this same schedule applied, whether maintained or not, between Ducktown and Cleveland during the eighties.

Mail carriers of that era were a hardy group. It required ruggedness, stamina, and determination to put the mails through, over roads that in winter were deep in mud, ice, and snow. On one trip between Ducktown and Ellijay, James Haren had his feet frozen in the stirrups. Bud Long, Kem Kell, and James P. Aaron were other hard-bitten carriers on this route. Twelve hours was the schedule between these two places, but on July 30, 1880, Long brought the Ducktown mail into Ellijay by 10:00 A.M. "Bud's roan mare is as good a traveler as can be found in North Georgia," said the news item in telling of the feat. Bud neglected to say, however, at what time he had left Ducktown on this particular trip.

It was late in the eighties when rocks from out of the darkness began greeting Evans, the Cleveland carrier, at night as he entered Hiwassee. Evans conferred with James P. Aaron, the Ellijay post rider, and they devised local postal measures for combatting this peril. The two carriers met one night and rode into Hiwassee together. The usual shower of missiles greeted them. Unlimbering two well-oiled six-shooters the intrepid mail carriers plastered the surrounding landscape with a heavy barrage of lead. No one was hit, but thereafter Evans cantered into the village unmolested and unafraid.

The long road between Hiwassee and Ellijay was lined in the springtime with violets; in the fall goldenrod glowed with a warmth that tempered the approach of frigid breezes. In the silvery sun of winter icicles sparkled along the route like diamond pendants gracing the neck of a fairy princess. But not every post rider who lurched over this trail was aware of these delicate manifestations of nature; for most of them there was only dust, mud, and fatigue. But to James P. Aaron, later to turn to the ministry, there were violets, goldenrod, and dazzling icicles along the way, because romance rode with him. This swashbuckling knight of the mail pouch would glide out of Ellijay, speed up to Boardtown, and come to a sudden stop beyond the divide where a lass named Mattie Thomas, daughter of W. F. Thomas, lived. Sometime later—perhaps hours later—the race against the schedule would be resumed, and in record-breaking time Aaron's steed would be rattling the planks of Rogers' ferry. At the opposite bank the ferry would be left with a rush as the wild dash to Hiwassee was resumed. The mail had to go through on time. Twelve hours was a gruelling schedule on this route for the horse—when his master was in love.

This romance of the post-riding era of Ducktown mails ended on schedule when James P. Aaron wed Mattie Thomas. And time has not obliterated some of the memories of those glamorous days. For instance, there was the time once on a sultry day in summer when, driving hard ahead of schedule, the swaggering young Aaron dashed up to Mattie's gate and found her standing before him—barefooted! It was too late for the embarrassed maiden to escape, and too mortifying for her to remain, thus exposed. An unbearable predicament was averted when the tactful suitor feigned more interest in a gourd of water than in uneasy barefeet. Then there was another time, when the icicles had formed, that unnoticed snow covered the mail pouches left on the porch while the confident courier reposed before a blazing parlor fire that Mattie had prepared for him. Each season had its hardships, but each had its enchantments.

After the flight of Dr. Augustin Gattinger from Ducktown during the war, J. D. Ketcherside was once again the only physician in the entire district. Late in 1865 J. E. Raht secured the services of Dr. A. Sylvester Aubright as company physician. Aubright, a graduate of the University of Pennsylvania and a surgeon in the Second Ohio Heavy Artillery Regiment during the war, was residing at Loudon, Tennessee, when he accepted Raht's offer to come to Ducktown. For several years both Aubright and Ketcherside were employed by Raht as physicians at the mines. Also both dealt extensively in real estate at Ducktown. J. D. Ketcherside left Ducktown about the year 1875, and Aubright left soon after the mines closed.

The elder Ketcherside was succeeded as company doctor by his son, J. N. Ketcherside. The younger Ketcherside had been engaged in private practice at Ducktown since his graduation from New York University some three years previously. Upon his return to Ducktown from the same university, H. A. Rogers succeeded Sylvester Aubright as company doctor and served as such during the waning days of mining operations. Other physicians at Ducktown during this period were S. M. Hunter, W. R. Marshall, Adolphus Brooks, and a Dr. Parks. A news item in the Ellijay *Courier* of February 2, 1882, stated that Drs. Hunter, Marshall, and Parks, of Ducktown, and Dr. Fain, of Murphy, had operated on John Falls's feet, which had been frozen while he was in the Morganton jail, and that one foot was amputated. Other than Adolphus Brooks, all of these physicians left Ducktown within a few years after the closing of the mines. Following the reopening of the mines in 1890, Hunter and Rogers returned to Ducktown where they remained for several years.

After completing the course of instructions at the Academy at Hiwassee, James R. Nankivell entered East Tennessee University, now the University of Tennessee. The youth, son of James Nankivell, was born in England March 21, 1854, and came to Ducktown with his mother, as previously related, just prior to the outbreak of the Civil War. Returning to Hiwassee in 1873 before graduating from the university, young Nankivell went to work in a machine shop with the intention of becoming a machinist. The following year, however, he and H. A. Rogers, upon invitation of Dr. J. N. Ketcherside, began the study of medicine under the doctor's tutorship. As Dr. Nankivell said: "At that time the law governing requirements for graduation from all reputable medical colleges, specified that before entrance a student must present a certificate stating that he had pursued a course of study of the first seven branches of medical subjects, under a competent preceptor, for a period of two years. By the fall of the year 1876, Rogers and I had completed our two years' study, and we then went to New York and entered the Medical Department of the University of New York. From this school we were duly graduated in 1878."

Upon his graduation, Dr. Nankivell began the practice of medicine at Benton, Tennessee. After a few months there he removed

Compressed Air Magazine

Hoisting ore by means of the windlass was an early method replaced by the whim (see following page).

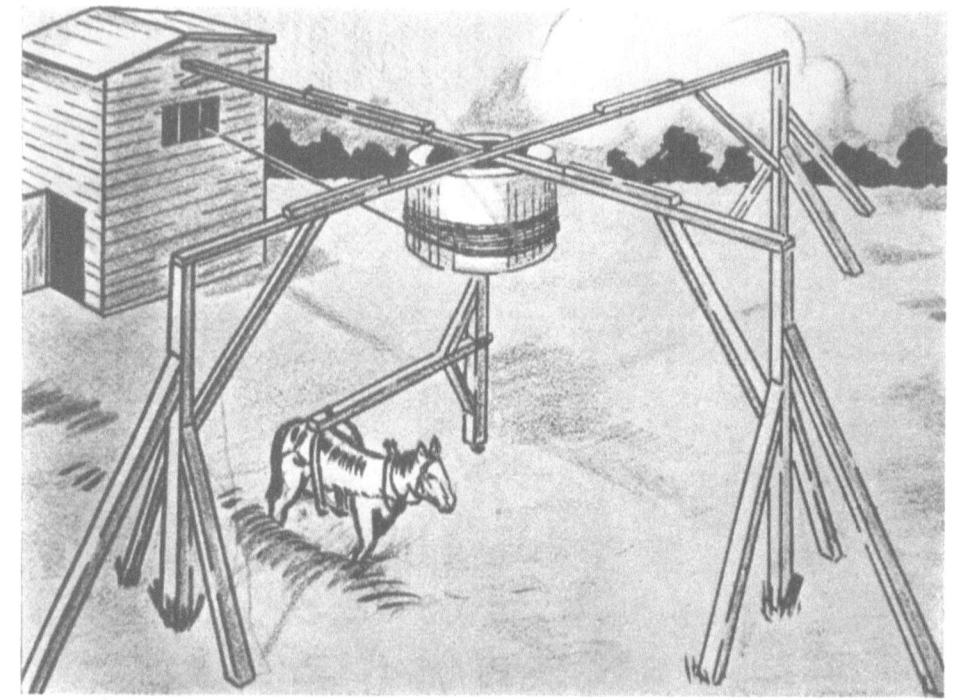

Compressed Air Magazine

The whim as a device for hoisting ore was widely used at the Ducktown mines. To operate the whim, the horse walked in a circle, winding the hoisting rope around the drum to which his harness was fastened. Whim animals often became highly trained.

to Springtown, a west Texas community that was settled largely by former Tennesseans. He remained in Texas for five years, then returned to Athens, Tennessee, where he opened an office in the year 1884. Dr. Nankivell remained at Athens and was active in his profession until his death on February 6, 1942.

There was ready, if excruciating, relief for aching molars and unsightly incisors at Ducktown during the seventies. Forceps were standard equipment of medical doctors, and it was usually known by the loud cries of pain emanating from doctors' offices when these dreaded tools were being put to use. But for more refined sieges of truly exquisite pain the citizens of the district awaited visits of itinerant dentists for more specialized dental work. Broad grins that revealed shining incisors and canines of red gold were left in the wake of these visiting dentists. In the Cleveland *Banner* of June 4, 1878, was a notice by W. C. Carson, dentist, stating that he was to return to Ducktown to complete his spring engagements. This advance notice allowed ample time for clients of faltering courage to be far removed from Ducktown by the time of his arrival.

Not only was Ducktown the industrial center of the county, but the district began to play an increasingly important part in inter-county affairs when a common law court was established there by a legislative act approved March 25, 1873. The court was established to serve the seventh, eighth, and tenth civil districts of Polk County. It constituted one of the courts of the fourth judicial circuit and was presided over by the judge of the circuit. The court, so it was claimed, served as a restraining influence upon the wayward element of the district. It was also of benefit in a material way. At each session it brought to Hiwassee a contingent of lawyers, court attendants, litigants, and visitors.

Previous to the establishment of the court at Ducktown, all litigation, however trivial, which arose in the district above the mountains, and which called for court action, required all participants to journey to the regular sessions of court at Benton. Likewise, all citizens of Ducktown summoned for jury duty were compelled to make the tortuous journey to Benton, in fair weather or foul. The trip to the county seat and return alone required two days. So manifest were these hardships upon the citizens of the upper end of the county, where the population was nearly one-half that of the county, that it was not difficult for them to secure a regular law court in their midst.

An attempt was made by J. E. Raht early in 1875 to have the

Ducktown Court abolished. He had four reasons for wanting this done: (1) The light dockets at the court at Benton did not justify two courts in the county; (2) so large a majority of the citizens in the district derived their livelihood from the copper mines that in court actions involving the companies impartial juries would be hard to secure; (3) too many employees were forced to serve as jurors; and (4) it would be but a question of time until taxes would be required to build a court house and jail at Hiwassee. Mining expenses, Raht said, were already so great that any additional taxes would be disastrous to the industry.

These objections to the court at Ducktown were sent out in letters to William R. Trewhitt, representative of Bradley and Polk counties in the state legislature, and A. Blizard, state senator. In a letter to Raht, dated Nashville, Tennessee, March 15, 1875, Trewhitt explained that bills to abolish the court had been introduced in both the Senate and House, as Raht had requested, but that both had been voted down. Trewhitt further explained that a petition signed by 433 citizens of Ducktown, praying that the court not be abolished, was introduced, as was a petition signed by 170 citizens living below the mountains, praying that the court be abolished. The representative told Raht that he presented the petitions, an act he was honor-bound to do, but that he made a speech favoring the abolishment of the court. However, the preponderance of sentiment in favor of retaining the court, as evidenced by the two petitions, made his efforts, Trewhitt said, of no avail.

The intense interest which Raht took in the Ducktown court affair is illustrated by a letter which he wrote to Harry Jory on March 5, 1875. Jory had been one of Raht's most trusted employees for several years. During the time that the court question was hottest at Hiwassee Jory committed, perhaps unwittingly, what Raht considered to be a disloyal act. In reminding Jory of his lapse of judgment, Raht displayed two of his outstanding characteristics, his boundless patience with those who erred and his ability to express himself in terms of simplicity beyond misunderstanding. The letter follows:

CLEVELAND, TENN., *March 5, 1875.*

DEAR HARRY:

Your quiet allusion on Sunday evening to a letter received by you from Hon. Wm. Trewhitt in reference to the Ducktown Law Court, and the course you took with that letter, did strike me not pleasantly, to say the least.

I cannot think that you deliberated with yourself before you turned that letter over to a citizen whose subsequent action you could easily foresee.

You knew my sentiments and the interest of the Mining Companies; you knew, furthermore, that I had been rather sensitive on this question, and that I had hardly got over my feeling about the quiet way in which the original petition had been managed at Ducktown.

Your attachment to myself after so many years acquaintance I deemed stronger in this particular instance than your ties as Mason, Methodist, or as one townsman to another.

Of course the measure is a popular one, especially in Hiwassee Town, but then your own opinion about it in relation to the interest of the Mining Companies, as you expressed it to me, should have dictated a different action on your part.

Yours truly,
(Signed) J. E. RAHT.

The court at Ducktown was finally abolished by the Legislature on March 26, 1879. But this was only after the mines had closed and the population of Ducktown was slowly dwindling away. That section of Polk County above the mountains was being written off as a county asset and was apparently henceforth to be nothing more than a thinly settled community whose wants and needs would diminish more and more as time went on. Certainly there was nothing then to indicate that either the court or the copper industry would one day be re-established.

Deserving of special mention because of the part it played in the long, rough journey between Cleveland and Ducktown, was the Half-Way House. Situated on the copper road just west of the mouth of Greasy Creek, the building, a two-story frame structure, was erected as a combination dwelling and tavern by James M. Charles in the year 1859. There was probably no connection between an experience of Charles while he was still a youth and the building of the tavern, except that he knew the fatigue and hardships, and sometimes danger, of long, unbroken stretches of travel in his day and time. Twenty-five years before he erected the tavern James Charles was a mail carrier between Dahlonega and Ellijay. Once, on what was referred to as the cold Saturday of February 7, 1835, when he was but sixteen years of age, he almost perished from cold on a trip from Dahlonega to Ellijay. The lad was barely able to reach Goodman's Mill, six miles from Ellijay, where he stayed all night. A searching party sent out to find him the next morning met him between the mill and Ellijay. The determined young mail carrier, with badly frost-bitten feet, was carrying two hound puppies in his bosom which, it was generally conceded, had kept him from freezing to death. The puppies had been secured at the home of Daniel Davis, presumably as a guard against just such a contingency.

Charles continued to operate the tavern at Greasy Creek until the mines at Ducktown closed in 1863. In that year he sold the property to Mrs. Matilda Mullins, and in 1866 J. E. Raht came into possession of it. Raht added to the facilities of the tavern and converted it into a fashionable stopping place. Located midway between Cleveland and Ducktown, the tavern came to be known as the Half-Way House. The place was a terminal where hack lines and mail carriers changed horses. Mine officials, drummers, and visitors, when traveling in private conveyances between Cleveland and Ducktown, usually began their trips so as to reach the Half-Way House before nightfall, where they remained overnight. The beautiful location of the house near the surging Ocoee, with its background of rugged mountains, and the house's comforts and sumptuous bills of fare were subjects aften dwelt upon by writers who were guests there.

One such article was written by the editor of the Cleveland *Banner* in May, 1874. The editor was in a party of six persons who stopped at the tavern on their trip to Ducktown.

A good house to stop at—Persons traveling to and from Ducktown will find the "Halfway" House a No. 1 place to stop at. The late visiting party to Ducktown tarried at it over night in going and coming, and found it all they could possibly desire. Everything was in real bon style, and the eating-doings were almost too good to talk about.

Mrs. Gibson, the landlady, knows exactly how to get up good meals, while 'Lias, the landlord, is unremitting in his attention to his guests. It is the very place to go on a pleasure excursion of a few days—the pure atmosphere, the mountain scenery, the fishing and hunting grounds in the immediate vicinity, and the good fare at the Hotel is not only real and romantic, but very inviting.

In fact, there is no place where more pleasure and comfort can be enjoyed than at the "Halfway" House. Suppose, when the heated season arrives, that some of our good citizens try it as a Summer Resort. We feel assured that they will be pleased with the experience.

Two popular landlords were Elias R. Gibson and Jacob Peck. The Half-Way House, as a hotel, passed out of existence soon after the mines at Ducktown closed. Its site was later covered by the Parksville lake.

Contemporaneous with the growth of schools, churches, and other like activities at Ducktown following the resumption of mining after the war was the development of merchandising and other forms of private enterprise. The village of Hiwassee burst through the gloom of war-days into joyous expectancy of permanent prosperity. Merchants and others with products to sell had suffered acutely from the effects of war conditions. There had been but few customers, for all sources of income in the district had been depleted. But with Raht's return to Ducktown with plans to reopen the mines, the business outlook brightened immediately.

Among the better known business houses at Hiwassee for several years following the war, in addition to the commissaries which Captain Raht operated in connection with his managerial functions, were the firms of Kilpatrick and Ketcherside (later Kilpatrick and Mosley), McCay and Marshall, Jacob Zodak, Samuel T. Waters, and I. J. Stamper. Pendleton Jones ran a small store in the Turtletown district, and McKinney's store at Chestnut Gap was of consequence in that vicinity. And while there were several other smaller stores in obscure places throughout the district, the stores at Hiwassee and Raht's commissaries remained the chief sources of varied lines of goods and produce.

Goods bought by Ducktown merchants were hauled by wagon from the railroad at Cleveland. Ample stocks were of necessity kept on hand. Not days but weeks often elapsed between the time an order was given a drummer and the receipt of the goods. Uncertain mail service and poor roads had to be taken into consideration by progressive merchants who endeavored to keep their inventories up to date.

The leading mercantile establishments at Hiwassee carried a varied assortment of wares. They supplied rope, axle grease, trace chains, salt, and green coffee to teamsters and farmers; brogans, workshirts, and chewing tobacco to miners; and cravats, derbies, cologne, cheroots, and hair dye to the men about town. For the fashionable lady shoppers they offered the latest in hats, bonnets, laces, cashmeres, chignons, switches, and curls—and a pure vegetable liver invigorator.

Visitors to Hiwassee until 1878 found comfortable accommodations at the Hunter House, or Mountain House, operated by Thomas A. Hunter. In his advertisements Hunter stated that he kept a hack, buggy, and saddle horses for conveying travelers to North Carolina and Georgia. During court weeks, especially, these hostelries were the scenes of lively gatherings where impending litigation received much unofficial pre-adjudication.

A regularly scheduled hack line was operated between Cleveland and Ducktown. Three round trips a week were made between the two towns. The hack left Cleveland at four o'clock each Monday, Wednesday, and Friday morning, and arrived at Ducktown the same day. Return trips to Cleveland were made on Tuesdays, Thursdays, and Saturdays. For several years during this period the hack line was operated by Thomas A. Hunter, who also had the mail contract on this route. Following the closing of the mines, when commercial travel between Cleveland and Ducktown virtually ceased, the hack line was discontinued.

The resumption of mining brought renewed activity in the rural sections surrounding Hiwassee. As had been true prior to the war, farmers throughout the region found a ready market at the mines for their surplus products. Those living within a radius of from four to six miles of the mines supplemented their inadequate incomes from farming by part-time employment at the works, and by furnishing wood, rock, and charcoal to the copper companies.

Many of the residents of the district who were able to retain their draft animals during the war suffered later from overanxiousness to come into possession of ready money soon after the close of the war when they sold their animals to cotton farmers in Georgia and Alabama, where an acute shortage of horses and mules existed. Not only did this result in a scarcity of such animals on the small farms of Ducktown, but Raht found it difficult to secure a sufficient number of wood, charcoal, and copper haulers when the mines were reopened. In his estimation of this policy of the natives' selling their chief means of livelihood, Raht remarked that "poor people have poor ways." He soon found it both necessary and profitable to buy mules and bring them to Ducktown where he resold them to disillusioned bargain hunters. Invariably the prices which they paid for these animals were higher than the amounts for which they had sold their original animals.

Notable among the many grist mills in this region was the McKinney Mill at Chestnut Gap. Originally known as the Hick's Mill, it was established on Fightingtown Creek in the early days of settlement of that portion of Fannin County. The mill was later acquired by Michael M. McKinney who established a small store there before the time of the Civil War. In the years following the war Chestnut Gap became a busy trading and mail center, and was a popular mid-day stopping place for travelers between Ellijay and Ducktown. The store, later operated by McKinney and Keller, handled a full line of merchandise. One of the seasonal products traded in was chestnuts. At one time the store had on hand about five hundred bushels of the rustic delicacies which were being prepared for shipment. A sudden drop in the price, however, proved disastrous—it took the last gust of wind out of the chestnut market. Only the worms profited from this calamity. Since that time a blight has destroyed practically every chestnut tree in this whole mountainous region.

Another large mill, on Grassy Creek, was originally owned by Martin and Joseph Menko, Jews. The Menko brothers left the district at about the time of the war, but the mill was operated for several years afterwards. Martin Menko later became one of the leading clothing merchants of Atlanta. Two other mills were situated in the immediate vicinity of the mines—on Potato Creek, north of Isabella, and on Davis Mill Creek near the present site of Coletown.

The tannery which was located just west of the East Tennessee Mine, at Ocoee Town, was operated by the Ocoee Leather Company possibly both before and after the Civil War. Another local industry was a wool carding machine erected by Erby Boyd on what is now known as Stuarttown Creek, about one mile east of Isabella. This plant, the only one of its kind in the district, was later operated by James Nankivell. Wool was brought to the mill from both Cherokee and Fannin counties. The owner of the machine collected as his toll one-sixth of the wool carded. Sawmills were numerous in the district.

A study of economic conditions at Ducktown during the period from 1865 to 1878 revealed that prosperity here was never of substantial proportions. Not only was this true of private business ventures, but, as will be learned in the following chapter, it was equally true of the local mining companies that struggled gallantly against heavy odds for thirteen years. The welfare and growth of Hiwassee fluctuated with the fortunes of the copper industry. Enterprises at Hiwassee were chiefly commercial and professional, and had as their basis of prosperity regular paydays at the mines. And no less dependent upon the mines for social and material betterment were the rural districts adjacent to Hiwassee. Although Ducktown did enjoy a measure of prosperity which was the envy of other towns and settlements in this tri-state region, yet the volume of wealth was always meager. There were four obstacles to an expanding economic order at Ducktown: (1) The inaccessibility of the district; (2) the limited scale of mining and smelting operations; (3) the quarterly paydays; and (4) Raht's commissaries. The dead-weight of each of these on Ducktown's prosperity will be briefly reviewed.

Inaccessibility of the district.—It is readily understood why the Ducktown district could never be developed to its potential limits of production so long as forty miles of rough road separated it from a railroad. Dependent as it was upon wagon transportation the copper industry, as well as every other form of business enterprise here, could be expanded only in terms of mule speed and wagon capacity. Even in an age that accepted inadequate transportation facilities as being a concomitant of the problems of industrial and agricultural development, the Ducktown district was hopelessly handicapped. Railroad facilities for the district was a lively subject of discussion for many years. However, the railroad that finally arrived came too late to be of benefit to the Ducktown of that era.

Limited Scale of Mining and Smelting Operations.—The spectre of a vanquished copper industry was always in the background at Ducktown. Inseparably bound up as it was with lack of transportation facilities, the industry was definitely limited in its operations. To add to the instability of feeling, the grade of ore each year became poorer, and the price of copper continued downward. Under these handicaps, plant facilities could not be greatly improved and wages and volume of employment could not be increased. While the Union Consolidated Mining Company operated continuously until 1878, yet the rate of operations fluctuated to a large extent with that of the price of copper. Further uncertainty over the future of the district arose, as will be seen later, when the break between Captain Raht and the Union Consolidated Mining Company came in 1875. Under so many adverse conditions it was inevitable that no permanent growth of the industry as a whole could be expected.

Quarterly Paydays.—Even when the mines were operating at normal capacity, and the question of transportation could be viewed objectively, there remained the long wait for paydays. These joyful days occurred but once a quarter, or four times a year. Only the most thrifty wage earner could stretch his earnings from one payday until the next, and only the most discriminating merchant could keep his charge accounts in satisfactory balance. Raht defended the quarterly paydays on the grounds that they tended to reduce lost time from payday celebrations and carousals, and that the fewer times the money was brought to Ducktown the less the chances were of hold-ups along the lonely stretches of the copper road. But the long lapse between paydays was an acknowledged drag on general business conditions throughout the district.

Raht's Commissaries.—Following Captain Raht's return to Ducktown in 1865, he consolidated his several stores located at the different mines into two large commissaries, one at Isabella and one at the Burra Burra Copper Company's smelters near McPherson Mine. Raht owned these stores personally, but had the privilege of collecting employees' accounts through the different payrolls. In this respect he held an unequal advantage over other merchants at Ducktown. Raht carried large stocks of goods. The quality of his merchandise was equal, and in many cases superior, to that of the general run of merchandise sold in the district. Admittedly a fair competitor as to both quality and price, Raht's sales were nevertheless always far in excess of those of his rivals. Enabled as he was to collect his accounts through the payrolls of the different companies, he received his pay first, and the remainder of the wages, which was usually not of much consequence, went to other creditors of his employees. It seems likely that even with the other three obstacles to general prosperity at Ducktown during that era, prosperity would have been more widespread had these commissaries not existed. On the other hand, had Raht not owned the stores they would most certainly have been operated by the mining companies and their competition with local merchants would have been none the less severe.

Speaking purely in the abstract, local interests at Ducktown had no more control over the distribution of the wealth that was created here than they had over its source or its volume. They were, in a literal sense, beneficiaries of an enterprise about which they knew nothing, so far as the influences under which it existed and strove for survival were concerned. They could anticipate future events that might affect them, but, humanlike, these anticipations could always be strained into an optimistic outlook.

We have already seen that moral conditions at Ducktown were on the upgrade by the year 1860. Following the resettlement of the district beginning in 1865, social and moral conditions continued on a high plane. There was frank intolerance of intemperance or of anything that smacked of worldly enjoyments. All forms of amusement and recreation sprang from and revolved around the churches. There simply did not develop off-shoots of society in the district, and especially in Hiwassee, that fashioned their social patterns outside churchly surveillance. Those who were not religious in fact were religious in act.

There were three contributing factors to the reign of law and order at Ducktown. The first of these was the natural passiveness of the native element. By far the greater number of inhabitants of this region were quiet, industrious, church-going folk. Many of them, through employment at the mines, gradually took on a more carefree mode of living. But this transition from rustic to industrial pursuits did not result in any marked abandonment of their inherent traits of simple respectability. This was due partly to an ancestry of companionable aloofness, and partly to forces in the district that did not accept rowdy behavior as being an inevitable companion of industrialism. The second factor, relating principally to the more urban society at Hiwassee, was the type of foreign citizen who came here. The foreign element was made up principally of English and German subjects, and many of them at once became leaders in school, church, and other polite affairs. The third factor, and the one which was most decisive in maintaining order in the district, was the strong character and restraining influence of J. E. Raht. A man could not become a nuisance in the community and hold a job at the mines or furnaces. The trouble-maker at Ducktown during that era was indeed a lone wolf.

Except at the town of Hiwassee, there was little cultural advancement in the Ducktown region between 1865 and 1890. A brass band was organized at Hiwassee soon after the war. The band first came into mention when it serenaded a prominent newspaperman who stayed overnight at the Hunter House in April, 1871. The visitor, in a later description of Ducktown, very graciously said: "Ducktown has good morals, fine schools, pretty women, healthy and robust children, and fat babies. There are no dram shops or loafers." The band was later one of the chief attractions at the big Sunday school picnics.

In March, 1882, eleven years after the visitor's appraisal of Ducktown, "Theseus," the local correspondent, said: "Ducktown has six churches, no whiskey saloons, and has had only two dances since the war. It is twenty-nine miles to the nearest still-house in the state, and there is not a drunkard to be found in the town, nor within a radius of two miles." Several months later "Theseus" told of a temperance convention at Hiwassee. Stirring speeches were delivered, and strong resolutions favoring prohibition and the nomination of a state ticket were adopted. And, concluded this self-styled namesake of the mythical Greek hero, "The people of Ducktown are right on the mark when a question of morals comes up."

Although there were no dram shops in Hiwassee, liquor was sold at two or three places in the district. The presence of these groceries, as they were called, was enough to keep the citizens of this citadel of morality alert to the dangers of strong drink.

There did, of course, develop a very definite higher class of society at Hiwassee. This polite circle went attired in the latest styles, did their culinary shopping daily, slept late on Sunday mornings, officered the church organizations, made up the literary society, discoursed upon the more timely topics of the day, and furnished much of the blast for the brass band. The literary society was organized in January, 1878, and news items for several years afterwards proudly proclaimed the flourishing condition of the society. Hiwassee's elite group was traditionally clannish. They strolled together, went horse-back and buggy riding in caravans, occupied the most conspicuous places in the choirs, played dominoes for excitement, spread their picnic dinners together in the coolest spots, and sipped their lemonades very daintily at the same stands.

They manifested becoming interest, too, in new developments in the district. An instance of this was the attention given the pontoon bridge which was built across the Ocoee River at Edwards' ferry for recovering cordwood being floated down the river. About the site of this unusual contraption it was said, "It is a place of fashionable resort on Sunday afternoons."

Forming the keystone supporting Hiwassee's social and cultural accomplishments, out of which grew the district's enviable reputation, were the merchants and professional men of the town, the men who in later years would have formed the local luncheon club. Although there were no individuals of great wealth among them, they nevertheless were men of solid character and respected ability. They were conscious of their influence upon the town's social order and took an active part in guiding its direction. For instance, it was said of I. J. Stamper that he would handle nothing in his store, including tobacco, that he could not with a clear conscience sell to the smallest child.

Hiwassee molded her social life in a definitely concentric form. That is, it developed and grew from within. With but few additions to their ranks from the outside world, the upper strata of society reproduced their own accessions to membership in their clan. Temporary additions were the estimable young gentlemen and ladies who came from North Carolina and Georgia to attend the Academy.

There was the faintest trace of a developing endogenous order at Hiwassee as the years of the shut-down lengthened. The tendency in this direction was, however, suddenly and effectively halted with the end of the industrial stagnation in 1890 when Ducktown's population was again greatly increased by newcomers seeking employment.

Although the closing of the mines in 1878 left the Ducktown district in extenuating circumstances, there was some basis of hope at Hiwassee that the mines would not remain idle indefinitely. In the summer of 1882 the district was visited by William Hutton, a civil engineer from New York, who spent some time in surveying and mapping the mining properties and in taking an inventory of the furnaces, machinery, and mining equipment that had been left here. And, too, owners of the old Union Consolidated Mining Company properties were spending a few hundred dollars a month in keeping the water pumped out of East Tennessee Mine and in keeping their machinery in order. However, the following year saw the few remaining employees dismissed and the mines deserted by their disillusioned owners.

Hiwassee never lost its courage. Despite the fact that its mines were closed, its law court abolished, and the Cleveland mail carrier would make trips to Ducktown only when enough mail would accumulate at Cleveland to make the trip seem necessary, the tenacious little mountain metropolis retained its spirit of determined hope for the future. A visitor to the district in the midst of the period of idleness reported that business at Hiwassee and Isabella was better than he expected to find it. The people were brisk and happy.

The Academy continued as the principal school of the region, Sunday school picnics each summer were high-spots of community enjoyment, and the literary society found more time for serious study. The smart set at Hiwassee, though not so numerous as in former years, lost none of its caste. Apparently, certain of Hiwassee's citizens turned to storekeeping in the absence of anything else to do, for the number of stores here increased from six before the shut-down to nine in later years. One explanation of the complacency at Hiwassee during the lean years of the eighties was offered by I. J. Stamper, who said, "We are learning to get along on little."

The prolonged period of idleness at the mines had the effect of reducing rural Ducktown to an economic status comparable to that of the decade of the 1840's. With the mines closed there was little local demand for farm products raised in the surrounding countryside. And transportation facilities to distant markets had undergone no improvement of note since the old copper road was built. Cattle and sheep were, however, raised rather extensively. There was definite advantage in raising live stock, as animals could be got to market under their own power. Much of the timber had been cleared from the central portion of the district, and wide ranges were available for grazing. Cattle and sheep were driven to markets at Atlanta, Dalton, and Cleveland. White beans and sorghum were hauled to these far away markets and sold for cash with which to pay taxes. Such trips usually required from one to two weeks. Taxes had to be paid, and means of raising the needed money locally were few indeed.

As late as the eighties many articles of clothing worn by native inhabitants were home-spun. Home-made shoes too were common. Many a gallant young swain took pardonable pride in his specially made, ornately decorated, high-heeled boots. These were carefully tallowed and preserved for such special occasions as camp meetings, church services, and matrimonial forays. Emerging from the age of puberty, Ferdinand C. Cochran, one of the more fastidious youths of the Camp Ground community, began finding the ill-fitting, home-made clothing increasingly vexatious to his discriminating taste. When he could secure cloth of a texture more delicate than that of the ordinary jeans, he would carry it all the way to the home of Betty Witt, at Isabella, where this expert seamstress would fashion the material into garments more befitting the young man's sartorial attainments.

The period of shrinkage into which Ducktown slipped upon closing of the mines ended only when the population had ebbed away to a point where it met the region's economic level of subsistence. But this downward trend came to a halt when railroad construction crews appeared and the long-awaited railroad followed in their wake. With the arrival of the first train at Ducktown early in 1890 came a new day and a new age for this district; and with the train's departure went an era that took with it nothing sacred—but memories.

CHAPTER 13

MINING, 1865-1878

IMMEDIATELY FOLLOWING THE CLOSE OF THE CIVIL WAR CAPTAIN Raht returned from Cincinnati and established his office at Cleveland, Tennessee. It was from this office that he thereafter directed the affairs of the copper companies at Ducktown. As soon as he could do so, Raht visited Ducktown for the purpose of ascertaining conditions at the mines. In a letter dated July 16, 1865, to Samuel Congdon, managing director of the Union Consolidated Mining Company, he reported as follows on the properties of that company:

On my return here I find that no serious damage has been done to our buildings and machinery; many of our houses have been broken open and somewhat injured, and some log cabins have been burnt; the material houses and workshops have been repeatedly plundered; the offices and storehouses have also been entered by the guerillas, and some property has been carried off, part of which we may recover again.

About the damage underground I cannot say as yet; but I think that the shafts and tunnels in the Isabella mine are crushed considerably. This may delay mining, but will not delay the pumping of copper water.... The tail race at the Isabella mine has filled up with mud, and is caved in near the water wheel, which is injured thereby. The dam is washed away, and the upper race needs cleaning out. A new set of troughs is required to precipitate in, and iron is wanted for this purpose. I recommend an immediate appropriation to start this work vigorously....

The blast furnaces at the Tennessee Mine need considerable repair, while those at the Isabella property are in good condition. There are about five thousand bushels of charcoal, and but little fire-proof rock on hand at these two smelting works.

Conditions at the mines and furnaces of the Burra Burra Copper Company and Polk County Copper Company were much the same as those at the works of the Union Consolidated Mining Company.

Four tasks confronted Raht in his efforts to resume work at Ducktown. All were equally important and all were attacked simultaneously. Probably the most difficult of these was his having to discover from the officials of the different companies just how vigorously they intended to prosecute operations and how willing they were to finance adequately the work. To secure this information, he was in constant communication with the officials of the three companies from July, 1865, until the latter part of the year. Conditions at the mines were in a discouraging state, but they were no less so than the conditions existing in the executive branches of the organizations. The defeat of the Confederacy rendered invalid, of course, the sales by that government of the properties at Ducktown in 1863, but several months elapsed after Raht's return to Ducktown before meetings of the dispersed directors of the Union Consolidated Mining Company, Burra Burra Copper Company, and Polk County Copper Company could be held and plans agreed upon. None of the companies had finances enough to furnish Raht with the amounts he needed at the mines, and one of his chief worries was whether they ever would have. The Union Consolidated Mining Company was the first to authoize resumption of work. The other two companies delayed such action for several months.

Raht's second task was in having the old copper road and the road through Cherokee County, North Carolina, put in condition for use. Both of these roads were unfit for heavy wagons. Since there were no funds in the treasury of the Ocoee Turnpike and Plank Road Company, Raht put men to work on the copper road and prorated the expense to the three copper companies. This work was begun immediately following Raht's visit to the mines, as he was anxious to begin moving the ingot copper stored at Ducktown. It was necessary that the road in Cherokee County be repaired, as it was over this road that fire-proof rock, or "cotton rock," was hauled for use in furnace construction. Raht reported that several bridges on the road were down, and that to secure the rock when needed he would be forced to pay for having the bridges rebuilt himself as the county was financially unable to do the work. These expenses were likewise to be borne by the copper companies.

Insofar as immediate needs were concerned, his third, but prime, task was in getting to market as promptly as possible the some two hundred thousand pounds of copper hidden in caverns at Ducktown. The revenue from this would go a long way in

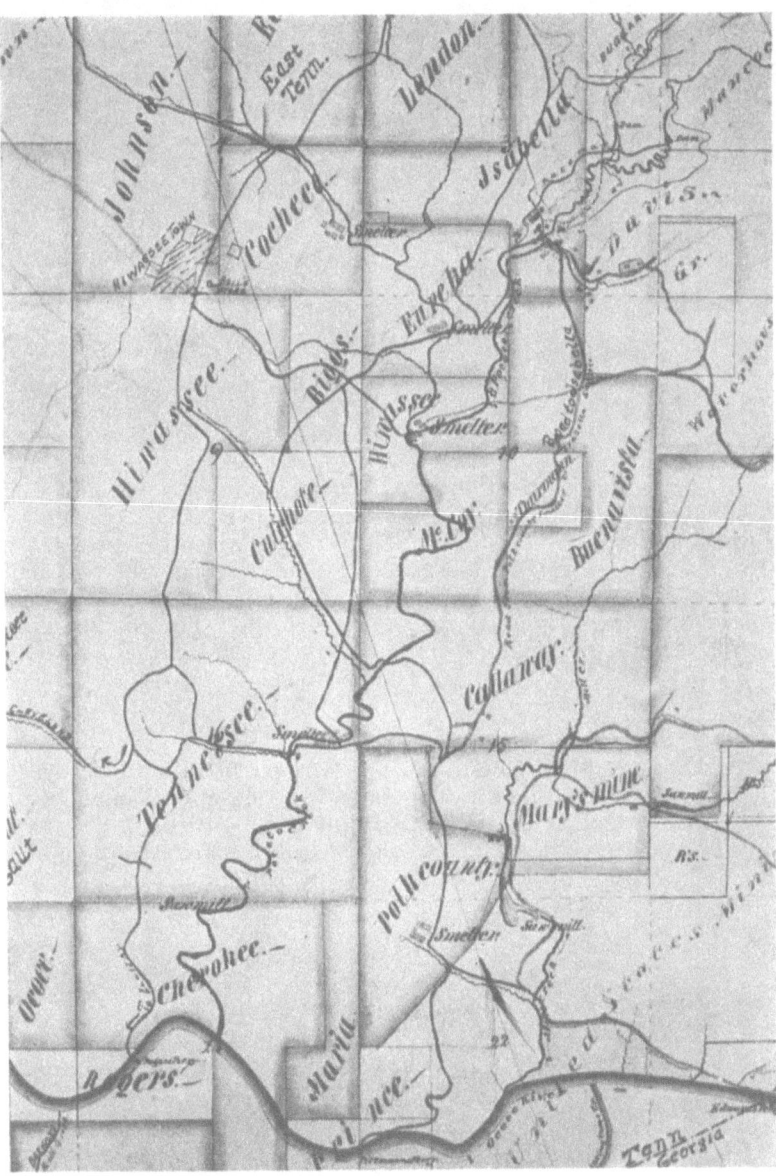

An old map of the 1870's showing the central portion of the Ducktown district. The names Tennessee, Callaway, etc., refer to mining properties. Edward's Ferry, in the lower right-hand corner, is the site of Copperhill. Hiwassee Town, at the upper left, is the present-day Ducktown. The Copper Road to Cleveland appears in the Tennessee Mine block, and the road to Ellijay descends along the left of the map, crossing the Ocoee River at Rogers' Ferry. The Tennessee smelter on Potato Creek was the first to be erected in the district.

The old copper road through the Ocoee Gorge, completed in 1853. This narrow strip of wagon road, over which copper was hauled the forty miles to the railroad at Cleveland, is hemmed in for a distance of 25 miles by steep mountains and the turbulent Ocoee River. It was Ducktown's only effective means of communication with the outside world until 1890. The portion of the road winding along the river looks just as it did in the nineteenth century.

McKinney's Mill, Chestnut Gap, Georgia, is said to be over a hundred years old and was operated by Michael McKinney before the time of the Civil War. Chestnut Gap, with its mill, general store, and tavern, was a popular stopover for travelers between Ducktown and Ellijay in the 1860's and 1870's.

relieving, at least temporarily, the financial stringency of the companies. But this was no easy task. In the first place guerrillas were still active; in the second place the copper road was almost impassable and, finally, wagons were virtually non-existent. Late in June, 1865, before Raht visited the mines, he had visited military headquarters at Nashville, Knoxville, and Chattanooga, and succeeded in having orders issued to the commander at Cleveland to let ten of his wagons, accompanied by a guard, make a trip a week to Ducktown to haul the copper to Cleveland. On July 16, however, he reported that the military commanders were shifted so frequently that the military "will or cannot assist us in hauling copper from the mines." Nevertheless, by the end of July the copper road had been repaired in part and enough wagons had been secured to start the movement of copper from Ducktown.

For shipment by rail from Cleveland the copper ingots were packed in barrels, each of which weighed when loaded about twelve hundred pounds. Ownership of the stored copper was divided among the companies, Raht, and the employees. Raht's interest in the copper was by virtue of advances made the companies prior to and during the war, while the copper owned by the employees came about by some of them having accepted the metal in lieu of money wages during the war. It was, therefore, a matter of much concern to a great many that the copper be taken to market as quickly as possible.

Rail service to the north and east by way of Knoxville and Lynchburg was not resumed until October, six months after the war had ended. During this interim the Ducktown copper that was shipped moved northward by way of Chattanooga and Nashville.

To expedite the movement of these cars of copper, after the East Tennessee and Virginia Railroad had been put back in operation, Raht sent Harry Jory to Lynchburg, Virginia, in November, 1865, to trace shipments and push them to their destination, and, said Raht, "he will push as hard as a little man can."

The fourth task confronting Raht was, naturally enough, that of repairing the furnaces and putting the mines in condition for producing ore. His first objective in this respect was to place the furnaces in operation in order to treat the ores already mined.

While Raht was engaged with the four major tasks just described, he was faced with other problems. One of these was ridding the mountainous region around Ducktown of guerrillas.

On August 8, 1865, he wrote to Major-General James B. Steedman, Commander of the Department of Georgia, at Augusta, and requested that a Federal post be established at Blairsville to protect the surrounding territory from raids by men wearing Rebel uniforms and carrying heavy pistols. A group of citizens of Union County, Georgia, had called upon the Federal commander at Cleveland, Tennessee, and requested that a scouting force be sent through Fannin, Gilmer, Towns, and Union counties to drive these brigands away, but their request had not been granted. Raht told General Steedman that the guerrilla bands were made up of north Georgians who at times extended their raids into nearby Tennessee, and that if an army post were established at Blairsville the robbers could in a short time be dispersed. Although military protection was not given, guerrilla activities in this region ceased within a few months after work was resumed at Ducktown.

No sooner had Raht returned to the mines than several of his former employees began harassing him for back wages due. A letter written by him to Edward Dunn, Greenfield, Ohio, on August 16, 1865, throws some light on this subject. The letter said:

> The companies for which I am agent are shipping copper to market now and will be able to pay their indebtedness with the proceeds of this copper sometime in October next.
>
> You may send me a statement of your account against the companies, and also state how many dollars you are willing to take for your claim in greenbacks.
>
> I told you, like every one of my employees, that I expect to act fair towards you and do what is right between the men and the companies. I did not force anybody to take Confederate money but I do not expect to pay as many dollars in United States Currency as I agreed to pay in Confederate money.
>
> I shall deal just as fair with you as with any other of my former employees, although you attempted to put me to unnecessary trouble at Cincinnati.
>
> Please notify any of your friends to send in their claims to me.
>   Truly yours,
>   J. E. RAHT, *Agent*.

Additional teams for hauling copper had to be secured; charcoal was needed for furnace operations, as was cordwood for stationary engines and for roasting ore, and mine timbers for repairing crushed underground workings. In regard to the shortage of teams, Raht, in a letter to Samuel Congdon, said that aid would have to be given the local citizens in buying animals and wagons. The people here were poor, he said, and the few who had remained at Ducktown throughout the war had lost about all they had ever owned.

Barrels had to be purchased for shipping copper. These were secured, for the most part, from breweries. Castings for copper moulds, rope for windlass and whim use, black powder, fuse and blasting caps, candles for use underground, picks, shovels, and many other similar items had to be secured and hauled to the mines.

One phase of the operation at Ducktown which could be started immediately was that of the recovery of copper from mine water. One of Raht's first orders to John Tonkin was to repair the troughs and place in them any scrap iron available. So anxious was Raht to obtain scrap that he said in a letter to Tonkin on September 7, 1865, "Poor Harry [Jory] was sent to Nashville to attend a sale of scrap iron and make purchases without having any money."

Thus has been outlined many of Raht's tasks and problems in reviving the copper industry at Ducktown following the close of the war. Not only was it left to him to initiate this work, but to him was left the larger problem of financing the industry until the directors of the three interested companies could formulate plans whereby operations could be placed on a permanent basis. In the following description of mining at Ducktown between 1865 and 1878, the narrative will continue to be divided into the part played by each of the three operating companies. As the Polk County Copper Company, Burra Burra Copper Company, and Union Consolidated Mining Company ceased operations and passed out of existence in the order listed, the story of each will be thus related.

POLK COUNTY COPPER COMPANY

Although owners of one of the richest copper mines at Ducktown, as well as of a smelting works that had been completed on Confederate money during the war, the Polk County Copper Company was never able to carry on sustained operations after the return to peace. For two or three years after resuming work, Raht utilized this company's furnaces in treating ores from some of the other mines in the district, and took a small tonnage of ore from the Polk County Mine during this period, but operations on the company's part were inconsequential and of short duration.

The death of William H. Peet during the war had removed one of the company's principal figures, and lack of finances thereafter inevitably led to complete failure.

The Polk County Copper Company emerged from the reorganization of 1859 indebted to John Caldwell, A. H. Keith, and the Mastin heirs for the purchase price of Polk County Mine. Keith and the heirs retained mortgage liens on their interests in the property pending payments of $34,831.94 to Keith and $25,065.00 to the heirs. It seems that Caldwell accepted stock in the company in payment of his interest in the property, and the amount owed to the heirs was finally paid, but Keith was paid only about one-half the amount owed to him. This latter obligation was instrumental in bringing about the final dissolution of the company.

In September, 1869, E. MacPherson, then president of the company, visited Ducktown. One purpose of the visit was to inspect the mine, idle at that time from lack of funds, and another purpose was to try to induce A. H. Keith to accept new, first-mortgage, 8 per cent bonds of the company for the balance due on his original mortgage. The mortgage at that time, including principal and interest, amounted to about $27,000. But with regard to reaching an agreement with Keith, the president reported to the board of directors: "I have satisfactorily ascertained that no settlement can be made with him, short of payment in money."

A lawsuit to force settlement of his claim was instituted by Keith in the chancery court at Benton in November, 1870. The case dragged on until January, 1874, when the court ruled that Keith was entitled to foreclosure, and sale of the mine property was ordered. However, an appeal was granted the company, but nothing came of it. The struggle next came to light when, on December 18, 1874, notice was issued by the United States District Court at New Orleans, Louisiana, that the Polk County Copper Company had been adjudged bankrupt upon its own petition.

Prior to sale of the Polk County Mine, Captain Raht corresponded at length with E. MacPherson and L. F. Generes at New Orleans. Raht was attempting to salvage what he could for the benefit of stockholders of the Polk County Copper Company, who, he said, had already lost heavily. Negotiations between the New Orleans parties and Keith were handled through Raht. Keith wanted the money owed him and not the mine; the parties at New Orleans wanted the mine, but they were unable to raise the necessary funds to satisfy Keith. At one stage of the negotiations Raht had almost succeeded in inducing Keith to accept $5,000 in cash and to wait a year for payment of the balance. Upon learning of Keith's apparent capitulation, L. F. Generes promptly took up the negotiations direct with Keith, whereupon Keith became suspicious of some ulterior motive and declined further attempts at settlement.

The sale of the mining property took place at Benton, as ordered by the chancery court, on May 12, 1875. Keith opened the bidding at $10,000. J. E. Raht, acting on behalf of his principals at New Orleans, next bid $20,000. Keith then bid $25,000, at which figure the sale was closed. This last amount was considered to be in excess of the mine's worth, not because of lack of ore, but because hope of a railroad's being built to Ducktown had been abandoned and the future of the entire district was indeed not bright. Despite the uncertainty of the future, however, Keith preferred possession of the mine to accepting settlement for any amount less than that owed to him. The ownership of the property still rests in his heirs.

BURRA BURRA COPPER COMPANY

Underground work was resumed by the Burra Burra Copper Company early in 1866. For some five or six years the ore continued to average from 10 per cent to 15 per cent copper. It was from this rich ore, located near the surface, that the company hoped to be able to realize profits sufficient to cover expenses until deep workings could tap the more abundant yellow ore. In June, 1869, with the supply of black copper nearing exhaustion, earnest efforts were being made to reach the yellow sulphurets and work was started on the MacPherson shaft. Unfortunately the shaft failed to strike the anticipated ore body, as did a cross-cut driven off the shaft for a distance of 110 feet. A steam hoisting engine of forty horsepower was installed, but about all it hoisted was muck and waste rock from the shaft and cross-cut.

The smelting works of the Burra Burra Copper Company, like those of the other two companies at Ducktown, had been completed during the years of the war. These consisted of nine furnaces, a forty-horsepower steam engine, and a waterwheel of four horsepower. An average of about one million pounds of copper was produced at these works annually.

The Burra Burra company employed normally about 160 men and boys, and its average yearly payroll was about $60,000. It consumed approximately ten thousand cords of wood a year, at an average cost of $3.00 a cord.

By the spring of 1872 the Burra Burra Copper Company was verging on collapse. Further financing was impossible and the poor results attendant upon sinking the MacPherson shaft left no immediate ore supply available. What transpired between that time and the summer of 1873 can best be described by quoting from E. MacPherson's report to the stockholders in August, 1873. In that part of the report dealing with the obstacles encountered at the mines, it was stated that:

> Instead of finding a good vein [in the new shaft] that would pay, we met with only narrow strips of mundic, or iron pyrites, associated with a little yellow ore, and separated by wide bars of gneiss and slate. This constituted the vein!
>
> Disappointed by its barren character at this point, and having worked out all the black ores that would pay for mining, at the extraordinarily low price of copper at that time, and which, up to April 1872, had furnished our working means, but one alternative presented itself for exploring at other points....
>
> Believing this might be done by means of a diamond pointed drill, an instrument then recently invented and used successfully on mining properties in the northern states to test the character of veins in depth at a comparatively small expense and in the shortest time, I determined at once to raise by voluntary subscription of stockholders of the Burra Burra Copper Company and the Polk County Copper Company a sum sufficient to purchase one and work one or both properties. After some effort I raised $5,500.00—a drill of the best construction was bought, with its necessary appendages and 500 feet of tubing, and on June 15, 1872 put it to work on the Burra Burra vein....

After reciting the repeated failures to find ores of necessary richness, MacPherson stated in the report that funds for further explorations and operations could not be raised with a mortgage debt of nearly $256,000 burdening the company. He concluded by saying that he had advised Franklin H. Delano, trustee, of the company's inability to continue in operation.

It will be interesting to look behind the scenes and learn something of the trials and tribulations of the officials of the Burra Burra Copper Company during the eight years they vainly tried to put the company's operations on a paying basis following the close of the Civil War. These years had been replete with hopes and disappointments. They had been filled with internal misunderstandings; with schemes at financing and refinancing; with planning, but mostly with hoping for, a railroad from Cleveland to Ducktown; with assisting in securing an increase in the tariff on copper; and, finally, with dissolving the firm.

A roster of the board of directors was not available for the entire eight-year period, but for a number of years the board was composed of E. MacPherson, president, and W. T. Williams, Albin Rochereau, H. H. Stanley, F. Camerden, and William Creevy. Of these men, E. MacPherson was the only one who was connected in an official capacity with the company from the time it was first organized until its active days were over.

Like that of the Polk County Copper Company, the history of the Burra Burra Copper Company reveals a struggle of several years against an old debt that became heavier with each passing year. This debt was in the form of a series of mortgage bonds, amounting to nearly $300,000, held by John M. Dow, Warren Delano, and Samuel F. Tracy on the old Cocheco and Hiwassee properties purchased by the Burra Burra Copper Company in 1860. These bonds first came due in 1866, but were renewed for a further period of five years. It was a memorable feat to keep the interest alone paid.

Fortunately there was enough copper stored at Ducktown belonging to the Burra Burra Copper Company at the end of the war to put the company's mines and smelters back into operation. But J. E. Raht immediately levied on ten thousand dollars' worth of this copper to reimburse himself for bonds of the company in that amount which he held, and which were declared to be fraudulent because they did not show on their face that they were second-mortgage bonds. Raht secured judgment against the company, and on November 21, 1865, the chancery court at Benton authorized him to sell copper produced by the Burra Burra Copper Company until his judgment was satisfied.

Early in 1866 Raht received a letter from Lyman W. Gilbert in which Gilbert inquired about the prospects of his receiving payment of $5,000 owed to him by the Burra Burra Copper Company. Raht's reply tempered any hope that Gilbert might have cherished in this respect when he confided to Gilbert that "our operations are rather small in proportion to our great name and the amount of our indebtedness."

In his yearly reports to the stockholders, E. MacPherson held to the lingering hope that the proposed railroad would be built to Ducktown. In his report for the year 1868 he very eloquently remarked: "In a word, this railroad built, the mines at Ducktown could make ingot copper and forward it to market at all seasons of the year at less cost than any other mines in the United States, and realize ample profits at prices that would compel the stoppage of those elsewhere." But the Burra Burra Copper Company could only hope for the best; it could never lend financial assistance to the railroad project.

Another factor contributing to the company's straitened circumstances was that of the declining price of copper. Raht apprised MacPherson of some of the reasons for the decline when he said: "The low price of copper has been attributed to the increased production of same in several parts of the world, and especially in California, and the decrease of its consumption—for example; in shipbuilding where iron vessels are taking the place of wooden ones which require no copper lining; zinked iron being used frequently now in lieu of sheet copper, and steel and iron cannon instead of brass ones." In his report for the year 1870 MacPherson said that the falling price of copper over the past five years had cost the company $150,000.

In order to bolster the price of domestic copper, the copper mining interests of the United States began laboring to secure an increase in the tariff on copper ores soon after the close of the war. On the other side of the fence, opposed to any such tariff on ores, were the copper refiners. As one of the refining companies said about the mining companies: "If copper is imported, then it is the duty upon ingots and bars that alone will benefit them."

In a "Memorial Upon the Free Admission of Foreign Copper Ores," addressed to the Committee of Ways and Means of the House of Representatives by S. T. Snow, agent of the Revere Copper Company of Boston, in February, 1867, it was said in part:

> An effort is being made, by parties interested in mining on Lake Superior and in California, to have an additional duty imposed upon the importation of foreign copper ores. This movement we must oppose by every proper means within our power. We go still further, and urge *the removal of the duty with which it is now charged.*
>
> The business of smelting copper ore was begun in this country a little more than twenty years ago. At that time England was the only country where ores were carried to be smelted....
>
> While *here* they were then admitted free.
>
> Since that time the duties *there* have been removed entirely; and

here the change has been in the other direction; they are now charged with 5 percent ad valorem, first imposed by the tariff of 1861.

England has been seeking to draw the vast trade of Chili and Peru to herself, by removing every obstacle in the way of an easy and attractive remittance for the commodities they must obtain from other countries, and the result is that, today, the considerable trade which had grown up between this country [United States] and the South West Coast is substantially at an end....

No ore, nor anything else in fact, are *required* in payment of our deliveries of merchandise exported to them, for the reason we now make no such deliveries. *A peculiar class of ores needed by the smelters here,* so as to work our own, mined either in California or in the Atlantic States, to the best advantage, *can only be obtained from Chili and Peru.* We can smelt our own ores by themselves, but only at a greater cost....

England is still the only country where copper ores are carried to be smelted; she has pursued such a course as really to absorb this business to herself, and at the present time she controls, for this article, the markets of the world. Occasionally, however, efforts are made in other countries to compete with her. Smelting furnaces have been erected and the business carried on to a small extent, enough to exhibit the fact that ores may be carried to any other country in the world, but the United States, free of an import duty.

Attention was then turned to copper-mining companies that were claiming that they had been forced out of business because of the poor price of copper. To these claims the memorial countered:

The companies referred to which have stopped work have not done so because of the unremunerative price of copper, but solely in consequence of the inability to show any such hopes of a profit in copper as would, under any circumstances, be likely to compensate for the assessments called for. An advance in the cost of working an unproductive mine has, in many cases, been the determining cause for closing it; a decline in the price of copper, never.

A mine producing any considerable quantity of copper will go on for years calling with great regularity upon its stockholders for further payments, but its abandonment may never once be contemplated....

This attempt by the smelting interests to clarify the copper situation in this country, and the efforts they made to lay the blame upon the miners for their own predicament, merely enlivened the controversy. And as to the contention that certain kinds of foreign ores were necessary in the treatment of domestic ores, the following letter, written by Carl Raht, secretary of the Union Consolidated Mining Company, to Congressman Maynard of Tennessee, will be revealing:

> I duly received your esteemed favor of the 18th inst.
> The bill proposed in the Committee of Ways and Means will give to the copper mining interest all the protection needed.
> The copper production of this country is fully equal to its consumption. Foreign copper, refined or in ores, is not needed in any branch of industry for which our own productions would not answer better....
> How the present tariff on copper ores—too low alike for protection and revenue—operates, became very apparent in last fall. Copper prices were then returning to something like a paying rate in this country, and holders could with some reason expect some further advance. There was much disposition to buy for future delivery in the expectation of better rates. At that period one of the largest smelting establishments on the coast stepped into the market and sold for future delivery large quantities of copper, which they then neither had refined nor in the ores. But they based their calculations for ability to deliver on the European market for ores, bought by telegram several cargoes of Chilian and other foreign ores, brought them here, smelted and delivered them and glutted the market to such an extent that prices went lower than ever.
> It cannot be asserted that this smelting industry deserves any particular fostering care by legislation or the omission of legislation.
> The amount of capital and labor employed in it are utterly inconsiderable compared to those employed in the copper mining interest of the country, while its producing capacity and power for ruinous competition are very great.

Evidently Congress knew, as did Carl Raht, that there were more copper miners than smelters in this country, for the proposed tariff law was passed by the House in December, 1868. Congressman Maynard was active in his support of the measure.

Before the Senate acted on the bill, which it passed in the following month, Captain Raht found it advisable to enter the fight in behalf of his brother, Carl. It seems from the Captain's correspondence that the Baltimore Copper Smelting Company had cast some unkind aspersions on Carl Raht's letter. They had seemingly designated him as being nothing more than a Wall Street broker who knew but little about copper mining. To refute these charges Captain Raht wrote to Joseph S. Fowler, Senator from Tennessee, and said in part: "Wall Street is admitted to be a bad place to hail from in many instances, but this circumstance will not detract anything from Mr. Chas. Raht's statements, when the statistical authorities and facts are on his side.... Any assistance you do give us will be duly appreciated, not only by us who are directly interested, but also by the whole surrounding country."

For a month after the Senate passed the tariff bill, it lay on President Andrew Johnson's desk, awaiting his action. During this period Captain Raht took several sarcastic digs at the President in letters to his brother. The Rahts were fighting the battles not only for the Burra Burra Copper Company but for the Union Consolidated Mining Company, themselves, and all others engaged in mining at Ducktown. The President's known opposition to the tariff law made him an object of Captain Raht's ire.

In one of his letters to his brother the Captain said, "Has Andy signed the copper tariff bill yet?" And again, "I hope the copper tariff bill becomes a law today, either with or without Andy." And, "There is only one Andy! If you had invited him to dinner before the Baltimore Committee reached him, he might have signed the bill...."

The President vetoed the bill on February 24, 1869, but the veto was promptly overridden by Congress. The next day Captain Raht wrote to his brother: "Your message reporting the action of Congress... came to hand last night, and was very timely as I had had the blues for the last day or two. Well, we must work ahead now and do our utmost to produce a large quantity of copper, get out of debt, build the railroad, and live contented...."

As finally passed, the bill increased the duty from 5 per cent ad valorem to three cents a pound on fine copper in ores; to four cents a pound on fine copper in matte and regulus; and to five cents a pound from two and a half cents a pound on ingot copper. The domestic price of copper increased somewhat following enactment of the bill, but by this time the Burra Burra Copper Company was too weak to respond to such artificial stimulants. What the company needed most was more money and less encouragement.

There were times when the Burra Burra officials could probably find surcease from all their worries, with the exception of the mortgage held on the company's properties by Dow, Delano, and Tracy. For instance, they reached an agreement with the mortgagees in 1867 whereby the time limit on the debt was extended for a period of five years. To do this, however, they needed $50,000, which they secured of their superintendent, J. E. Raht. This resulted in the Captain's taking possession of all copper produced until the debt was repaid; consequently the company's treasury remained bare during this interim. Apparently hopeful that some miracle would occur which would allow them to receive another payment, the creditors stayed immediate action when the renewed mortgage was not paid. But the miracle stage had passed, and in the latter part of 1875 Henry L. Pierson and Franklin H. Delano, trustees of the mortgage holders, moved in and instituted foreclosure proceedings.

The closing chapter of the active history of the Burra Burra Company was written in 1877. Foreclosure proceedings had been completed and sale of the company's properties was scheduled to be held at Benton on June 14. Raht had told MacPherson that Warren Delano, of New York, and Daniel S. Printup, of Rome, Georgia, attorney for the bondholders, would attend the sale, but that if the New Orleans parties interested in the property desired to act, he would be glad to carry out their instructions. But MacPherson had had enough, and at the sale Warren Delano bid in the entire real estate and mining properties of the Burra Burra Copper Company for the nominal sum of $25,000.

As a parting tribute to E. MacPherson let it be said that for nearly twenty years he labored faithfully and diligently to make a success of the interests he represented at Ducktown. With better transportation facilities he might have succeeded.

UNION CONSOLIDATED MINING COMPANY

There was no litigation involved in reclaiming possession of their properties by the Union Consolidated Mining Company after the end of the Civil War. Titles to these, which passed to William H. Peet when the properties were sold by the Confederate Government in 1863, faded away with the return of peace. And while Captain Raht was busily engaged in putting the mines and smelters at Ducktown back into operation in the fall and winter of 1865, the executive branch of the company at New York was undergoing reorganization. The new board, finally elected in 1866, was composed of the following members: John Thomas, president; Charles Raht, secretary; J. E. Raht, superintendent at the mines; and John Thomas, J. Eager, Charles B. Tatham, Samuel Congdon, E. W. McGinnis, G. C. Bogert, F. A.

Kirtland, J. A. Alexander, C. B. Payne, George S. Cameron, and J. E. Raht, directors.

One of the first acts of the new board was to prepare a report to the stockholders, informing them of conditions at Ducktown, and assuring them that the future of the company was bright. Following are excerpts from the report, showing that the effects of the war on the company's position had not been very bad after all:

> If, since 1860, your Board of Directors has only now called a meeting of stockholders, the reasons are obvious. The breaking out of the war had placed the mines beyond the control of this Board, and even beyond the reach of information, and here the affairs of the Company were therefore kept in a state of suspense.
>
> When, at the close of the war, we examined the condition of the mines and the financial status of the Company, we found not only that we might have fared much worse, but that in some respects our position was materially improved. It is true the mines had been worked to some extent during the war, and our stock of ores diminished, but there had also been new developments made which have vastly enhanced the value of the mines, by proving, beyond the most sanguine expectations, the existence of a solid and inexhaustible supply of ores. The yellow sulphuret of copper, which had first been discovered in the East Tennessee mine immediately before the war, has been proven to form a lode of uncommon dimensions and of uniform richness....
>
> Shortly before the beginning of the war we had passed resolutions advising the erection of Refining Works, jointly with the Polk County Copper Co. and the Burra Burra Copper Co., and we had also authorized the erection of new Smelting Works on the Isabella property. These works, upon the return of peace, we found finished and available for immediate operations.
>
> Even financially our affairs have improved, and the ores taken out and disposed of during the war do not prove an absolute loss; for, in the settlement effected with the parties who controlled the mines during the war, we have in last February wiped out the debt of $80,000 we owed to the Treasurer before the war, have secured a one third interest in the United Refining Works, and have obtained good and collectible claims—since partly collected—for about $39,000, besides freeing our properties from two different liens of as large an amount. The nominal balance then remaining to the credit of our Company from the sale of copper during the war was $372,431.02....
>
> The war has greatly depopulated our mining district. The remaining people are impoverished; produce and feed are scarce and high, and consequent thereon, labor, transportation and fuel, from 50 to 100

per cent. higher than before the war. It is hoped that the growing crop of cereals will improve the condition of the surrounding population, and that after next fall labor and transportation will be lower.

From that time until 1878, echoes of what transpired within the sacred confines of directors' rooms reached the public in carefully prepared reports and statements. Becoming executive demeanor and reticence lent glamor to losses and dignity to gains, though there were but few instances of the latter. But there was confidence, and it extended all the way to Ducktown where it was reflected in the thriving village of Hiwassee, in the buying and selling of real estate, in enlarged and better schools, in new homes, in Sunday school picnics, in more and bigger stores, and in employees taking pride in their jobs and in what they hoped to be able to do for their families. The mines and furnaces were visible; the ore supply had hardly been touched; and at Ducktown there was a feeling of assurance too that somewhere back of deepening shafts and smoking roast piles was a group of officials capable of enlarging and perpetuating their mutual industry. Difficult it was, indeed, to visualize this region ever again being abandoned. There was too much copper ore here and too much machinery at work on it, and copper was a product that seemed to be always in demand.

It has been shown that both the Polk County Copper Company and Burra Burra Copper Company suffered because of old debts for mining properties that could never be retired. The Union Consolidated had a somewhat similar though not so vital a problem caused by an interest in the Isabella Mine held by H. B. Henegar. At the outbreak of the war Henegar, Thomas H. Callaway, and Euclid Waterhouse held sizeable interests in the mine which it was the intention of the Union Consolidated to purchase. During William H. Peet's control of the mines in 1863-64, he purchased the Callaway and Waterhouse interests which, according to Raht, were assuredly the best investment that could have been made on behalf of the company. As soon as Raht returned to Cleveland he began negotiating with Henegar for the purchase of his interest in the Isabella Mine. Raht was, of course, acting for the Union Consolidated Mining Company, and he found Henegar a wary and cautious trader. Henegar's lien was a rather unique one in that Samuel Congdon had obligated himself to discharge it, but in the event that he failed to do so the debt was to become an obligation of the company. After judgment was secured by Henegar to force the issue, a sale of the property was held at Ducktown by Robert N. Fleming, clerk and master, on August 5, 1865. At Raht's request the property was bid in by John Tonkin on behalf of the Union Consolidated Mining Company, but as Henegar refused to recognize the sale the whole matter reverted to its former status. Henegar's distrust of anything to which Congdon was a party rendered Raht's efforts at settlement more difficult. The case was finally settled out of court, however, during the following February when Raht paid $21,215.96 in legal tender notes to Henegar. Not only would Henegar not accept anybody's check in settlement of his claim, but he would not even accept one that had been certified. When he was paid, it required a satchel for him to carry away the greenbacks received from Raht.

For several years after the company's reorganization in 1866 the subject of a railroad from Cleveland to Ducktown held the attention of the directors of the Union Consolidated company. It was not until well into the seventies that hope of securing the railroad was abandoned. It was this hope of eventual rail facilities that led the company, beset by financial difficulties though they often were, to put back into the business at Ducktown every dollar they earned instead of issuing the money in dividends. Even after it became apparent that the railroad could not be built, operations were bravely, or foolishly, continued for a number of years. Records of the company, written by hands long since stilled in death, reveal a sublime faith in the potential profits at Ducktown, provided that the ordinary facilities required by any industrial enterprise were present.

The Union Consolidated Mining Company owned five mines, the East Tennessee, Isabella, Mary's, Callaway, and Cherokee, any one of which was capable of producing all the ore that could be treated at the company's smelting works. Therefore, after his inspection trip to Ducktown, Raht decided upon the East Tennessee Mine for his ore supply until more furnace capacity could be provided. Considerable retimbering was first necessary to repair underground crushing that had occurred in the mine since the shut-down in 1863. Hoisting of ore was begun in the fall of 1865. The mining method pursued was described as underhand stopping, and the general character of the work bore a striking resemblance to the working of a Cornish mine of a century previous.

The whim method of hoisting was continued at the East Tennessee Mine until late in 1868. As the whim had to be used for pumping water from the mine as well as for hoisting ore, it was difficult to keep a sufficient quantity of ore at the smelting works. To overcome this handicap Captain Raht contracted with Thomas Webster and Company of Chattanooga for the erection of a steam hoisting-engine at East Tennessee.

Drilling by hand was continued until 1872 when several machine drills were purchased by the Union Consolidated Mining Company for use at the East Tennessee and Mary mines. Before the advent of machine drills there came into local usage a term called "dyking," which carried with it a stigma abhorrent to any good miner. As it was used, "dyking" meant letting a hand drill become stuck so that it could not be lifted and turned slightly between blows of the hammer. The origin of the term was obvious. A miner named Powell had as a helper a man named Dyke. When it would come Dyke's turn to hold the drill he would frequently fail to shift the position of the drill point often enough, which would result in the drill's becoming stuck. Hence, a miner who permitted his drill to stick fast in the hole was guilty of "dyking."

One of the most difficult items to secure following the war was drill steel. For sometime after the war it was bought in Boston, but shipments were often delayed, and Raht was frequently writing to his brother Carl, secretary of the company, at New York, to have shipments expedited as much as possible. Once he wrote that the steel ordered from Boston had not arrived and that a duplicate order should be placed. "But," said he, "have it sent by the 'Crooked Line' as the [Virginia and Tennessee] 'Air Line' won't do!"

Dynamite supplanted black powder for mining purposes here at about the same time machine drills came into use. Considerable ingenuity was required to blast in a wet hole with loose black powder. The practice was to force clay into the hole to hold back the flow of water until the powder could be fired. Dynamite made blasting much easier. It was, of course, the discoveries of Alfred Nobel, Swedish inventor and philanthropist, that led to the manufacture of dynamite. He discovered in 1865 that nitroglycerin could be made to detonate violently by the explosion of a very small quantity of fulminate of mercury and in 1866 he found that liquid nitroglycerin, when absorbed in kieselguhr, could be placed conveniently and safely in paper cartridges, thus rendering it reasonably free from unexpected detonation. The latter invention led to the manufacture of commercial dynamite, and the new product was at once employed at the mines at Ducktown. Sticks of dynamite were known at Ducktown as "doolies." One brand of dynamite used here was "Neptune's Cartridge" and another was Dualin, manufactured by Laflin and Rand Powder Company. It seems probable, therefore, that "doolie" was a local vulgarism of the word Dualin.

Mention has been made of the degree to which animals used in whim service became trained. A notable example of this was furnished by a stolid, mouse-colored mule that for several years after the war operated a whim at one of the shafts at East Tennessee Mine. The mule would start, stop, and reverse according to the signal bell. But especially was it noted for its actions when the miners were preparing to do their blasting at the end of the shift. It learned when shots were to be put off by the sound of drill steel being piled up at the bottom of the shaft. At such times the animal had to be firmly held, for it was as anxious to be away as a race-horse at the starting post. When the "go" signal would finally come it would race around its path until the large ore bucket in which the miners were riding came to the surface. As soon as the last man was safely aground, the mule would wheel and make several hurried laps until the bucket on the other end of the rope was hoisted high enough in the shaft not to be damaged by the explosions.

For underground illumination each miner was given two candles, rolled in clay for convenience in handling, at the beginning of the shift. After the steam hoisting engine was installed, small tram cars of about one-ton capacity were used instead of ore buckets. These were hoisted to the surface in cages, dumped, and returned underground.

Ore from East Tennessee Mine was hauled to the furnaces at both Isabella and Burra Burra by wagon until 1868. In that year a railroad of thirty-three-inch gauge was built from the mine to Isabella. The loaded ore cars, each with a capacity of 4,500 pounds, rolled by gravity the mile and a quarter from the mine to the furnaces. A small saddle-tank locomotive was purchased to handle the cars around the smelting works, but the dinkey was unable to negotiate the steep grade to the mine. The empty cars were drawn back to the mine by mules.

By the end of the year 1872 the East Tennessee was a rather completely equipped mine. Its hoist and pumps were steam powered, drilling was done to a large extent by pneumatic drills, dynamite was used instead of black powder, and a railroad connected the mine and furnaces.

Occasional pockets of black oxide, yielding from 15 per cent to 25 per cent copper, were found for several years after the mine was reopened. The yellow sulphide ore averaged about 10 per cent copper in 1866. The grade dropped gradually each year until 1878 when it averaged between 4 per cent and 5 per cent copper. Ore production at the mine from 1865 to 1878 averaged about six thousand tons a year.

Because of the passing of the Burra Burra Copper Company with its annual production of about one million pounds of copper and of the increasingly poor grade of ore at East Tennessee Mine, the Union Consolidated Mining Company made an effort to increase its own output of copper when it reopened Mary Mine in April, 1872. This mine was equipped with a steam hoist, machine drills, and ore-dressing works. The works consisted of a new type of Blake crusher, a revolving screen and revolving picking table, a self-feeding six-hundred-pound, ten-stamp battery—from which the pulp flowed into a "Rittenger" grading box of three compartments, which in turn fed two continuous fine-grained jigs—and one continuous revolving buddle. The machinery was systematically arranged, the feeds and discharges being automatic. The power was derived from a turbine wheel which had an ample head and supply of water. The narrow-gauge railroad was extended from the Isabella furnaces to Mary Mine in 1874-75, and another small locomotive was purchased. Over $80,000 was spent on these improvements.

Between four and six thousand tons of ore was mined at Mary Mine annually. As at East Tennessee, the grade of ore at Mary Mine decreased from 10 per cent and higher to as low as 4 and 5 per cent copper by 1878.

E. Mueller served as mine captain at Mary Mine until 1876. He was succeeded by John Spargo, and upon the death of Spargo in April, 1878, James Bailey, former mine captain at Burra Burra, was transferred to Mary Mine.

Both the Callaway and Cherokee mines were worked intermittently in the last years of the Union Consolidated Mining Company's operations. The Isabella Mine, however, was allowed to remain idle. From this distance it seems strange that the mine was never worked after the war. The ore supply was abundant and the mine was situated within a hundred yards of the Isabella smelters. The chief value of the Isabella Mine in the years immediately following the war, as it had been prior to the war, was the copper recovered from its mine water. Old records of the Union Consolidated Mining Company of that period show that several thousand pounds of fine copper were produced monthly at Isabella Mine by the precipitation method. The production was often dependent upon the quantity of available scrap iron. As an example of a month's production of precipitated copper the record of November, 1868, follows: gross pounds, 15,254; per cent moisture, 16.7; net pounds, 12,707; per cent copper, 79.5; pounds of fine copper, 10,102.

Of the two major phases of operations at Ducktown, mining and smelting, the former, which involved only the extracting of the ore, was much easier than the latter, the reducing of the ore to the fine copper stage. The chief problem at the mines was the grade of the ore; at the smelting works it was recovering as much as possible of the copper contained in the ore. Under the best possible smelting arrangement there was an unavoidable loss of much copper in the several stages through which the ore passed.

While the Union Consolidated was smelting at both the Tennessee and Isabella, the refining works remained at the old Polk County smelters. This necessitated much expensive hauling of both ores and matte until refining facilities were erected at Isabella in 1871.

In organizing his smelting department after the war Raht hired Henry Zisch to attend to the reverberatory furnaces at the refinery, and August Raht, a brother of the Captain's, was made superintendent of the smelting department.

For sometime after the war the same process of smelting that had been in vogue at Ducktown prior to the war was continued. A notable improvement in treating not only the Ducktown ores, but all metalliferous ores containing sulphur, arsenic, or antimony was effected when William L. Raht, of Baltimore, a brother of J. E. and August Raht, patented the process of passing air through the molten metal in the year 1866. This process of bessemerizing copper matte was invented by August Raht, but probably as a matter of convenience he permitted the patent (No. 57,376) to be issued in his brother's name. William L. Raht had moved to Baltimore during the war and did not return to Ducktown until after the issuance of the patent.

In 1867 Captain Raht did some experimenting with a Dr. Seaton's method of expelling sulphur from copper ores, but found it ineffective when applied on a large scale. Some further experimenting, this time with the Monier process for the wet extraction of copper, was done in 1873, and two years later the Hunt and Douglas copper-process was investigated. Raht had A. Thies, plant chemist, to make some test runs with the prescribed formula, but no further steps were taken.

UNITED STATES PATENT OFFICE.

WILLIAM L. RAHT, OF BALTIMORE, MARYLAND.

IMPROVEMENT IN TREATING METALLIFEROUS ORES.

Specification forming part of Letters Patent No. 57,276, dated August 21, 1866.

To all whom it may concern:

Be it known that I, WILLIAM L. RAHT, of Baltimore, in the county of Baltimore and State of Maryland, have invented a new and useful Improvement in Treating Ores; and I do hereby declare that the following is a full, clear, and exact description thereof, which will enable others skilled in the art to make and use the same.

This invention relates to a new process for treating mat or regulus run from metalliferous ores containing sulphur, arsenic, or antimony; and the invention consists in forcing atmospheric air or other gas through the liquid fused mat obtained from such ores in such a manner that by such air or gases the sulphur, arsenic, or antimony contained in the mat is vaporized, and a pure metal is obtained.

In the usual process of treating ores of copper, nickel, lead, silver, gold, &c. in short, all metalliferous ores containing sulphur, arsenic, or antimony—the surface only of the melted mass is exposed to the air or other gases, and it is obviously very difficult, and in fact impossible, to reach by this process all the sulphur, arsenic, or antimony which may be mixed with said melted mass.

In my process this difficulty is obviated. I force the air or gases through the melted mass in a similar manner to Bessemer's process in treating iron, and thereby said air or gases are disseminated throughout the entire mass, and every particle of sulphur, arsenic, or antimony is reached and expelled.

I do not claim, broadly, as my invention to pass air or gases through metalliferous ores when the same are in a melted state, as this process is described in Bessemer's patents for treating iron ore; but

What I claim as new, and desire to secure by Letters Patent, is—

The within-described process of expelling from metalliferous ores sulphur, arsenic, or antimony by treating the mat or regulus run from such ores in the manner set forth.

The above specification of my invention signed by me this 3d day of March, 1866.

WM. L. RAHT.

Witnesses:
M. M. LIVINGSTON,
W. HAUFF.

A copy of the patent covering the invention of an improved method of treating ores similar to Bessemer's process. Although the patent was issued to William L. Raht, the process was really the invention of his brother, August Raht.

The *Engineering and Mining Journal* of July 1, 1876, carried the following almost complete description of the Union Consolidated Mining Company's smelting works:

The Isabella Smelting Works, the only smelter now in operation in the district, is connected with the Mary and East Tennessee Mines by a narrow gauge railroad. The works are systematically built, the furnaces being located on both sides of a little valley, the bottom between being occupied by roast-piles. The smelting process, as carried out, included the following operations:

1st. Roasting the ore.
2d. Smelting for first matte.
3d. Roasting the first matte.
4th. Smelting for second matte and black copper.
5th. Smelting for blister copper.
6th. Refining.

The roasting of the ores and first matte is carried out in piles of 500 and of 50 tons respectively.

The material to be roasted was thrown on a bed of cordwood laid on a stamped clay floor, and fire applied to the corners of the pile. The roasting of the ores is conducted in the open air, which must entail considerable loss by leaching. In fact green pools of water collecting about the roast yard after a heavy rain bore ample witness to this fact. The ore and matte smelting was carried out in small square furnaces about twelve feet high. Two tuyere holes are placed in the back wall, and the furnaces blown with noses. Of course the only fuel available is charcoal. A "Pilz" [Pilz-Mansfeld] furnace which was tried a year ago gave poor results owing to the rapid accumulation of iron sows in its crucible. This furnace is now being repaired and fitted with water tuyeres, and will shortly be blown in on matte, and will be the first trial of water tuyeres in this section. The experiment is certainly worthy of the trial the intelligent managers are willing to give it.

The blowing cylinders, producing the wind for the shaft furnaces, are placed in a vertical frame and a horizontal steam engine geared to their crank shaft. No attention seems to have been paid to economy in the use of steam and fuel in the building of these engines, nor in fact in any of the steam machinery in use about Ducktown. But this is by no means an isolated instance in American metallurgy and mining. Many of our Western mills waste even more fuel and money by cheap (?) steam machinery. If Nothern mills and furnaces find it profitable to buy costly compound or high expansion condensing engines with fuel comparatively cheap, the same course of reasoning must apply with still greater force to mining districts depending on expensive cordwood as its only fuel.

The blister and refining furnaces are reverberatories, fitted with a gas generator instead of a grate, and all connected by underground flues with one stack. The furnaces are well built in every respect and seem to give excellent results. They are lined with soapstone, and the arch is built of the same material. The soapstone, locally termed cotton rock, answers every purpose and is far superior to the best firebrick.

The bottom of the furnaces are, as usual, built up of layers of beaten sand and slag. In the blister furnaces blast is made use of to facilitate the operation. As soon as the matte and black copper are molten an iron nozzle is introduced through a side door, and the blast directed on the surface of the liquid mass. Heavy fumes escaping from the stack of the furnace are the best evidence of the success of this method.

In the refining furnace no blast is used. The refined metal is ladled into copper molds, which are a great improvement on the old cast iron pattern, are far less costly, and prevent spitting of the metal.

The smelting processes are, on the whole, well carried out, and experience has undoubtedly suggested any deviations from the usual course. Most of the modern improvements have been given a fair test, or are to be tested, and if the company would inaugurate a similar policy in its mines, it would have a bright future, and financial success would be reasonably certain.

The Union Consolidated Mining Company employed between six and seven hundred men and boys. In 1872 the number of employees was 562 men and 80 children. The annual payroll exceeded $200,000. Miners received a company-time rate of from $40 to $45 a month, while the common-labor rate was from 75 cents to $1.25 a day.

Typical of a year's business of the Union Consolidated Mining Company are the figures shown in the company's report for the fiscal year 1874-75, reproduced on the opposite page. The operations that year were admittedly not profitable, but the exact amount of the loss was not readily determinable from the manner in which the report was constructed.

A definite turn in the history of the Union Consolidated Mining Company occurred in the fall of 1875 when a conflict between Captain Raht and the company over financial matters resulted in Raht's services with the company being brought to a close. This conflict, the details of which will be recounted later, is mentioned here only as an explanation of the turn of events leading up to the complete industrial shut-down in 1878. E. G. Duvall, who, as secretary of the company, had been instrumental in bringing about Raht's departure, succeeded him as superintendent late in 1875. August Raht left the position of smelter superintendent and was succeeded by Arthur F. Wendt.

August Raht's wife had died of pneumonia on December 29, 1874, and was buried in the Southern Methodist Cemetery at Ducktown. After leaving Ducktown he moved to the West and

MINING, 1865-1878

THE FOLLOWING IS A STATEMENT OF RECEIPTS AND DISBURSEMENTS DURING THE PAST YEAR:

To Balance, June 1st, 1874	$26,525 85	
" Materials as reported on hand, June 1st, 1874 $14,822 29 Less Materials charged to expenses of fiscal year 1873–74 $9,300 00		
Receipts during fiscal year 1874–75	5,522 29	
To Live Stock	175 00	
" Rents	3,101 87	
" Copper	250,009 00	
" Cordwood and Timber from Company's Timber Lands, valued at	15,121 54	
" Accounts and Bills payable	113,337 13	
	$413,792 68	

By Balance due at Mines, June 1st, 1874	$42,239 54	
Disbursements during fiscal year 1874–75:		
By Eureka and Isabella Mines	1,579 07	
" East Tenn. Mine, Dead Work	15,949 91	
" East Tenn. Mine, Ore Mining	43,567 89	
" Mary Mine, Dead Work	8,428 95	
" " " Ore Mining	11,703 32	
" Isabella Smelter	146,556 02	
" " Dressing Works	5,492 67	
" Mary Mine " "	1,879 16	
" Diamond Drill	494 00	
" Machine Drills	58 32	
" Cutting Cordwood and Timber from Company's Timber Lands	12,304 50	
" Materials	30,656 55	
" Cleveland Expenses	7,740 96	
" New York Expenses	10,155 13	
" Insurance	751 69	
" Transportation	19,333 74	
" Storage	42 75	
" Brokerage	1,070 81	
" Interest	4,306 07	
" Ores	43 70	
" Ocoee Turnpike Company	828 15	
" Cleveland and Ducktown Railway Company	106 75	
" Mary & East Tenn. Mines R. R.	10,390 49	
" House Improvement	3,712 47	
" Permanent Improvement	12,427 93	
" Mortgage Bonds payable	4,000 00	
" Cash	17,972 14	
	$413,792 68	

became associated with the American Smelting and Refining Company of New Jersey. Following his retirement as head of this company he resided in San Francisco, where he died suddenly on Christmas Day, 1916, at the age of 74. He was born in Germany, graduated at Freiburg, and came to the United States in 1864. It was said that so strong was his preference for San Francisco as a place of residence that he had instructed his two daughters that upon his death his body be cremated and the ashes spread upon Monterey Bay. They complied with his request.

There was a general feeling of unrest at Ducktown when Duvall arrived to take charge as superintendent. It was felt that the Old Master's going forebode evil days for all. Schools were temporarily suspended in the district, and memories of the lean years of a decade ago were revived. Duvall was referred to locally as the Cotton Broker Miner and as the Moses who had come to lead the district to greener fields.

It was not until the Union Consolidated was definitely in a weakened condition that they at last began operating a commissary. They purchased Raht's Isabella Store in June, 1876, some six months after he had left their services. However, the acquisition of this business, with its attendant profits, had been too long deferred to be of material assistance at this stage of the company's history at Ducktown. It was somewhat like resorting to first-aid treatment after the failure of a major operation.

For nearly three years Duvall kept the works in operation. During this time the idea of a railroad to Ducktown was abandoned; the price of copper continued its downward trend; fuel became so scarce that wood had to be floated down the Ocoee River from Fannin County; and the trouble between Raht and the company was being contested in the courts. Especially was the price of copper discouraging. From an average price of twenty-eight cents a pound in 1873, it dropped to an average of nineteen cents a pound in 1877, and by the summer of 1878 it was about sixteen cents a pound. Copper mining was definitely becoming a poor avocation for an aspiring Moses.

With losses continuing and with no prospects that the business could ever do much better, coupled with the fact that Raht was getting the better of the company in their legal tug-of-war over which was to pay the other a large sum of money, a decision to cease operations was reached and in June, 1878, the travail of the Union Consolidated Mining Company at Ducktown came to an end. Edward Mueller was appointed receiver on August 20 and

J. E. Raht's first warehouse and store at Cleveland, opened in 1865, served principally as a source of supply for the mining industry at Ducktown. The Captain is standing at the right of the man with the outstretched arm. Notice the copper wagon, drawn by a six-mule team, at the left. The picture was taken in 1866.

The Isabella Smelting Works in 1875. The first furnaces at this site were erected by the Union Consolidated Mining Company before the Civil War. In 1871 many improvements were made in equipment. "The Isabella Smelting Works... is connected with the Mary and East Tennessee Mines by a narrow gauge railroad," read a description of 1876. "The works are systematically built, the furnaces being located on both sides of a little valley, the bottom being occupied by roast piles." The large brick building to the left of the tall chimney is the Isabella Store.

A rare old bank note issued by the Ocoee Bank, Cleveland (Cleaveland), Tennessee. The fine script following the name of the bank reads, "Will pay to Bearer on demand ten dollars at their Bank in Cleaveland, Jan. 1, 1860."

A sociable interlude at the Polk County Mine. The scene shows the conditions under which mining was carried on at Ducktown during the 1870's. Notice the adit entrances at the center and right, and the hoist house at the shaft entrance on the hill. The small tram car seems to be loaded to capacity with mining dignitaries.

continued the smelting operations only long enough to treat the ores then in process of roasting and smelting. Thus, for the first time since 1850, with the exception of the Civil War period, every mine at Ducktown was idle. Furnace operations under the receivership came to a close in the spring of 1879.

The annual production of copper by the Union Consolidated from 1865 to 1878 was as follows:

YEAR	POUNDS
1866	257,304
1867	632,377
1868	1,013,883
1869	1,006,146
1870	1,466,847
1871	1,441,941
1872	1,390,511
1873	1,267,863
1874	1,376,512
1875	1,305,931
1876	1,300,000 (est.)
1877	1,271,235
1878	2,145,626
Period of Receivership	1,000,000 (est.)
Total	16,876,176

Estimating the copper production of both the Burra Burra Copper Company and the Polk County Copper Company during their years of operation at 7,000,000 pounds, the total copper production at Ducktown during the above years was approximately 24,000,000 pounds.

However far-reaching the consequences of the shut-down at Ducktown might have been, it was but another short news item to the editor of the Ellijay *Courier*, for he tersely stated: "The Ducktown Copper Mines have busted." But the editor of the *Courier* at that time was a rather matter-of-fact commentator. A little later he came out with another squib, more voluble than that on the mines, in which he said, "We have named our shotgun 'Doctor,' because it hardly ever fails to kill."

When it was announced that the mines were to be closed, a rumor spread that the company was only threatening a shut-down in order to induce the employees to trade up their earnings at the Isabelle Store. However, the store was closed and only charcoal and wood haulers with the most wages due them were admitted. The news of this spread quickly and immediately a throng of several hundred gathered at the store. A clamor went up that all be let inside and so menacing did the crowd become that the doors were opened and all rushed in. It was never known how many received the exact amount in merchandise that was due them in wages.

The following anonymous poem, written at the time the mines closed, brings out many hitherto undisclosed events, some portentous, some unimportant, of that gloomy day at Ducktown in the summer of 1878:

> Come listen awhile and I'll sing you a song,
> How the Ducktown Mines are getting along,
> The hardest of times that have ever been known
> Has surely been here since Duvall has flown.
>
> It's old rusty bacon and coarse corn bread
> And that is the way the miners are fed
> They'll talk about rations and then about work
> And for twenty-five cents they'd kill any clerk.
>
> But the Clerks did their best, as every one knows
> Worked early and late till the Office was closed.
> The Office was closed by the Sheriff they say
> And the Clerks couldn't give all the miners their pay.
>
> There is Duvall a cunning old chap
> He never was made to be caught in a trap
> He'll talk about mortgages, then about bonds
> When danger comes in you'll see he absconds.
>
> The people here thought he was doing quite well
> Till he fled in the night with Mr. Becknell,
> His wife, she soon followed and then in her hack
> Went all those New Yorkers and never came back.
>
> There is Jim Witt at the head of the store,
> Gives bread to the rich as well as the poor
> When Cornwall and Stevens ran away in the night
> Jim kept his position and came out all right.
>
> There is John Williams I'll bring on the stand
> I believe he possesses the heart of a man
> But as a Clerk he was not thought the best
> When Duvall played out he had to go west.

There is Hard Ramey I'd like to've forgot
I'm inclined to believe he's the best of the lot
He'll tell you to work if you feel so disposed
And advises you to quit if the Office is closed.

There is Bell Witt we must not forget
I believe in my soul he's the meanest one yet
He'll tell you to wait you're sure of your pay
But takes what is due him in the Office that day.

And there is Joe Stuart a Kinsman of Witt
Took lots in the store and owes for it yet
And Mr. Nankivell is not like other fools
He made himself safe by hiding his tools.

There is Humphrey Kimsey had nothing to say
But hammered away on his anvil all day
He waited for some, took some in the store
And said he had plenty he'd worked for before.

There is Will Hutsell who never got mad
He said if they stopped him he'd go home to his dad
And there is Will Cannon who's black in the face
That said he'd eat bread without any grease.

There is Mug Ledford contrary to rule
He carried off rations and killed his old mule
And there is Jim Ledford, a brother to Mug
Got twenty-five dollars to stop up his jug.

Now Capt. John Tonkin we'll bring on the stand
I think he indeed is a very good man
He advised the boys with a sorrowful face
If they saw any chance to get a new place.

Now in sadness though hope I'll close up my song
Though brief I've endeavored to bring all along
But it's my true opinion 'twill all come to naught
Unless they procure the assistance of Raht.

The wife of Duvall, who soon followed her trail-blazing husband, and in whose hack fled "all those New Yorkers and never came back," was the former Elizabeth Williams, comely daughter of John H. Williams, of Hiwassee. Duvall was considerably older than the Hiwassee belle he wooed and won, but love, like copper mining, has a thousand precedents from which to choose.

GEORGIA MINES

The Number 20 Mine was worked on a small scale at different times between 1865 and 1878. The ore was sold to the Union Consolidated Mining Company. James Phillips did some mining there in 1866, as did A. H. Moore in 1877. Memory lingers of Moore's leaving the district without paying his employees the final amounts due them.

Soon after operations had been resumed at the other mines at Ducktown, the owners of the Mobile Mine began contemplating its reopening. On April 8, 1867, N. H. Brown, of Mobile, Alabama, inquired of J. E. Raht his opinion of the wisdom of this. Raht replied that he had never been underground there, but that he had learned that just about all of the discovered ore at Mobile had been taken out. He told Brown, too, that the fire at the mine just prior to the war had done only minor damage to the steam engine and blast cylinders, and that the calcine and blast furnaces were in good condition. But he probably dampened Brown's enthusiasm when he said that $25,000 would be required to explore for new ore and, should this be found, another $25,000 would be necessary to begin mining and smelting. This put a quietus on the Mobile owners for some time.

Interest in the Mobile Mine next came to light when, on August 23, 1872, the Georgia Legislature granted a charter to the Mobile and Atlanta Mining Company for a period of twenty years. This company, successor to the Spring Place Mining Company, was incorporated by N. H. Brown, George A. Tuthill, W. D. Berry, T. T. Tyree, M. H. Bransford, Carey W. Stiles, E. H. Bacon, and W. W. Strother. T. T. Tyree was president and George A. Tuthill secretary of the company. Fully organized and empowered to proceed, there remained but one requisite for the Mobile and Atlanta Mining Company to begin operations—a supply of ore. And as this did not exist at the Mobile Mine the company disappeared down the trail followed by so many other companies at Ducktown—to the shadows of comforting oblivion.

CHAPTER 14

THE BOARD OF DIRECTORS

To NEGLECT THE ACTIVITIES OF THE EXECUTIVE BRANCH OF THE Union Consolidated Mining Company would be to omit from the post-war history of mining at Ducktown some of its most interesting and revealing features. For several years the principal office of the company was located in New York City at 66 Wall Street, but after 1872 the address was changed to 35 and 37 Broad Street. The capitalization of the company remained at $2,200,000, represented by 220,000 shares of stock at $10 each. Of this number of shares 24,000 were never issued. Occasionally, when it was deemed prudent to add a little weight to the annual financial statements, the $240,000 in unissued stock would be hauled out and exposed to the eyes of interested readers. Verily, any mining company that had a permanent nest-egg of $240,000 in unissued stock was in no immediate danger of collapse from lack of funds.

The directors of the Union Consolidated, exercising their influence over affairs at the mines by their annual droning of "whereas" and "resolved that," tried vainly for years to place Ducktown at the forefront of copper mining in this country. That they eventually failed is not surprising; that they lasted as long as they did is inspiring. Although this phase of the history of the Union Consolidated reveals the unusual condition of a large corporation being virtually dependent upon its mine superintendent for financial support, the executive branch of the company was always attempting action, hopeful but hopeless though it often was. The directors' frequent inability to act with promptness and authority was caused by the company's obnoxious habit of remaining perpetually near the financial breaking point. And if their superintendent was a thrifty fellow who could save a little money and would use it to finance the business when necessary, they were willing, yea, eager, that he do so. But their superintendent, Captain Raht, was anything but a confiding philanthropist for wavering corporations. He was simply sagacious enough to know that his continued prosperity was dependent upon the operations at Ducktown, and to the continuance of these operations he lent his every energy and resource. It was a clear case of all sink or swim together, and it was to the best swimmer that all the others clung.

An integral part of the business though he was, Raht nevertheless labored always with a feeling of futility about the ability of a corporation to function with the singleness of purpose characteristic of a business controlled by one man. He so expressed himself in a letter to Charles Raht, during the time he was sales agent. "It is useless for me to make a proposition to work Consolidated out of debt," he said, "because any plan based upon sound principles does not suit stock corporations.... I cannot manage it like I would manage my own."

John Thomas, who was elected president of the Union Consolidated Mining Company in 1866, had been associated with the mining interests at Ducktown since long before the war. He owned a plantation in Georgia, his investments at Ducktown were large, and he was thoroughly familiar with conditions in the South and at the mines at Ducktown. Thomas was residing at La Grange, Georgia, at the close of the war, but made his residence in New York soon afterwards. He was a firm believer in Raht's ability, and the relations between the two were cordial enough. Another factor contributing to the amicable relations between the superintendent and the president was the selection in 1866, when the company was reorganized, of Charles Raht as secretary of the company. Charles Raht had been in his brother's employ at Ducktown prior to the war.

One of the most important positions in the organization of the Union Consolidated Mining Company was that of sales agent. This position carried with it the implied ability and willingness to furnish the company with funds needed at the mines when sales of copper were slow. Jennison Eager served in this capacity until his resignation in 1867. Although extremely reluctant to do so, Captain Raht accepted the sales agency upon Eager's withdrawal. Raht explained his reluctance several years later, in July, 1872, when, in a letter to John Thomas, he said: "I hesitated some time, though the commissions were high and the security placed in my hands ample; but I had to go in debt to raise means to continue the mining operations, while I never yet had been in debt in my life." In placing Raht in charge of sales, the company transferred to him virtual control of the whole business. He produced the copper, shipped it in his own name to his brother Charles, who sold it and remitted direct to him. The monthly expenses for which Captain Raht had to provide funds amounted to about $25,000. When sales were under that amount he had to make up the deficit. When receipts exceeded expenses, and the company was not otherwise indebted to him, he returned the profits to the New York office. Under this anomalous condition it was difficult to determine who was the employer and who the employed.

The company could never for long remain out of debt to Raht. Despite the fact that they had settled with him in full at the end of the war, they owed him again, in May, 1867, the sum of $36,943.57. This quickly mounted to nearly $85,000. The debt fluctuated thereafter: on January 1, 1869, it was $124,596.98, but by June 1, 1872, Raht had been paid in full and was in arrears to the company by $1,253.10. At this time he surrendered the notes and first-mortgage bonds he had been holding as security. So refreshing was this exotic air of non-indebtedness that the company decided forthwith to attempt to manage their own sales departbent. It seems that they could never let well-enough alone.

A committee composed of George R. A. Ricketts, N. S. Ray, and Jennison Eager visited the mines in 1867 and at that time recommended the discontinuance of the sales agency, stating that: "If the President and Secretary of the Company make the sales of the copper, which your committee claim they should do, without extra compensation, it will result in a saving of $12,000.00 to $15,000.00 per annum." This recommendation was not acted upon until 1872 when the debt to Raht had been fully paid. In September of that year another committee, composed of John Thomas, president, and J. L. Macaulay, William G. Smith, Addison Cammack, and Alfred Kimber, directors, visited Ducktown. They "... found all operations going on with the regularity, system, and economy that they had been led to expect under the able management of our superintendent, Mr. J. E. Raht." They thereupon reappointed Raht as superintendent until January 1, 1874, but broached the subject of cancelling his contract as sales agent which did not expire for another year. They offered him $6,000 for the contract, but Raht countered by agreeing to cancel the contract for $18,000. They compromised on $12,000, which was about the amount of commissions on sales of copper for a year. After the committee had returned to New York, Thomas and

Raht exchanged letters discussing the company's straitened circumstances up to that time. Raht concurred with Thomas in that the company had been poor, but, said he, "This was known only by themselves and not by the public."

For a year or two following the company's taking over the selling of copper they seemed to have held their own fairly well. Just to be on the safe side, however, they had a standing agreement with Raht whereby he was to furnish funds for payrolls and supplies when the money was not available at the New York office. As a result of this arrangement they gradually became again heavily indebted to their superintendent.

The secret of Raht's strong financial position was, of course, his ownership of commissaries at the mines. It was from this source that he derived a large portion of the funds used by him to tide the company over their frequent periods of financial stringency. He repeatedly pointed out to the officials of the company that his store business was a profitable one and that it would be to the company's advantage to own and operate it. Furthermore, a portion of the report of the committee made up of Ricketts, Ray, and Eager, who visited Ducktown in August, 1867, was devoted to this subject. The report stated that two-thirds of all disbursements of the company for labor, fuel, and other materials were paid for through Raht's stores, and it was strongly urged that the company operate their own store and garner the large profits for their own use. But from the beginning of mining at Ducktown not one of the many companies that had operated here had owned its own store. This privilege had been granted to local agents and superintendents, and it seemed that the Union Consolidated was determined to follow this precedent even if it meant that they must go broke in doing so. It was not until after Raht had left their services that the company at last entered upon the business of merchandising.

The year 1872 proved to be a more fateful one for Ducktown and the Union Consolidated Mining Company than was apparent at the time. A new board of directors elected that year was composed of John Thomas, president, and James A. Alexander, John L. Macaulay, William G. Smith, Addison Cammack, William R. Travers, and Alfred Kimber, directors. Charles Raht was reelected secretary, but he served only a few months, resigning on October 1. Gone too were Samuel Congdon, Charles B. Tatham, Jennison Eager, George S. Cameron, and others who had been associated with Captain Raht for many years. Five members of the new board, Thomas, Macaulay, Smith, Cammack, and Kimber later that year visited the mines and while there purchased the sales agency contract from Raht. While the new board of directors did not immediately manifest a hostile attitude towards Raht, there did not thereafter seem to exist in the organization a feeling of mutual trust and confidence.

Just prior to the arrival at Ducktown of John Thomas and the four directors, Captain Raht inquired of August Raht whether he thought they could make money on 5½ per cent ore. The reply was "No!" Not unless the railroad was built; not unless copper continued to rule at the then average price of about twenty-six cents; and not unless a plant could be built at Ducktown for the production of sulphuric acid. Without these wholly necessary additions and conditions, "Ducktown," said August Raht, "is gone without redemption!" Perhaps Raht was thinking of his brother's sound appraisal of the Ducktown industry when he relinquished the sales agency soon afterward for $12,000.

Of constant perplexity to Captain Raht was the seeming inattention of the directors to their mining interests at Ducktown. Not only was he left alone year after year to manage the plants and properties of the company as he saw fit, but he was often forced to make decisions for the company involving matters of corporate and financial policies. That this finally became a matter of concern to him is shown in the following letter:

Cleveland, Tenn., Feb'y 16th, 1872.

John Thomas, Esq., President,
New York:

Dear Sir,—Your two favors of the 13th inst. came to hand by last night's mail.

It is very nice and even flattering to me that you and the Board of Directors have the utmost confidence in me, but it is also very necessary that you should have confidence in your local agent. You will please excuse me for stating, however, that this does not release you, as President of the Company, from coming here sometimes and looking after the interests of the Company; in fact, I think, that I have the right to demand this.

It has been very unpleasant to me that I had frequently to assume responsibilities, as agent of the Company, which properly belonged to higher authorities, and to decide also upon questions wherein I was personally interested. I trust I have acted not to the injury of the Company.

I beg to request you to come here about the end of next month or early in April; it will be very well for a Director or two to come with you, but, if you cannot persuade any one to come with you, I think the President ought to come anyway.

With much respect,
Your obt. servt.,
J. E. RAHT,
Supt.

It would not be possible to furnish a more striking illustration of how completely the Ducktown operations were left in the hands of Raht than the foregoing letter. This same condition had prevailed since he was appointed superintendent in 1858 and with but one or two exceptions it continued thus until 1875.

There seems to have been no reason for fault-finding by the board of directors until late in 1874. New furnaces were being constructed at Ducktown during the summer of that year, and when they were not completed as scheduled the board placed the blame on Raht and passed a resolution penalizing him accordingly. The penalty was in the form of a reduction to 7 per cent in the rate of interest being paid on the indebtedness to him. Captain Raht was in New York when the resolution was passed and did not make known his acceptance of it until after he returned to Cleveland. His letter to John Thomas in regard to the board's action and several other letters that passed between the two over the following several months were merely preludes to an explosion that both felt would not be long in coming. Raht was in no mood to accept any penalty or censure from the directors; he offered to sell his commissaries to the company and suggested that the debt owed to him be paid at once. Thomas, on the other hand, was earnestly endeavoring to patch up the dissension, for without Captain Raht to stand between the company and adversity, he was fearful of the future for both himself and the Union Consolidated. Thomas could not forget that Raht had once reminded him that he (Raht) was about the only source of credit the company had.

At Ducktown and elsewhere in this section of Tennessee it was generally understood and taken for granted that Raht constituted about all the existing governing power of the Union Consolidated Mining Company. But this fact was not so apparent to those who kept themselves informed of the company's status only through the yearly reports issued by the directors. Other than that there were no dividends declared, there was no reason for unwary stockholders to deduce from the annual reports that the company was not enjoying normal growth.

THE BOARD OF DIRECTORS 165

There was one item of $300,000 which never found its way into the annual reports. This was a mortgage on the real estate of the company held by the Farmers Loan and Trust Company of New York, from June, 1868, until November, 1874. However, the stockholders' equity being in profits that might accrue from operations, matters of higher finance such as mortgages on the property were probably deemed to be none of their business.

The disadvantages and restrictions under which the Union Consolidated had been laboring for several years began taking their inevitable toll in 1875. The annual report for that year stated that the operations during the past year had been unprofitable. Three principal reasons for this were given: The price of copper had dropped from the anticipated price of 23 cents to 19.5 cents a pound; an alarming loss in copper inventory had been reported; and the grade of ores had been disappointingly low. Despite the rather poor showing, the report ended in an optimistic tenor, "Your Directors," it said, "feel encouraged as to the future... we still anticipate a decided improvement in our condition."

Especially did the loss in copper inventory prove to be of far-reaching consequence. This loss, discovered on May 1, 1875, amounted to 568,172 pounds. Appended to the annual report was an explanation by August Raht, smelter superintendent, stating the causes of the huge shortage. It was simply that the 1 per cent loss that had been allowed was insufficient on 5 per cent ore. Raht enumerated the principal sources of loss as ore slag, iron salamander, dust blown out of furnace stacks, matte slag, roast piles, and shovelling and carting the material. Although these reasons for the loss were sound enough on ores that passed through so many stages of treatment, and though it was admitted in the annual report that the loss was an accumulation over a period of two years, the directors were by no means disposed to pass the matter off as a mere inadvertence.

The copper incident occurred at a time when Captain Raht was endeavoring to secure settlement with the company. In an attempt to allay discontent at New York over the staggering loss that would have to be absorbed, John Thomas visited Ducktown soon after the annual meeting. Upon his return to New York he wrote to Raht and said: "After my visit to the mines, I can say with entire confidence and frankness that in my judgment you have managed the affairs of the company generally well." But several of the directors did not share Thomas' good opinion of Raht. At their meeting on July 13, 1875, they not only refused to arrange for settlement with him, but instead dispatched E. G. Duvall, their secretary, to the mines to report more fully on Raht's conduct of the business. Thomas was decidedly dubious regarding Raht's reaction to Duvall's visit. Also Thomas probably did not fully approve of the mission, in view of his recently expressed approval of his superintendent, and he might have felt that he too was not meeting with the board's approbation. However, he tried earnestly through correspondence to put the Captain in the right frame of mind about the secretary's errand. But the secretary was charged with a duty and he entered upon it with enthusiasm. However, it was espionage and not co-operation that Raht was fully expecting.

After Duvall's return to New York, Raht tried vainly to secure a copy of his report. In a letter to Thomas written September 4 he said: "Simple justice to your Superintendent dictates that you should send me a copy of the Secretary's report, formal or informal; while I am the Company's representative here, I do demand it. Unless you do act openly with me, I cannot serve you any longer." There was too much subversiveness to suit Raht. On the other hand, Duvall and members of the board felt that their superintendent had already done far too much clog dancing on their figurative spines for an unwarranted number of years.

While Raht was denied access to Duvall's report at that time, he did later come into full knowledge of its contents when everything that had transpired between him and the company was given a thorough airing in the courts. A portion of Duvall's lengthy report dealt with such prosaic things as drill cores, mine development, and the supply of cordwood coming down the Ocoee River. With the subject of mining disposed of, however, he warmed up to the subjects about which he was principally concerned, J. E. Raht and the commissaries.

> I cannot refrain from expressing to you my most decided opinion that it is a waste of your substance and a sacrifice of your ores to continue to work under the present organization. Nothing but rich ores and high prices of copper all the time can make you any money or save you from disaster and the total loss of your property. I judge that your superintendent will continue to make such advances for dead work only as he may see clearly will be speedily returned to him in copper, with the addition of a large profit through his stores....
> I recommend, as an absolute necessity for the safety of the company, that you immediately devise some plans to change the present damaging condition, get possession of the store house, or its business, at the

earliest possible moment.... It is safe to conclude that the two stores have paid for the last three years $100,000.00 per year, which would have enabled you to make handsome dividends on your stock, or build your railroad, or open and develop your large mining property.... Instead of that, the business has been conducted on such a purely philanthropic basis as to contribute to one man the entire profits of the whole property for years... simply to secure a superintendent to visit the mines once a month to make contracts for supplies to be paid for in his own goods, at just such prices as he chooses to charge. His information about the mines is mainly obtained from his subordinates, as you are aware. I believe that any good practical business man can easily take his place.

In this last sentence Duvall was plainly putting in a good word for John. And there was no mistaking the John he had reference to—he, himself, being a good practical businessman.

The secretary continued by informing the directors that Raht was reported to be the richest man in Tennessee. He estimated that their superintendent had cleared $1,000,000 over the preceding ten years, "while the company is brought in debt, and the stockholders to grief." Thus the report continued. The gist of it was that Raht be disposed of and that the store business be acquired by the company. In his closing remarks Duvall made a statement that Raht had evidently falsified his statements and agreements and that as a result he was liable in equity to the company for every dollar he had made over and above 10 per cent net profit. This profit was later estimated to be $1,000,000 and that was the amount which the company endeavored by litigation to recover from Raht.

Obviously John Thomas was in no hurry for Raht to read Duvall's report. Thomas himself was in an uncomfortable position because of his continued faith in Raht. The president was treading as softly and cautiously as he could, but the superintendent felt no need of such restraint on his own part. Thoroughly aggrieved now at the directors' attitude, wholly disgusted at Duvall's visit and his inability to secure a copy of the report, reasonably convinced that the company did not intend to pay him the $108,789.34 then owed to him, and satisfied that his days of usefulness in his present position were at an end, Raht began legal action to force settlement with the company he had served since its founding nearly twenty years before.

Following Raht's action, E. G. Duvall was sent to replace him as superintendent; John Thomas resigned as president of the company; and the days of copper mining at Ducktown were definitely numbered. At the next annual meeting of the directors A. G. Black was elected president and served in that capacity during the remaining life of the company. Black and Francis W. Williams were associates in the firm of Williams, Black and Company, of New York.

It is necessary to go back some three years in the history of the Union Consolidated to find one of the contributing causes that led to the resignation of John Thomas. About the time Thomas and his committee visited Ducktown in 1872, he was searching for cash with which to refinance his own affairs. The company had just liquidated their debt to Raht and were looking forward to better days. Thomas no doubt thought that this would be a propitious time for him to rearrange his personal finances and at the same time move into position to buy additional shares of Union Consolidated stock. The stock at that time was selling at about one and a half, and he was anxious to buy more of it before the price advanced beyond his reach. He estimated that about $12,500 would be sufficient to allow him to carry out his plans, and he approached Raht on the subject of a loan in that amount. The loan was granted and as security Raht took a mortgage on Thomas' plantation in Worth County, Georgia. Thus the situation stood in 1875 when the rift between Raht and the company occurred. To add to matters that were already bad enough for Thomas, his loan secured of Raht had become known to the directors and he was accused of being in collusion with the scheming superintendent. His resignation followed soon after Raht began his court proceedings against the company.

That holders of Union Consolidated stock were becoming alarmed over the trouble that was brewing between Captain Raht and the company is illustrated in a letter written to Raht by P. M. Bartlett, president of Maryville College, on August 11, 1875. Bartlett said: "We hold 400 shares of the Union Consolidated Mining Company, John Thomas, President. Please tell us if this company is good. If it is, what is the stock worth now? What the prospective value?" Unfortunately Raht's reply is not known, but it probably caused a sudden shake-up in that school's theory of "Economics, or the Benefits of Investments." The stock, however, continued active in a speculative way for a year or more after that at a price of between one and two dollars a share.

After disposing of Thomas and Raht the Union Consolidated Mining Company secured another loan of $300,000 from the

Farmers Loan and Trust Company in December, 1875, giving as security a mortgage on Ducktown properties similar to the one given in 1868. In June, 1878, just prior to the shut-down, two other mortgages aggregating $110,000 were given Andrew J. Macaulay and Francis W. Williams. These mortgages were on all ores and minerals on the surface. Later, just to make it unanimous, a deed to all other company property, both real and personal, was made to E. G. Duvall. It was intended that Macaulay and Williams take charge of the smelting works and all wood and charcoal on July 31. Raht declared that these recent maneuvers simply constituted a "freezing-out" process on the part of four or five directors who designed to secure for themselves everything of value at Ducktown and thus render fruitless any action on the part of stockholders or creditors.

Raht's claim of over $100,000 against the Union Consolidated had been decided in his favor the previous year, but at that time the case was under appeal. His only hope of recompense was in the supply of ores ready for smelting, and he feared that unless Macauly and Williams were forestalled they would continue operations at the smelting works, getting away with the copper and leaving him and other legitimate creditors of the company with worthless claims. Accordingly an injunction was secured forbidding the removal of any ores, copper, or other property belonging to the company. From this point the works passed into the hands of the receiver and he began turning out copper to pay the company's creditors. This campaign came to a close the following spring.

Named as defendants in the creditors' bill which came up for hearing in December, 1879, were the Union Consolidated Mining Company of Tennessee, the Farmers Loan and Trust Company, Andrew J. Macaulay, and Francis W. Williams. Named as plaintiffs were wholesalers, supply dealers, wood and copper haulers, and former employees, numbering in all nearly three hundred. Macaulay and Williams came in for a cut of the proceeds when they withdrew their claims as mortgagees of the company and were entered as general creditors. Shortly thereafter the Ducktown properties were sold to Francis W. Williams for $120,000 and the money was distributed among the creditors.

CHAPTER 15

THE TRIAL

OF SUCH MAGNITUDE WAS THE TRIAL STYLED *J. E. Raht* vs. *The Union Consolidated Mining Company of Tennessee* and *The Union Consolidated Mining Company of Tennessee* vs. *J. E. Raht* that it was said: "The pleadings and proof make a transcript in the Supreme Court of 6,000 pages, and, together with the exhibits, make a record which surpasses in size any record ever seen in the Supreme Court of Tennessee." * So minutely in detail were the depositions, pleadings, exhibits, and decisions that they embraced virtually the entire history of Raht's seventeen-year reign at Ducktown. Although transcended in interest by no other phase of the early history of copper mining in Tennessee, it will be possible to touch but briefly on the more important aspects of the trial, which was the climax of so many things that meant so much to so many people. Ironically enough the lawsuit violated one of Raht's basic principles, that of avoiding litigation, because, as he once said, "most lawsuits result in losses to all but the lawyers."

It has already been stated that the litigation between J. E. Raht and the Union Consolidated Mining Company grew out of the company's indebtedness to Raht, which was renounced by the company in 1875. The last settlement between Raht and the company had been consummated on December 1, 1874. At that time it was agreed that the balance due Raht was $84,711.61. To secure the debt and subsequent advances a lien on the company's personal property, including the production at the mines and smelters, was given Raht. By the following August the debt had increased to $108,789.34. For some time previous to this Raht had been insisting on payment or additional security, as the large loss discovered in the copper inventory in May, 1875, rendered his lien

* A. S. Colyar's reply to the arguments of Judges John Baxter and John L. T. Sneed.

of doubtful value. Not only was additional security not forthcoming but, to Raht's surprise, the board of directors early in September passed a resolution denying any indebtedness whatever to him. He promptly countered with his original bill of attachment in the chancery court at Benton on September 20, 1875, and a big-time law suit was on its way.

An answer and cross-bill was filed by the Union Consolidated Mining Company on October 15, 1875, and on October 30 an amended answer was filed. Raht's answers to these were filed on November 19. The receivership, with himself as receiver, which followed Raht's original action, was terminated in a decree by Chancellor Bradford, at Athens, Tennessee, on November 27, 1875. Some of the points decided by Chancellor Bradford were: (1) That a receiver was no longer necessary or proper in this cause; (2) that the rights and equities of the receiver and company were antagonistic; (3) that the receiver appointed be no longer retained and that he be removed; and (4) that the company be authorized to replevy the personal property on which the attachment remained. Soon thereafter the company deposited $114,000 to replevy its properties, Raht was dismissed as receiver, and E. G. Duvall took over management of the mines and smelters at Ducktown. Later, on September 18, 1876, another amended cross-bill was filed by the company. The company was suing Raht for $1,000,000 of which it was alleged that he had deprived the company through fraud, overreaching, mismanagement, and violation of trust.

In the meantime a suit similar to that brought against Raht in Tennessee was instituted in the supreme court in New York City against J. E. Raht, John Thomas, and Charles Raht by the Union Consolidated Mining Company for $1,200,000. This suit, begun on February 4, 1876, hinged upon a resolution entered in the minute book by Charles Raht, secretary, at a directors meeting held on June 19, 1872. It was charged that this entry, stating that Raht was indebted to the company at that time to the amount of $1,253.10 and that this was to be the basis of future settlements with Raht, was a fraudulent entry made by Charles Raht without the knowledge or approval of the directors. This case, however, soon "went out of court without a struggle" when Charles Raht produced a memorandum of the resolution, written by James A. Alexander, one of the directors, from which the entry was transcribed on the minute book. Alexander acknowledged having written the memorandum, apologized for having signed an affidavit stating that he had not written it, and thereafter took no further part in the proceedings against J. E. Raht.

While both parties to the suit in Tennessee were maneuvering into position, the board of directors of the Union Consolidated Mining Company issued to the stockholders, on June 21, 1876, a scathing denunciation of Captain Raht. This was done, no doubt, for the purpose of preparing the minds of the stockholders for the legal battle that was to follow. The diatribe reviewed Raht's long years of service, explained how he had by malfeasance and inefficiency brought the company almost to ruin, and how, now that he was disposed of, the operations would prove profitable and the courts would restore to the company the money that Raht had unscrupulously turned to his own account. The following are quotations from the promulgation, which was signed by Alfred Kimber, secretary:

For the past seventeen years the mining property of this company has been managed by J. E. Raht, its Superintendent, who entered its employ, without means, but with the reputation of being a skillful miner.

Recent investigations have developed the fact that he is a skillful appropriator of the company's funds but an unskillful miner and an unfaithful agent. This company while producing largely of copper under his management has paid no dividends, but *he* has amassed a fortune estimated at several millions of dollars, and developed the mines solely for his own benefit and advantage. The property of this company being located 800 miles from New York was seldom visited by the various Boards of Directors, but having confidence in their superintendent Raht they relied upon the correctness of his statements and accounts and upon his frequent plausible letters which always glimmered with hope in the future, and profits about to be realized, which he knew full well could be realized with an honest management, but which he systematically contrived to absorb himself.

He was constantly harping upon and advising the building of a railroad from Ducktown to Cleveland.... and it now appears that the railroad would benefit him much more than the company, as he owns nearly all the available property for forty miles between Ducktown and Cleveland.

The report went on at great length and enumerated practically all the charges that were later brought against Raht in the trial. It effectively laid the groundwork for united opposition to Raht by all who held Union Consolidated Mining Company stock—

those trusting souls many of whom had bought the stock on the basis of dividends yielded by some other copper mine in some far-off land.

One feature of this suit was the large number of depositions taken. Scores of depositions were taken at Ducktown, Cleveland, New York, in Fannin and Cherokee counties, and at iron and other kinds of furnaces in Tennessee and Alabama. Both parties to the suit spared neither time, effort, nor money in gathering evidence that would strengthen their cases. For eighteen months a squad composed much of the time of S. P. Gaut, A. S. Jarnagin, and Edward Mueller, for Raht; and S. A. Kendall, W. H. Wimberly, and B. I. Lowe, for the company, took depositions at Ducktown, Murphy, and Morganton. This was a trying ordeal. The men travelled by horseback and buggy, in winter and summer, and their lodging accomodations were often barren of comforts. Raht accompanied his counsel occasionally, and on December 30, 1876, he wrote, "I am getting ready to start in a wagon for Morganton; we have a heavy snow and cold weather...."

Throughout these excursions Gaut kept Raht informed of their progress. Despite the hardships and monotony of interviewing an endless procession of witnesses, Gaut retained a superb sense of humor. In his letters to Raht he often facetiously remarked on attempts of the opposing counsel to instruct witnesses "who had never seen any arithmetic in the intricacies of finance and percentage." He applied high-sounding titles to his opponents. They were Chancellor Kendall, Corporal Wimberly, and Brigadier-General Lowe. Kendall was often incapacitated by illness which to Gaut was nothing but the "blind-staggers."

In examining witnesses at Morganton, Georgia, in September 1876, the company's lawyers were trying to prove that Raht had paid an exorbitant price for charcoal so as to profit the more through supplies furnished the colliers through his store. The price paid at the time in question was six cents a bushel. As a rule the colliers averred that they could have furnished coal cheaper had they been paid all in cash every month instead of part in supplies and part in cash, with paydays every three months. In his cross-examination of two of the witnesses at Morganton, Gaut had them give a detailed account of the actual expenses of coal delivered at the Ducktown works. One of these showed a total cost of 6.6 cents and another of 8.9 cents a bushel. Gaut exultantly conveyed this information to Raht, and added that neither Kendall nor Wimberly had seen the point. These inconsistiences were later brought out in Gaut's pleadings before the chancery and supreme courts.

Included in the long list of depositions were those of Samuel Congdon, John Thomas, Alexander Tripple, Addison Cammack, John Tonkin, Edward Mueller, C. L. Hardwick, E. M. Kilpatrick, Pendleton Jones, G. W. Lindsey, J. M. Withrow, James Jory, Jr., George C. and Paul Parks, Aaron Mathews, H. T. McCay, James Phillips, A. A. Campbell, F. F. Passmore, I. J. Stamper, A. M. Arp, George Barnes, B. K. Dickey, D. M. Collins, E. M. Weeks, John Amburn, J. R. Hyatt, A. C. Hunter, Erby Boyd, W. L. Ledford, H. P. Ramey, William Prince, and M. M. McKinney.

To draw a comparison between the price paid by Raht for charcoal and the prices paid by other users of this fuel, the Union Consolidated Mining Company had depositions taken of Samuel Noble, manager and superintendent of the Woodfolk Iron Company; W. Warner, president and manager of the Tecumseh Iron Company; A. G. West, president and general superintendent of the Cherokee Iron Company; and George T. Lewis, styled Tennessee's iron master, of the Grange Iron Works, Stewart County, Tennessee. Evidence furnished by these depositions was not presented by counsel for the company because, in every case, prices paid for charcoal at these works were higher than Raht had paid at Ducktown. Raht's counsel did, however, use the comparisons to good effect.

Practically all of Raht's attention between the time of his original bill and the time of the trial was directed to the task of perfecting his defense and weakening the offense of his opponents. He was present at many of the sessions when depositions were being taken and frequently assisted in preparing questions to be asked deponents. At the preparation of his own deposition at Benton in May, 1876, Raht was quick to take full advantage of the latitude offered him in one of the questions to bring out certain facts irrelevant to the question but not to the case. Objections to his answer were promptly offered by John Baxter, chief counsel of the company. Writing about the incident a few days later, Raht said: "I got all down I wanted. Colonel Baxter then wrote his exceptions to the answer, which is all right; the Chancellor has to read it all. We got on all right, Colonel Baxter had his way and I had mine."

It was not Raht, however, who initiated the long campaign of deposition-taking. Nor was it he who prolonged it. He chafed at the delay in bringing the suit to trial and frequently expressed regret at the time and money that was being wasted in this procedure. He said, "They want to take depositions of every woodchopper, collier, wagoner, laborer, miner, smelter, carpenter, blacksmith, etc. etc., who has ever done a day's work for me, all for the purpose of delaying and annoying." He stated in effect, that the company was pursuing a wearing-down process, but that he was determined not to be "wore down." Depositions in his behalf were more in the nature of rebuttals than in efforts to adduce new evidence. The evidence upon which he relied had long since been written into the company's records.

At different times throughout the years of the trial, Raht expressed regret that the courts were having to settle the affairs between him and the Union Consolidated Mining Company. He said that it was disagreeable to him to be at law with his old employer, but, after all, it was a stock company and had no soul. And, he once added, the whole thing could have been settled by arbitration had he been dealing with sensible men. Events later proved that this indictment was well founded.

It was not until twenty-one months after the date of J. E. Raht's original attachment that the litigation between him and the Union Consolidated Mining Company came to trial. The case was opened on Monday, June 18, 1877, before Chancellor W. F. Cooper in the chancery court at Benton, Tennessee. So voluminous were the books of records, affidavits, depositions, and exhibits used in the trial that the clerk had resorted to common goods boxes for storing these papers. All week Chancellor Cooper sat and listened patiently to arguments of the opposing counsel. The case was argued by A. S. Colyar, P. B. Mayfield, and S. P. Gaut for J. E. Raht, and by John Baxter, S. A. Kendall, and W. H. Wimberly for the company. Raht had added D. M. Key to his legal staff, but Key, having been appointed United States Senator to succeed Andrew Johnson, had been of little assistance. Key withdrew entirely from the case when he was later appointed Postmaster General by President Hayes in 1877.

In reporting on the decision in what came to be known as East Tennessee's Great Lawsuit, the Chattanooga *Dispatch* of June 27, 1877, said: "The Chancellor, after a most patient examination of the case, sustained the contracts and settlements, and dismissed the cross-bill, and gave Raht a decree for the amount claimed. The case was appealed to the Supreme Court, and it is said it will take the Clerk and Master one year to make out the record." The seriousness of the decision against the company was mitigated to some extent, however, by all costs of the case being adjudged against Raht. Chancellor Cooper's reason for fixing the costs against him was explained by Raht as being "... in consideration of the many advantages and profits I had had from the company."

Chancellor Cooper's conduct of the widely advertised lawsuit won for him much favorable comment. The trial was attended by many visitors, and before the week was ended Cooper had gained among both visitors and natives the affectionate appellation "The Little Chancellor." His fitness for the supreme court of the state became a general topic of conversation and was acquiesced in by much head-wagging and learned grunts of approval around the court house and general stores at Benton. And it came to pass that "The Little Chancellor" had succeeded to this position before Raht's case reached that body two years later.

No sooner was Raht back in his office at Cleveland following the favorable decision at Benton than he began by letters and telegrams notifying friends of the outcome of the trial. To William A. Bartlett at New Orleans he wrote that he had won the case, but that it had been appealed to the state supreme court. He added, however, that this would amount to nothing, as the decision was rendered by the most eminent chancellor in Tennessee.

It was Raht's opinion that the testimony of the four directors who testified did their cause more harm than good. He also expressed some surprise at Duvall's failure to testify. Not only was Duvall not used as a witness by the company's counsel, but no part of his lengthy, confidential report on Raht was adduced. Raht predicted that Kendall would place the blame for failure on John Baxter for going into the tiral unprepared. He said that Kendall would probably think that much more valuable evidence could have been picked up around Morganton. But as to his own conduct while on the witness stand, Raht found considerable satisfaction in the fact that he had comported himself in such a manner that he had no regrets. He said that several, including Chancellor Cooper, had expressed surprise in that he had not been more vehement in his denials of the many charges filed against him. The composed, restrained manner in which he testified proved to be, as he said, just as effective as would have a lot of arm-waving and loud swearing.

East Tennessee's Great Lawsuit did not reach the state supreme court until the fall of 1879. During this interim the whole future of both Ducktown and the Union Consolidated Mining Company had gone into total eclipse. The mines had been closed and abandoned, the company had gone into bankruptcy, and J. E. Raht had passed away. Despite these misfortunes and tragedies, the pending lawsuit was carried to the higher court and there fought out as bitterly and as exhaustively as though closed mines, failure, and death were but momentary diversions in a court of eternal session.

The case was argued before the supreme court at Knoxville, Tennessee, from October 14 to October 17, 1879. The court was composed of Chief Justice Deadrick and Associate Justices R. J. McFarland and Peter Turney, with Jordan Stokes of the Lebanon Bar sitting as special judge in place of Associate Justice W. F. Cooper. Justice Cooper was rendered incompetent because of his having heard the trial at Benton in 1877. Arguing the case were A. S. Colyar, P. B. Mayfield, and S. P. Gaut for the executors of J. E. Raht, and John Baxter, William Baxter, and John L. T. Sneed for the Union Consolidated Mining Company.

In his argument before the supreme court, P. B. Mayfield reviewed the charges filed against Raht in both the company's original and amended cross-bills. Following is a digest of these charges: (1) Raht's wealth in the space of ten years had increased from little over nothing to over $1,000,000, while enlarged powers had been given and full confidence reposed in him; (2) he had purposely and fraudulently withheld that his store privilege was very valuable; (3) he had shown bad faith in every respect, violated every promise and condition upon which contracts were granted, and made false statements in monthly reports as to production and costs; (4) inequality in prices paid for down- and backhauling between Ducktown and Cleveland; (5) he manipulated wages so as to enable himself to absorb the entire earnings of employees; (6) he kept employees on the payroll when their services were not needed; (7) the debt due him on August 31, 1875, was for interest on alleged advances, none of which were made; (8) his representations that the company did not have sufficient capital to carry on its operations, by which he obtained several sales agency contracts, were fraudulent; (9) his misrepresentation of facts and conditions induced the company to purchase his sales agency contract; (10) he bought supplies in excess of the company's needs, hindered its operations, discredited its ores, and embarrassed its finances, with a view to the ultimate appropriation of its properties.

The amended cross-bill filed on September 18, 1876, reiterated the foregoing charges, with minor corrections, and then further added the following charges: (1) that Raht charged the two company physicians 10 per cent for collecting the one dollar a month paid to them by each employee, or by the company; (2) that he appropriated the scrip dividends on insurance on copper shipments; (3) that he bought timber lands for the purpose of reselling them to the company at a profit; (4) that he should have contributed to the purchase and upkeep of the Ocoee River road; (5) that he made 10 per cent on the cost of constructing the road from Greasy Creek to Parksville; (6) that he appropriated for use on his farm wood ashes that should have been used in fertilizing the company's own properties; (7) that he used the company's scrap iron during his receivership; and (8) that he failed to account for proportionate loss on his and Burra Burra ores used in fluxing. Another charge alleged that he was paid $57,000 as reimbursement for expenditures by him at the mines during the war.

Taking up where the charges left off, John Baxter launched into an argument in behalf of the company, and to the disparagement of Raht, that was so extended it filled a closely printed booklet of eighty-two pages. He opened his pleadings by saying: "This record is an interesting one. It displays a capacity for original, intricate and far reaching fraud, beyond anything that has hitherto come under the judicial observation of this court." And not once thereafter did he veer from his theme that Raht was, or had been, nothing but a conniving culprit intent upon the ruin of his employers. It is apparent that Baxter endeavored to beat out of the heads of the justices all their judicial training, perspective, and reasoning, and to picture Raht as having been so vile and cunning that they would be incapable of recognizing or desiring facts and records presented in his behalf.

To illustrate the vituperation which Baxter injected into his pleadings, excerpts from some of these statements, which followed his opening remarks, follow: "It is clear that there is a point in business matters when a fraud, like gravitation, turns the other way and vests a right...." "But defendant Raht, in his grasping, eager cupidity, has drawn the line of demarcation at the wrong place...." "No man could exist under his shadow and prosper except under his auspices...." "He never neglected an opportunity to drain any and every one that came within his reach...." "But, notwithstanding his great personal purity, his elevation of character, his boasted disinterestedness, self-sacrificing disposition

Old Burra Burra furnace sheds at McPherson, as they appeared in 1892. Seven similar smelting works were, or were being, erected at Ducktown by 1860. The small furnaces required four months to produce metallic copper. The impure copper was then refined and cast into ingots at the United Refining Works.

Prospecting for ore with a diamond drill. Ducktown's first diamond drill was used to test the Burra Burra vein in 1872 and was bought for $5,500, raised from stockholders of the Burra Burra and Polk County companies.

Interrogatories of the Receiver. One of the first moves by the Confederacy toward sequestration of Ducktown enterprises under northern ownership was the serving of this paper upon J. E. Raht in November, 1861. The marginal notes were made by Raht.

THE TRIAL 179

and incorruptible nature, he permitted himself to be tempted, and fell a melancholy example of man's fallibility and utter incapacity to serve God and mammon at the same time...." "Everybody was required by force of the circumstances surrounding them to drop their mite with uniform regularity into his capacious maw to propitiate his favor...."

From the beginning of the litigation Raht had relied for relief upon his regular monthly statements and reports of operations, duly executed contracts and agreements, and faith in the impartiality of the courts of justice. And it is doubtful if ever attorneys entered upon a case in which a client furnished them with more printed and recorded evidence favorable to his own cause than was true in this one. Raht had rested but lightly upon the buttressing evidence as brought out in depositions. These latter instruments had been the bane of his existence since institution of the proceedings. And to cap the climax he had been charged with the expenses which the company incurred in their heedless quest of every individual who would testify that he had wronged him. But that he was strong where the real stress would fall, Captain Raht had never doubted.

As a matter of fact the case against Raht was based almost wholly upon hypotheses, or wishful thinking. The Union Consolidated Mining Company was suing him on account of a vague feeling that they had been grievously wronged, but just how or to what extent it was difficult to prove. In all candor it must be said that the company would have accepted a million dollars of him in simple faith that he owed them that amount from profits they believed he had surreptitiously realized at his Isabella store up until 1875. They cried liar, thief, and interloper at him in childlike sincerity, but when called upon by disinterested judges to prove their charges, they became confused and uncertain. To support their tenuous accusations, counsel for the company inevitably resorted to questionable statements regarding Raht's character, motives, and principles. They were patently evading a cardinal principle of law that "where you charge fraud you must state the facts upon which you allege fraud and prove them strictly."

On the other hand, Raht's counsel was at no time forced to resort to detracting and scurrilous dissertations as substitutes for matters of fact. Consequently their defense of him was as morally sincere as it was judicially ethical and determined.

It would be incorrect to infer that Raht's counsel found no appropriate openings for the display of their store of sarcasm. It was William G. Smith, John L. Macaulay, and Alfred Kimber, directors of the Union Consolidated Mining Company, who, as P. B. Mayfield said, were the motivators of the suit against Raht. And it was against these three individuals that Colyar, Mayfield, and Gaut occasionally loosed denunciatory outbursts. It was alleged by these directors that eleven letters written by Raht to John Thomas, president of the company, from 1872 to 1874, bearing on policies and practices at the mines, had been suppressed by Thomas. It was further alleged that Thomas was in collusion with Raht by virtue of his having borrowed money from him and that had the president made known to the board of directors the contents of the letters, future events would have been otherwise. Colyar proved, however, that the company's cross-bill contained extracts from these letters, which obviously would have been impossible had the letters not been available. Said Colyar: "The company's lawsuit—its claim—is founded on certain facts, fraudulently concealed at the time of the settlement [December 1, 1874]. This is supported by the swearing of the three directors who own the stock, that certain letters containing important facts were suppressed, but this is disproved by the production of their own books, and the three witnesses stand before the court stultified, condemned, without explanation, and without a palliating circumstance.... It is manifest there is no escaping the conclusion, that they brought a false charge and swore to it, which contemplated the recovery of a large sum of money from Julius E. Raht...." And thus the haranguing continued for four days.

The decision of the state supreme court was rendered at Knoxville, on March 16, 1880, by the Honorable Jordan Stokes, the special judge. This was five months after the case was heard by the court, and nearly five years after it was first instituted. Judge Stokes began by saying:

> It is apparent, from a careful examination of the record, that the parties have spared no labor or pains in the preparation of the case in the inferior court. They have furnished us with a large mass of proof, both oral and documentary, upon all the issues in the pleadings, as well as a large amount which lies outside of any issue legitimately presented. The arguments of learned counsel on both sides have displayed great ability, and legal learning and research, and have been full and exhaustive upon all the questions of law and fact. Nothing has been left undone by either of the parties, which could aid the court in arriving at an accurate and satisfactory conclusion. We have given to the case, as a whole, and in detail, the consideration which

its interest and magnitude seem to demand, and have, upon careful examination and deliberate reflection, arrived at a conclusion which meets with the unanimous approval of the Court.

After reviewing the circumstances leading up to Raht's appointment as sales agent, and his relinquishment of this position, the court next took up the question of his monthly reports:

> It is admitted that Raht made out and forwarded to the board of directors, during the whole period of his superintendency and agency, excepting three years during the Civil War, monthly statements of his accounts, showing, with great minuteness of detail, the expenditures for labor, materials, hauling, et cetera, for the preceding month. These statements gave every item of expenditure, the names of the employees, and the amount paid to each; the number of bushels of charcoal bought, and the price paid for it per bushel; the number of cords of wood bought, as well as the number of cords cut on the lands of the company, and the price per cord paid in each instance, and the amount and price paid per hundred pounds for hauling from the mines and works to Cleveland, and from Cleveland back to the mines and works. No complaint was ever made, before the commencement of this litigation, that these statements were not sufficiently full and minute in the detail of items....

Thereafter the several charges were taken up and the proof in support of each, and the rebuttals thereto, commented upon. In each and every one of the charges it was the opinion of the court that insufficient evidence had been produced and that the allegations were too general and indefinite to sustain the charges. For instance, with respect to the charge that Raht had amassed a fortune during his years of employment at Ducktown and that enlarged powers had been given and full confidence reposed in him, the court observed as follows:

> Great emphasis in the pleadings and arguments is placed upon the facts that Raht accumulated a large estate during his agency, while the conditions of the company was not materially improved, and that he acquired the unbounded confidence of the directors, and exercised a controlling influence over them in all the business matters of the company. If it were shown that his agency for the company, and his management of its mines and works, were his only source of profit and gain, then, the fact of his amassing a large estate would create some suspicion of his integrity and fidelity, and awaken greater care and caution in looking into and determining his motives and purposes in his dealings and transactions with the company. But the force of this argument is greatly weakened, if not entirely overcome,

by the concession that he was the owner of two valuable mills, two productive farms and two or more mines, was agent for other companies, and extensively engaged in the business of merchandising and trade generally, from all which sources, his great activity, business talent, and close economy enabled him to realize handsome profits. If the directors had reposed unbounded confidence in his integrity and fidelity, and had followed, without question or dissent his suggestions and recommendations, it could not, most certainly, be alleged against him as a fault; but the minutes of the board do not show any such blind confidence or implicit obedience to his advice. No doubt many things which Raht recommended, and the board adopted, turned out in the end to be unprofitable to the company; but in view of the character of the company's enterprise and business, and the frequent changes and improvements which experience, science, and perfected skill were daily making, it would be most wonderful if no mistakes, no miscalculations, no unwise and unprofitable alterations had been advised and adopted during the long reign of his agency. We do not think either branch of the argument can be properly used to sustain the claim of the company, or to disparage that of the agent, Raht.

Captain Raht knew some law, too. Four years before the supreme court's opinion he had said: "If an agent keeps his employer apprised of his acts... no fraud can be established then, although the management may have been ever so bad. I kept my employer apprised of everything, most assuredly."

Despite the many charges and allegations, it was apparent that they served merely as feints for the attack on Raht's store privilege. The supreme court recognized this, of course, and prefaced their opinion on this angle of the case by remarking: "We now proceed to consider the main ground for relief under the cross-bill. The company claims the whole net profit of the store carried on at the mines under the name of Raht, and for his individual benefit, from the commencement to the termination of his general agency." It was a matter of record, as the court pointed out, that the store privilege was a form of compensation in lieu of salary; that the contract was renewed year after year; that it was common knowledge to all and Raht had admitted such to the company at different times; that the store was a source of much profit to him; that the store question was never mentioned in the many settlements between him and the company; and that the company did not incur any liability or run any risk in the operations of the store. Although they reviewed the case at great length, not once did the court find any grounds for relief of the company in respect to Raht's merchandising business.

In the closing paragraph of the court's opinion, preceding the decision, it was stated: "Serious complaints are also made in the cross-bill, upon the grounds that Raht invested large amounts of the company's money in lands during the Civil War, and at its close paid back the same in worthless Confederate notes and Southern bank-notes of but little value, and that he claimed and collected, at the same time, from the company a false and fraudulent debt, amounting to fifty-seven thousand dollars. There is not a scintilla of proof in the record to establish either one of these gross charges...." After briefly describing the efforts Raht made to continue operations during the war, and his success in conserving so much of the company's property during that time, the opinion was brought to a close by the following statement: "This summing up shows wonderful success in operating so extensive and complicated an enterprise during the period of a fierce civil war, and no doubt, the success is, in the main, attributable to the indomitable energy and activity and strict fidelity and good faith of the general agent and superintendent."

The Court's decision, which was by now obvious, was as follows:

We think, upon a careful and deliberate review and consideration of the whole case, that the decree of the Chancery Court, dismissing the cross-bill of the company, and granting the relief prayed for [by Raht] in the original bill, is correct; but we do not concur in opinion with the learned Chancellor on the subject of costs. The general rule on the subject of cost, adopted in the Court of Chancery, is the same as in a court of law, that the costs follow the result of the suit; but the former court may, under certain circumstances, excuse the unsuccessful party from the payment of costs to his opponent, and even in exceptional cases, actually throw his own costs upon the party succeeding. Cases of the latter class, however, are very limited, and seem to be confined to cases where the unsuccessful party is in no fault whatever.

We are unable to see any sufficient reason or circumstance to take the present case out of the general rule. It may be true that a demurrer to the cross-bill would have dispensed with the necessity of taking proof upon many of the issues imperfectly and insufficiently stated, but the intrinsic difficulty of making a demurrer, standing alone or combined with an answer, a full, satisfactory and complete defense, when general allegations of mistake, fraud and unconscionable advantage are interwoven with the whole texture of the adverse pleading, may well excuse, not to say positively deter parties, acting under the advice and direction of learned counsel, from resorting to it. It is further laid down as a settled rule in courts of equity, that a party introducing unfounded charges of fraud, will be made to pay the costs occasioned thereby; though he may be successful in the suit, or the other party may have acted in such manner as to give reasonable grounds of suspicion.

In view of the charges in the cross-bill, and the failure of the Company to make out a case for relief, under any one of these charges, we think it is highly reasonable, just and proper to adhere to the general rule in the disposition of costs. A decree will be entered in conformity with this opinion, dismissing the cross-bill of the company, and giving the relief sought in the original bill, with a reference to the Clerk of this Court, to ascertain the amount due to complainant Raht.... The Company will pay the costs in the Chancery Court and the costs in this Court.

CHAPTER 16

"THE RICHEST MAN IN TENNESSEE"

It seems to the author that he is sacrificing a potentially remarkable book by abridging the story of Captain Raht's life in two chapters and including it in a book devoted largely to another subject. But as the Captain and Ducktown were almost synonymous terms for so many years, it is entirely fitting that the stories of both be told together.

The story of Raht's life as herein recounted covers a period of twenty-five years. During this quarter of a century there were times when, no doubt, life to him was nothing more than a humdrum affair. But reduced to the pages of a book, with such static periods omitted, his life with its philosophy, determination, and success reveals a swift-moving panorama of personal achievement that should rank high in the annals of American biography.

The winter of 1853-54 was slowly melting into spring. Dogwoods were putting out their sprays of white along bleak hillsides at Ducktown. Speculators were busy checking on deeds to properties and misdeeds to purchasers. Fortune-hunters and curiosity seekers were resuming their trek into the district, and the winter's enforced idleness at the different mines was giving way to bustle and confusion. John Caldwell's new road down the Ocoee, completed but a few months before, was being put in preparation for the heavy wagons that would soon begin rolling down to Cleveland with boxes and barrels of black copper. Hacks and other lighter vehicles were arriving with increasing frequency at Hiwassee and dumping their cargoes of cramped humanity into the welter of a full-fledged mining boom. From one of these vehicles there one day emerged at Hiwassee a stockily-built young man whose accent instantly labeled him as a foreigner—undoubtedly a German. Judging from the bulges at the knees of his trousers and the accordion-like creases in the back of his coat, he had evidently been traveling for several days. Tarrying in the muddy streets of the busy little village only long enough to be directed to the destination he was seeking, he set off immediately, valise in hand, on the two-mile walk through the woods to the Polk County Mine. As he neared the mine he shifted to within easy reach a letter he was carrying, addressed to the superintendent. Upon arriving there, he delivered the highly-prized missive and stood impassively by while the letter was read. It was from an official of the company at New York instructing the mine superintendent to give the bearer a job at the Polk County Mine.

The thoroughly composed young man who came to Ducktown bearing the letter of introduction was Julius Eckhardt Raht, less than four years out of Germany. Entering upon his duties at the Polk County Mine, he quickly displayed a degree of training and experience that led to his promotion within a few months to the position of mine captain. It was here that he earned the title "Captain," by which he was afterwards known.

Julius Eckhardt Raht was born in Dillenburg, Duchy of Nassau, Germany, on June 26, 1826. Upon completion of his preparatory education he attended Bonn University during 1844 and 1845. He then transferred to the University of Berlin where he remained until 1847. The courses he pursued at these universities included, he later said, "Chemistry, Mineralogy, etc. etc."

For several years Raht's father was president of the Appellate Division of the Court of Justice at Dillenburg. Political persecution of his father by the Duke of Nassau, which led to the elder Raht's banishment from Dillenburg, was undoubtedly a contributing factor in the arrival in America of Julius E. and his brother Charles (or Carl) Raht, "by the good ship Bavaria," on September 26, 1850. From what has already been learned in previous chapters of J. E. Raht's intense love of freedom of speech and action, there remains no conjecture as to why he turned to the free land beyond the seas for a home and career. Incidentally, three other sons of the persecuted Raht, August, William, and Edward, the latter a noted architect, also made their way to America.

Captain Raht's education in the sciences had been supplemented by sound instruction in the English language. Written documents of his as early as 1856 revealed few ambiguities in his use of English. There was, however, a steady improvement to be noted in his handwriting in this language. Particularly noticeable was his early familiarity with legal matters, especially those pertaining to deeds, contracts, and agreements. No doubt it was from his father's profession that he had absorbed a natural penchant for things legal.

The young German immigrant did not delay long in his decision to become an American in his own right. He made his declaration to become a citizen of the United States, before the circuit court of the District of Columbia, on August 20, 1853. He was later "... admitted to the full enjoyment of all the rights and privilegs of a naturalized citizen of the United States of America..." by the circuit court for the county of Polk (Tennessee), on the twenty-second day of May, 1856.

Immediately upon his arrival in this country, Raht moved westward in quest of the mining industry. He went to Missouri and, as he said, "took my chances at very practical work at a mine...." From there he moved to a lead mine near Dubuque, Iowa. After another short sojourn, this time in Wisconsin, he returned east where he had charge of mining work at Harper's Ferry, Leesburg, and Jamestown, Virginia, and at Guilford, North Carolina. Young Raht had indeed ridden the mining circuit of the country when he finally reached Ducktown in the spring of 1854.

The spell of Ducktown was soon upon Raht. Obviously, there was enough ore here to last a lifetime. Fortunes could be made in this typically-situated copper region. "Why seek ye further when at your feet lie that for which ye were trained to master?" Thoughts such as these probably held the young German as he watched the sun at eventide as it slowly sank behind the distant rim of Big Frog Mountain. But he had come to Ducktown only half prepared. He began making plans to complete his arrangements for an indefinite stay in Tennessee. This meant a long journey back to Europe. The journey was made that summer for, in August, 1854, J. E. Raht and Mathilde Dombois were married at Freindiez, Duchy of Nassau. His mission to Germany fulfilled, Raht departed immediately with his bride for Ducktown.

The family of Raht's wife, like that of his own family, had suffered persecution in Europe. The Dombois family were French Protestants who had fled to Germany to escape religious persecution by French Catholics. Raht and his bride left Europe never to return permanently. Henceforth they were to be Americans at home in America.

From cultured surroundings in staid old Nassau to the coarse ways of a boisterous mining camp in the hills of Tennessee was indeed a bewildering transition for Raht's young wife. But with the stoicism of a professional pioneer she moved into her new home, a hastily constructed shack of rough boards near the Polk County Mine, and took up her duties with a courage not surpassed by that of her youthful mine captain.

Although much has already been told of Captain Raht's life, it is deemed advisable to add here an explanation of his financial condition at the time he began his eventful career at Ducktown. After his break with the Union Consolidated Mining Company in 1875, that company never desisted in their charge that he was penniless when he came to Ducktown, and that he had prospered at their expense. Colyar's brief in the trial disclosed, however, that "Mr. Raht was not in poverty when he commenced business for this company; he had been charged by the Government from which he came, though a very young man, with a responsible trust, involving questions of science. He had been likewise charged with a trust of much importance in New York before coming to Tennessee, and his fidelity in that trust put him at the head of the Ducktown enterprise." This latter trust undoubtedly was in connection with his having charge of the mines in Virginia and North Carolina for the New York interests who later sent him to Tennessee.

Local legends of Captain Raht maintain, of course, that he was just a poor miner looking for a job when he came to Ducktown. This is natural, because there is nothing like having "one of the boys" grow up and hold his former employer's nose to the grindstone rough. Most assuredly Raht was not rich when he came to Tennessee; had he been he would not have come to Ducktown and gone to work at the mines. But neither was he merely seeking a job; he was a capable young man in search of opportunity—and was astute enough to know when he had found it.

For four years following his return to Ducktown with his bride, Raht lived at the Polk County Mine on Copper Hill. This was in the vicinity described by Elizabeth Barker as being a place where there was much drinking, fighting, and debauchery. To augment his salary of $125 a month as mine captain, he opened a small store to serve employees at the Polk County and Mary's mines. Much of his spare time was spent at his store and in bartering and trading throughout the district. By August, 1856, the multiplicity of his transactions made the keeping of a balance sheet necessary. In that month his assets exceeded his liabilities by nearly $2,300. His cash on hand included $97.50 in gold, $10.00 in silver, and $496.00 in paper money. He began investing in real estate in 1856. His principal purchase in that year was the 480-acre farm of L. L. Threewitt, which he afterwards referred to as his Turtletown farm.

In May, 1857, Raht's balance sheet showed that his wealth had increased to over $3,700. In addition to his stock of goods and cash, he owned a carriage; three horses named James, Mo, and Fanny; a mule named Jaques; four steers named William, Tom, Dick, and Jerry; and a bull named John. Also, two cows and calves, one boar, three sows, two shoates, fourteen pigs, fifteen geese, some chickens, furniture, linen, and a host of lesser items.

The crust of routine affairs was first broken for Raht when, on January 1, 1858, he was appointed by Samuel Congdon to take over the management of the Ocoee Turnpike and Plank Road Company. On March 1 of that year he was also employed by Alexander Hamilton, president of the Davis Copper Company, to take charge of that company's properties, to lease its improved lands, and to rent the tenements thereon. He moved very definitely into the forefront of affairs in the district when he succeeded Samuel Congdon as superintendent of the Union Consolidated Mining Company soon after the company was organized in January, 1858. The following year he was hired as superintendent of the Polk County Copper Company, and in 1860 management of the works of the Burra Burra Copper Company was placed in his hands. Thus Raht, at the age of thirty-four, had attained to the position of chief of operations of all mines and smelting works at Ducktown.

After his appointment as superintendent of the Union Consolidated Mining Company, Captain Raht moved into the house vacated by Samuel Congdon at the Tennessee Mine. He purchased Congdon's household goods and also Congdon's commissary at the mine. In addition to hiring Raht as superintendent at a salary of $2,000 a year, Congdon, who was returning to New York, also tendered to him the store privilege and dwelling and store house free of rent. It was here that the groundwork was laid for Raht's subsequent success in the field of merchandising. But to Mathilde Raht it was the more comfortable dwelling and furniture that proved the most prized possession of all that came out of the deal.

When the right to operate commissaries on his own private initiative was granted to Raht, he became the owner of the best paying business at Ducktown. He catered particularly to employees, of course, and their store accounts were always the first deductions made from their earnings. In every way but one the stores were a part of the copper industry—the profits went to Raht instead of to the companies. But this was not an arrangement of his own making. He merely fell heir to its lucrative results.

Raht's personal business expanded rapidly. The tone of his balance sheets changed from that of a faltering tenor to that of a pompous baritone. There began appearing on the credit side of his ledger such items as farming lands, town lots, bonds, interest, mortgage loans, and pounds sterling. He also began buying four- and six-mule teams which he placed in copper hauling service. With one purchase of a six-mule team from Stephen Jones of Morgan County, Georgia, in 1859, he purchased the driver of the team also, a Negro slave named Edom. He paid $2,400 for the team and slave. In October of that year, however, Raht presented Edom a deed granting him his freedom to take effect on October 1, 1861, or sooner should Raht die or move from the state. The deed stated that Edom had been a loyal and faithful servant, that he had more than paid for his freedom through his labor, care, and faithfulness, and that it was his master's intention that Edom should never serve another.

With his influence in the district widening, Raht began increasing the number of his commissaries. In addition to the ones at the Tennessee and Mary's mines, stores were established by him at the Hiwassee, Isabella, and East Tennessee mines. His total merchandise inventory on January 1, 1862, was slightly less than $7,000. Some idea of the class of merchandise that was in demand by employees at Ducktown at that time can be had by reviewing some of the articles Raht carried in stock. For instance, the inventory of flour was, in even dollars, $2,300; sugar, $400; salt, $700; pork, $500; lard, $18; linsey, $140; shoes, $1,400; hats, $15; and drawers, $7. Store-bought underwear did not at that period flutter from every clothesline in the district. Raht must have put on a Christmas sale of men's hats at his Mary's store in December, 1861, as he sold thirty of them, at $1.50 each, which completely depleted his stock at this store.

Since the Captain was possessed of a tremendous capacity for work and a sublime patience for intricate matters of detail, his shadow fell athwart the headwaters of every stream of revenue that flowed through Ducktown. Spirited, methodical, ambitious, honest, he was no less a stern taskmaster in his own behalf than he was a loyal employee of those in whose interests he served. Young enough to be undaunted, he was at the same time sagacious in his plans and their execution. It required the poise of an executive and the bruskness of a shift boss to erect furnaces and develop mines in a locality where corporation existence was as fleeting as the wind. Between the years 1858 and 1861 stockholders of the Union Consolidated Mining Company, Polk County Copper Company, and Burra Burra Copper Company were confidently expecting the fabulous dividends promised them by the directors. The directors in turn were depending upon Raht to produce these dividends, and mindful of the trust imposed in him, he was making herculean effort to start a steady stream of copper ingots on their way to eastern markets. At the same time, however, he was keeping the candles burning in his commissaries until a late hour and was adding to his real estate and other holdings at opportune times.

Eight years after he had come to Ducktown bearing the letter of recommendation for a job, Raht estimated his net worth as being over $100,000. He was drawing salaries amounting to $600 a month from his different positions; his commissaries were showing gratifying profits; and he had purchased some three thousand acres of farming and mineral lands for which he had paid over $27,000. Not only this, but he held a lien on the personal property of the Union Consolidated Mining Company, which had become over-ambitious in 1860 and declared a 5 per cent dividend that not only left the company "broke" but left it unable to secure funds through customary channels. Upon earnest solicitation Captain Raht agreed to assist the treasurer in his efforts to raise the money needed for current payrolls and supplies, and in return he was given a lien on the personal property of the company. His potential power and influence was thus much greater than was reflected in the bare figures of his balance sheets. This phenomenal son of the old Fatherland was indeed safely enmeshed in the magic carpet of wealth.

Under his supervision the Ducktown industry too was close to realizing its just expectations of profits from Tennessee copper. This was the goal for which Raht was eagerly striving, because it was the accomplishment expected of him by men who had faith in his ability and who in return were held in high esteem by him. The coming of the war, however, upset his well-laid plans and left him hanging frantically to the fraying edges of his magic carpet. The predicament in which the Captain found himself following the beginning of hostilities and his attempts to keep the copper industry intact until he was forced to desert Ducktown late in the war, have already been related.

Raht's contribution to the South's war efforts apparently outweighed for some time his considered potentialities as a fighting man. However, he came up for consideration as a unit for the army when his name was entered on the "Muster and Descriptive Roll of Conscripts Enrolled in the State of Tennessee, and Detailed" at the recruiting office at Knoxville, on January 15, 1863. At this time he was detailed to keep the copper mines in operation, but within the next two months Raht found it necessary to furnish the army a substitute for himself, as the following document, executed on March 4, 1863, reveals:

> Know all men by these presents, that I, D. Wallis, of Polk County, Tennessee, am held and firmly bound unto J. E. Raht, of same county and State, to the sum of five thousand dollars to be paid to the said J. E. Raht, his executors, administrators, or assigns, for which payment well and truly be made, and I bind myself, my heirs, executors, and administrators and each of them, firmly by these presents:—Now the condition of the above obligation is such, that if the above bounden D. Wallis shall proceed to the Camp of Instruction at Knoxville, Tennessee, this week, and be mustered into Confederate service as a substitute for J. E. Raht; or, provided he is found sound, and J. E. Raht pays him twenty-five hundred dollars in Confederate money, then after he is mustered in, and D. Wallis enters the service as such substitute, then the above obligation is void; otherwise to remain in full force and virtue.

The end of Raht's value to the South's copper industry must have been in sight when it became necessary that he furnish the military forces with a substitute for himself. At this time the output at the works was gradually decreasing; the mining properties were in the process of being sold by Confederate authorities; and events that might follow thereafter were matters of serious conjecture.

As the fateful approach of Federal forces into lower East Tennessee brought a climax to the operations at Ducktown, and as the caravans of refugees from the district began crowding the copper road to Cleveland, Captain Raht too began making preparations to leave Ducktown. Despite the fact that a rifle and a double-barrel shot gun furnished by him to the Confederates in 1861 were then in use against the Yankees, that he had supplied the South for over two years with large quantities of copper, and that a substitute for him was then in a rebel-gray uniform, Captain Raht was neither stranger to nor enemy of certain influential Yankees. Therefore, when he departed from Ducktown in January, 1864, he took with him practically all his household goods, as well as some forty horses and mules. The animals he sold to the Federal forces at Cleveland, and from Major-General George H. Thomas he received a passport for himself, family, and household goods to Cincinnati.

Not knowing how long he would be forced to remain in the city, he immediately purchased residence Number 187 on Baymiller Street, for which he paid $4,500; and to keep in touch with conditions in East Tennessee, he subscribed to the *Knoxville Whig and Rebel Ventilator*, published by W. G. ("Parson") Brownlow.

When he left Ducktown, Raht also took with him the books and accounts of the Union Consolidated Mining Company. He proceeded to New York with these and while there a settlement was effected between him and the company for advances he had made the company since early in 1861. The amount due him was $31,004.34, for which payment was made in fine copper stored at Ducktown. There was no gamble whatever in this arrangement. There was a distinct possibility that the copper could never be claimed. On the other hand, if the metal could never be recovered the company would certainly be unable to repay him and both would be equally heavy losers.

After establishing himself at Cincinnati, Captain Raht spent much of his time during the next year and a half in writing letters. One of his first impressions of that city was the glaring difference that existed in economic conditions in the North and the South. In a letter addressed to Henry Jory at Ducktown on March 1, 1864, Raht said that he was living in "Porkapolis," because, he added, there was more pork stored at Cincinnati than there was in all Dixie. Cincinnati, he continued, was prosperous; the people there displayed little interest in the rebellion and were enjoying only the good effects of the war.

He also took occasion to tell Jory that "new recruits here receive about $500.00 in Greenbacks as United States, State, County and Ward bounty; in New York as high as $677.00 at present. Veterans receive $100.00 additional."

Two days later he wrote to Samuel Congdon that he had met a gentleman from Athens, Tennessee, who had brought thirty-six bales of cotton from that place to Cincinnati by railroad. Raht said that if the copper stored at Ducktown were in the East Tennessee valley they could get it to northern markets very soon. But with Confederate forces stationed at Murphy, North Carolina, and Ellijay, Georgia, he said that it could not be removed from Ducktown unless a special expedition of Federal soldiers protected the movement.

It might be well to explain briefly the route of travel between East Tennessee and Cincinnati at that time. Previous to the war there was direct rail connection from Chattanooga to the east by way of Knoxville, Bristol, and Lynchburg. However, to reach Louisville and Cincinnati from this section it was necessary to go by way of Chattanooga and Nashville. At that time, and for several years afterwards, there was no railroad from East Tennessee through Kentucky to Louisville and Cincinnati. Therefore, it was not until Federal forces had gained control of the East Tennessee and Georgia and the Nashville and Chattanooga railroads from Cleveland to Nashville late in 1863 that Captain Raht and the other refugees from Ducktown could reach the North by train. They could not move out by way of Knoxville and Bristol as Virginia was still held by the Confederates.

In the aforementioned letter to Congdon, written on March 3, 1864, Raht told him that train service under Federal control had been re-established from Nashville to Chattanooga and as far north of Chattanooga as Loudon, but that United States mail service had not then been extended further than to Chattanooga. Thus it was that the gentleman from Athens was able to ship his cotton from that place to Cincinnati by the circuitous route of Chattanooga, Nashville, and Louisville. And it was thus that the copper could have been moved northward had it been possible to haul it from Ducktown to Cleveland.

The foregoing will serve to explain too how Raht was able to correspond with the mines. He sent John Tonkin some United States postage stamps for his use in replying, as Tonkin at that time, and until the war ended, could secure only Confederate postage stamps at Ducktown.*

There was every reason why Captan Raht should suffer protracted fits of agony, as he did, over the copper at Ducktown. The price of the red metal was increasing steadily. On June 6, 1864, he wrote to John Tonkin and inquired about the prospects of hiring teams to begin hauling the ingots to Cleveland. This was an inquiry born of desperation for, as he knew, there were simply no such teams available. In the following month the Captain's

---

* Valuable information on the postal service in the South during the Civil War can be found in August Dietz, *The Postal Service of the Confederate States of America* (1929).

The Cleveland National Bank building, erected in 1872 and designed by Edward Raht, architect. The bank was organized by J. E. Raht, who served as its president for several years.

The old church and school building at Isabella, financed by J. E. Raht, who liberally supported schools and churches in his district. It was erected shortly after the Civil War.

The J. E. Raht residence in Cleveland, Tennessee. The house and farm were purchased in 1861, but the Raht family did not occupy the house until after the Civil War. The house is no longer standing.

Ocoee Street, Copperhill, looking east. The town, located on the Tennessee-Georgia line and called McCaysville on the Georgia side, serves as the metropolitan area of the Ducktown district. The combined population is approximately five thousand, about half the total population of the Ducktown Basin.

feet rested flat on the bottom of the slough of despond when the price of copper climbed to fifty-five cents a pound, the highest price at which the metal has ever sold in this country. The price of copper for the year 1864 averaged forty-seven cents a pound in good United States money. And during all this time there lay at Ducktown, beyond the reach of the mine owners, some two hundred thousand pounds of the precious metal, stored in secret caverns at the Mary's and Tennessee mines.

In his letter to John Tonkin, Raht said also that it had just been learned that General Schofield had destroyed the Etowah Iron Works in Georgia. The Confederate government had, he said, advanced over a million dollars in keeping these works in operation and their destruction was a blow to the Confederacy from an economic as well as a military standpoint. On the other hand Raht could glean some satisfaction from the fact that the Confederate government had never been financially involved in the copper mines at Ducktown, and for this reason he did not contemplate their being destroyed by Federal forces. Especially was he satisfied that the properties of the Union Consolidated Mining Company, owned largely by northern interests, would not be molested.

Of the many problems faced by Captain Raht during his enforced absence from Tennessee the welfare of those who remained at the mines was one of the most important. He communicated frequently with John Tonkin in an effort to keep himself informed of conditions at Ducktown. He kept Tonkin supplied with funds, part of which he furnished personally and part of which he secured of Samuel Congdon. In apprising Congdon of the straitened circumstances of those who were remaining at the mines at his request, he said that it was their mutual duty to send financial assistance when needed. He told Congdon that he did not see how a man with a family, or even one without a family, for that matter, could remain at Ducktown in safety. He felt that he was in honor bound to see that those at the mines did not suffer, and this duty he did not shirk.

Upon learning of the flight of Dr. Augustin Gattinger from Ducktown in March, 1864, Raht wrote Tonkin inquiring how they were getting along without a physician. Whether Gattinger's departure left the district without the services of a physician or whether Raht was referring to the absence of a company doctor at Ducktown is not clear. Sometime later he wrote Tonkin that he should not require much money for provisions so long as there were plenty of strawberries, blackberries, milk, and cream to be had.

In his efforts to aid those at Ducktown, Raht had, of course, been concerned chiefly with those still employed at the mining properties, for until the summer of 1864 a force of several men had been retained. By this time, however, guerrillas were becoming increasingly menacing, no means of securing fuel to keep pumps in operation were left, and hope of moving the copper to Cleveland was abandoned. In view of these conditions, Raht advised Captain Tonkin on July 4 to remain at the mines only if he considered it safe to do so and to retain Edward Mueller, "Uncle Jimmy," and A. S. Hoffman, but to cut off all other workers. It turned out that Tonkin and his three associates remained at Ducktown, and it was these four families only that Raht thereafter made provisions for.

Throughout his residence at Cincinnati Captain Raht was unremitting in his efforts to secure release of the copper belonging to the Union Consolidated Mining Company that had been captured by Federal forces at Cleveland, Tennessee, and had been moved to Cincinnati. On April 23, 1864, he wrote to Major General George H. Thomas, at Chattanooga, asking that the copper not be disposed of until the parties in interest could be heard. But no assistance in the matter was possible on the General's part, as the copper had been removed beyond his jurisdiction. Raht next wrote to Samuel Congdon as follows:

CINCINNATI, OHIO,
April 29, 1864.

S. Congdon, Esq.,
  General Agent,
    New York.

DEAR SIR:

I have called upon the United States Treasury agent at this place in reference to the copper which has been seized at Cleveland, as the property of Mr. Wm. H. Peet, and been shipped here to the Treasury Agency for the purpose to sell it like all other confiscated property.

The regular sales day of the Government is the 3rd Monday in next month, May 16, when the copper will be sold unless otherwise directed by the Secretary of the Treasury; the officers here have no discretionary powers in reference thereto.

The Agent thought there would be no difficulty to get so much of the ingot copper released as the northern stockholders were entitled to, according to their interest in the joint stock company—to which I remarked that, unfortunately, no division could be made, because the company owed a great deal more than that to loyal citizens and to some very poor people, and, although the indebtedness had been created during the rebellion, you had very generously passed resolutions authorizing me to pay these claims.

Mr. Chase will surely not object to release the copper to pay the company's liabilities to loyal citizens, when you tell him how many hundred thousand pounds the southern stockholders have received and kept for themselves without giving you your proportionate part.

An early decision is desirable; 1—to prevent a sale by the Government, and 2—to discontinue the expense of storage.

No doubt you have taken steps at Washington ere this which will bring forth this—Please advise me of the price of ingot and sheet copper.

Yours,
Very Respectfully,
J. E. RAHT

As time passed with no indications that their claims were being considered, Raht again wrote to Congdon and with pronounced asperity said: "What business has the Government with your property; they should give up your property which is here and can be proven as wrongfully seized. If they needed the copper, and had made use of it, then we would have to come into a court of claims, but this is not the case. Our proof is very plain, and if the Government is at all disposed to do right, they can do it now."

As a matter of fact, the government was probably justified in doubting all that was said about who owned the metal. Soon after Peet's death some foreign gentlemen, as Raht said, appeared in Cincinnati with claims to the deceased man's portion of the copper. Peet's southern sympathies being well known, government officials undoubtedly pondered the shenanigans whereby a large quantity of copper had come to be owned jointly by loyal, rebel, and foreign citizens. At any rate the metal was finally sold at public auction June 19, 1865, but it seems likely that the Union Consolidated Mining Company was eventually reimbursed for their portion of it.

In April, 1864, Raht secured an interview with General Sherman, who was visiting in Cincinnati, for the purpose of interesting the General in protecting the Ducktown district from guerrillas. Not only did his mission prove futile, but he learned some facts concerning his own activities from the General that both surprised and dismayed him. Almost before he had presented his plea in behalf of this little spot of Yankeeland in Dixie, the General brought Raht up suddenly with the bland assertion that he, himself, deserved to be executed. Continuing, Sherman reminded Raht that he had produced the copper that the Confederates had used in making cannon with which to shoot at him, and ended by saying that had he, Raht, been captured while at the copper works he would most certainly have been executed. In describing this unexpected excoriation at the hands of General Sherman, Raht said, "My reply was short, the more so since his Lady was in the same room." Loaded muskets around the premises might, too, have contributed to Raht's stifled reply.

Contrary to Sherman's belated indictment, Raht was seemingly never in danger of Federal punishment. Actually, he was beyond Federal reach at Ducktown so long as East Tennessee was held by the Confederates. When the Union army overran this section, he immediately placed himself under their protecting wing and applied for passage to the North. He was undeniably using higher diplomacy here, feeling confident that the South was doomed to defeat, otherwise he could just as well have moved farther southward. On the other hand, had the guerrilla menace not existed, he could have remained safely at Ducktown. While it is true that General Sherman might have under the circumstances dealt summarily with Raht, it was General Thomas who saw to it that the copper-mining captain and all his household goods received transportation to Cincinnati. A mutual esteem grew out of this association between General Thomas and Raht. The General visited the mines after the war, and in this instance it was Raht who played the part of the perfect host.

The adage that it never rains but it pours probably found a solemn subscriber in J. E. Raht when the news of William H. Peet's death reached him in May, 1864. Raht was laboring with all the might of his busy pen trying to maintain co-operation within the ranks of those interested in the Ducktown mines when Peet's death occurred. In the light of conditions as they existed at that time, this unfortunate stroke could very well have meant virtual dissolution of the Polk County Copper Company, Burra Burra Copper Company, and Union Consolidated Mining Company. For the next several months Raht assumed the burden of co-ordinating efforts that were being made to liquidate Peet's estate in such a manner that the rightful ownership of the Ducktown properties would not be disputed.

The commanding position held by Peet in the Tennessee copper industry, especially during the early part of the war, was brought out in an earlier chapter. Although this position became more figurative than actual with the South's gradual capitulation, the fact remained that with Peet, wherever he sought refuge, went records of evidence of his interest in the copper mines at Ducktown. Had there been reason to believe that the South was winning the war at the time of Peet's death, complications enough would have resulted in settling his estate. As it was, the South was gradually weakening and Ducktown already was within the Federal orbit.

Some light on the complexity of the affair can be shed by stating here that of the twelve or fifteen individuals who were active in the management of the copper industry perhaps half were southern and half were northern adherents. At no time, however, did their adherence to their respective sections overshadow adherence to their properties and associates at Ducktown. Therefore, when William H. Peet bought the shares of stock of his temporarily estranged northern associates at the Confederate sale of these securities in 1863, he did this not for the purpose of securing permanent ownership of the business, but instead for the primary purpose of keeping ownership of the properties from falling into strange hands. With their interests thus protected, former owners of the Ducktown mines could look forward with reasonable certainty to the privilege of resuming operations after the war, regardless of its outcome.

So long as Federal agents did not trouble themselves to investigate ownership of the deserted works, from whence had come much of the South's copper supply, and so long as Peet remained free, there was little to fear that unpleasant eventualities would ensue. But Peet's untimely passing precipitated consternation within the ranks of the Union Consolidated Mining Company. Peet had died a rebel, said Raht, and should it come to light that his properties were held jointly by northern and southern sympathisers, then indeed would inextricable difficulties follow. What Raht feared was that Peet's holdings at Ducktown would be confiscated by Federal authorities and vested in his heirs or relatives, all of whom were loyal to the Union cause. It so happened, of course, that this did not occur, and the matter of untangling Peet's affairs was left in private hands. In a letter to Samuel Congdon discussing the settlement of Peet's estate, Raht said, "I only wish an honorable settlement among parties in interest. Although of very different political opinions men may be, there is no reason why they should not settle money matters honorably.... We all have to attend a day of reckoning, no matter if we are Protestants or Catholics, anti-slavery or pro-slavery, etc."

The death of Peet was announced by William Bartlett from Nassau, Bahama Islands, where Bartlett had sailed with a cargo of cotton. This news was relayed to Raht, and his correspondence over the next several months in relation to Peet revealed the extent of Peet's activities. His interests had been varied and extensive, although confined principally to dealings in copper, cotton, and sugar. Much of his tangible property consisted of stocks and bonds, which he had carried with him in trunks. As his opportunities became more restricted with Union encroachment upon the South, he undertook the risky business of running the Federal blockade with cotton. It was Raht's belief that the venture engaged in at the time of his death was to have been Peet's last attempt at blockade-running, after which he was to come within the Union and make proper amends for his wayward conduct as a "rebel."

While Raht was deeply touched by the death of his friend, and felt much concern for all who might suffer financially from the tragedy, he did not forget those who were more intimately connected with Peet. He so expressed himself once by saying, "I am the more sorry for his good old mother, who was so anxiously looking for the return of her son, Willie." The cause of Peet's death was also of much concern to Raht. He finally learned that Peet "died of neuralgia which started in his head and moved down to his stomach, causing him much suffering, no doubt."

To Peet's mother, Mrs. Sahah A. Peet, at Norridgewock, Maine, Raht also wrote a letter of condolence, saying, in part, "Of course we wish that he would have lived for many years yet, as we do wish for all our friends and relatives, but in his case I wish in particular that he would have been permitted to remain at least long enough to have paid you a last visit.... Your son had a great many friends while in prosperity and, I trust, some will continue to act as friends, although he is no more...." Peet was born in Norridgewock, Maine, June 7, 1820. His father was a minister there for over forty years.

As a final tribute to William H. Peet, let it be said here that from the record he established in the few but tumultuous years he was active in the mining industry at Ducktown, and from Raht's high regard for his ability, it is altogether probable that had he survived the war, the history of both the Burra Burra Copper Company and Polk County Copper Company might have ended with less disastrous consequences for those who had invested their funds in these two companies. Thirteen years after Peet's death, at a time when the industry at Ducktown was in very dire circumstances and Raht and the Union Consolidated were suing each other, Raht said in a letter to his brother Carl: "If we had a Mr. Peet among us again, we might make one grand combination, and peace, too!"

Another event that was of vital importance to the Union Consolidated Mining Company was the escape, as Raht described it, of George S. Cameron, who fled from Dixie soon after Peet's death to make his residence in the North. Cameron's action was of importance because it brought within the folds of the Union the last remaining individual who had been connected financially with the Ducktown enterprise. Cameron, who was president of the Bank of Chester, South Carolina, had, as Raht said, maintained faith in Confederate currency so long as the government debt did not exceed a thousand million dollars, but now "he has convinced himself and left."

Despite the uncertainty of postal communications between Cincinnati and New Orleans during the war, Raht endeavored to keep officials of the Burra Burra Copper Company and Polk County Copper Company at New Orleans apprised of conditions at Ducktown. Of interest is a letter by him to John G. Gaines, written June 2, 1864, excerpts from which follow: "The affairs of the Burra Burra Copper Company, of which Mr. Wm. H. Peet was President, are in my humble opinion, in a rather critical condition and I take the liberty to call your attention to this and state that some steps have to be taken soon to prevent a serious disaster." In this he was referring to the lien on Burra Burra properties held by Dow, Delano, and Tracy. He continued, "... I expect that these gentlemen will foreclose their mortgage as soon as the officers of the civil courts in that part of Tennessee can resume their functions again.... The treasury Agent of East Tennessee will demand a list of our stockholders.... Will you be so kind to furnish me a list... and also a memorandum in reference to the loyalty of the parties who have taken the oath, and who are aliens, besides Northern citizens."

As the summer of 1864 drew to a close without apparent progress being made by the Federal Army, Raht expressed himself regarding the conduct of the campaign around Richmond. He was not in favor of wasting time trying to capture the Confederate capital. He said that if the Wilmington harbor were taken "where would the Confederate ammunition come from?" Powder mills were at Augusta, but, he asked, "Where would the salt petre come from with north Alabama and East Tennessee in possession of the Federals?"

Neither could Raht view with complacency the proceedings of the Republican convention at Chicago. In a letter to Lyman W. Gilbert on September 12, 1864, while the convention was in progress, he said that while he respected General George B. McClellan, he favored the nomination of Abraham Lincoln. But he preferred Lincoln merely because McClellan was his only serious opponent. He went on to say that he was sorry Lincoln did not withdraw in favor of a statesman, but that if he were nominated he favored his re-election, for it would be unwise at that time to elect a new President. He was a little ambiguous here about his political preferences, but so would any copper miner have been who had several carloads of copper that could not be got to market with copper selling at 55 cents a pound.

The refugee Captain could feel that he was privileged to express himself on military and political affairs for he had taken the oath of allegiance to the United States of America since his arrival in Cincinnati, as well as having paid into the Treasurer's Office at Hamilton County, Ohio, the sum of $4.00 "for commutation for fines and penalties for neglect to perform military service, except under calls to prevent or repel invasion or suppress insurrection."

The prolongation of the war was vexing to Raht on another account. In one of his many letters to Samuel Congdon during the summer of 1864, he told Congdon that his family was dissatisfied with living at Cincinnati and he confided, "My wife, I fear, will want to return to Germany if she is not permitted to return to East Tennessee this fall." Truly the good man was beset by troubles both martial and marital.

Throughout the year 1864 Captain Raht kept up a steady flow of correspondence. The confiscated copper, conditions at the mines, Peet's death, a seeming stalemate in the war, uncertainty about the future of Ducktown, the attitude of the different directors toward resuming operations when conditions permitted —all these were subjects upon which actions and decisions could be determined only by exchanges of letters with many individuals. His residence at Cincinnati became the headquarters of the disorganized copper industry at Ducktown. To this address came letters from every strata of the personnel making up the industry. At no time during his long reign at Ducktown was he more the central figure of the forces engaged in copper mining in Tennessee than he was during this period.

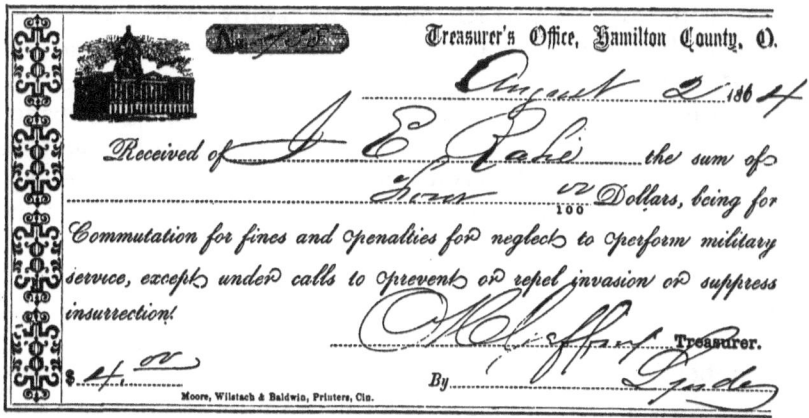

Receipt from the Treasurer's Office, Hamilton County, Ohio, for fine paid exempting Raht from military service. It was secured by Raht after he moved to Cincinnati during the Civil War.

In the early part of 1865 Raht's health was affected by a disease of his eyes. So grave did the condition become that he was unable to read or write. In March of that year he returned to Germany, had a successful operation performed on his eyes, and returned to the United States in May. Although his sight was restored, the operation left a slight peculiarity in the physical appearance of his eyes that was noticeable until his death.

The Atlantic Ocean probably seemed no wider to Columbus than it did to Raht on his journey back to America. The reason for this was that the Civil War had ended while he was in Germany, and in the far-away hills of Tennessee were the broken threads of a golden pattern that he was desperately anxious to take up again and weave to completion. And in Ducktown, too, were many war-weary people longing for his return and the resumption of peacetime activities. Within two months after he had arrived back in this country, he had sold his home at Cincinnati, had moved his family back to their beloved East Tennessee, and was feverishly communicating the glad news to his scattered forces to reassemble at Ducktown.

Pressure from within the family circle probably led Captain Raht to move back to the South when he did. He had purchased the Thomas H. Callaway residence and farm at Cleveland in 1861, and it was here that he decided to make his permanent home and establish his office upon his return to Tennessee. However, the residence was being used as Federal military headquarters in July, 1865, when the happy family arrived at Cleveland. Furthermore, several weeks passed before the house was vacated by the military. Raht was aware of the fact that his residence was being used as headquarters, and that the occupancy might be continued indefinitely, but to his nostalgic wife temporary discomfort and inconvenience in East Tennessee was preferable to the permanent comfort and convenience of Cincinnati.

Upon returning to Cleveland, Raht found his property to be in a sad state of repair. Four miles of fence, a large barn, a carriage house, a two-story spring house, the shade trees in the yard, and timber from forty acres of land had been destroyed. All these, he said, with the exception of about half a mile of rail fence that had been destroyed by Confederate troops, had been consumed as firewood by Federal forces since January, 1864. Only one gate post was left standing as a relic of the war. In reporting these damages to Colonel John H. James, chief quartermaster, at Chattanooga, Raht said that eighteen different companies had been quartered on his premises, and that officers ranking from major to major general had occupied his residence. Major General Steedman was quartered in the house when Raht returned with his family. In filing a requisition for lumber and materials to repair the damages, he informed Colonel James that he had already spent $1,000 on repairs to his residence, as he could not wait for this work to be done by the government. He expected, however, that he be reimbursed for this amount, and that all damages to his farm be repaired at government expense.

For nearly two years the Raht family were kept painfully aware of the insidious effects of troop concentrations on their premises. As late as the spring of 1867 Dr. Strickland Aubright, mine physician at Ducktown, was prescribing treatment for Raht's children, who were suffering from an excessive richness of the blood and from a persistent skin disorder. To tone down the blood, Aubright recommended a very small teaspoonful of cream of tartar every morning and night for a week or ten days. With regard to the skin irritation the Doctor wrote Raht: "Like yourself, Mr. Raht,

I can see no cause for this complaint in the children, unless it be that they have received it from the grounds of your place. You know soldiers were quartered there, covering almost every foot of ground. And, I think, I know, that this disease resembles that which soldiers are subject to, and is caught by camping on bare-ground. It seems it remains in the ground, and is always catching —one may catch it from another."

In preparation for setting up housekeeping the Captain wrote to John Tonkin at Ducktown to send him his two clocks, his baby carriage, and his children's dog, Fidel, that had been left there. He told Tonkin to send the dog if he could manage it with his little ones. This was done, for sometime later he wrote to Tonkin that Fidel was well and the children still "weller."

Raht began preparing for the winter of 1866 by writing to his brother Carl to have the New York tailor who had his measurements to make him a good winter coat—"and," said he, "when I say good I mean good." His brother had just sent him a pair of pants. In acknowledging their receipt he said that they fit all right, except that they did not come up high enough in the waist, were too short, and when buttoned they were drawn out of shape. Carl was doing a great deal of shopping for the Captain at that time. One of his purchases was a watch, which the Captain described as a fine timepiece but, alas, it was too small and delicate for a "mountainboomer" like him.

It was some two or three years before Raht had completely rehabilitated his farm and furnished his home. Late in 1868 he wrote to Carl and said: "This morning we gave our horses and the pony an introduction in the new barn. It looks all well. I do not regret to have spent the money here and enjoy it, while I have so much invested with Consolidated which I may not enjoy." He continued: "While at Cincinnati I bought some costly parlor furniture, more so than I ought to have done, but men get reckless sometimes, and then I thought, it is perhaps only once in a lifetime. I was tempted and could not withstand it. I have been a spendthrift in 1868."

Family affairs were not long in settling down to an ordered routine. Other things then came up for attention. Early in 1868 Captain Raht instructed his brother at New York to go ahead and buy the shawl for his wife, about which he had previously written. His wife was threatening to go visiting, he said, but of course could not go until she had a shawl. Carl was instructed to buy one that cost $100 or more, because "such a shawl should be for a lifetime." But we wonder. Mathilde was definitely true to her sex.

Shortly thereafter the question of ear-bobs rocked the tranquility of Raht's home. He again turned to his brother for assistance. After describing the jewelry to be purchased, the indulgent Captain disclosed why the trinkets were necessary. Mathilde had until recently been wearing a set of excellent ear-bobs, but she had confessed to having given them away. There was nothing to do now, of course, but to buy new ones.

When the curtain rang down on the copper industry at Ducktown in 1863, Captain Raht's personal wealth was estimated at slightly over $100,000. The principal items making up this total included his inventories of merchandise, real estate in Polk and Bradley counties, an interest in the London Mine, a lien on the personal properties of the Union Consolidated Mining Company, and $10,000 in bonds of the Burra Burra Copper Company. Other than his stock of goods at the mines, much of which probably was consumed by those who remained at Ducktown after the shutdown, practically every asset of his was virtually unimpaired when he returned to Cleveland to begin business anew. The copper mines were reopened and he was, of course, continued as manager of these properties. Endowed as he was with perspicacity, ability, determination, and ambition, Captain Raht was also bountifully endowed with just plain every-day luck. Despite the fact that he exercised astuteness to a superlative degree in the many decisions he was forced to make during the war, it is nevertheless undeniably true that events over which he had no control turned in almost every case to his advantage. The mammoth nest-egg from which he was forced to flee early in 1864, he found to be in a perfect state of fertility when he returned to it a year and a half later.

Much of that part of Raht's life which he devoted to the interests of the copper companies has been related—how he was repaid in copper the sum owed to him by the Union Consolidated Mining Company at the end of the war; how he levied upon copper belonging to the Burra Burra Copper Company to recover the $10,000 invested by him in fraudulent bonds; how he was finally forced to sue the Union Consolidated Mining Company; and how he won the suit.

But aside from his connections with the copper industry, Raht at the same time built up a formidable empire of his own. The two piers supporting the arch of his success were, first, his favorable position in the copper industry at Ducktown and, second, his own qualifications in the fields of finance and management. The keystone of his arch of success was his commissary business. Superimposed upon his training and experience in mining and mineralogy was a natural penchant for trading and bartering. Had he been denied the privilege of operating commissaries at the mines, where the great majority of his customers' accounts were deducted from their wages, it seems doubtful that his wealth should have grown to the proportions it did. Nevertheless, he was a born money-maker. Had he not been so fortunate as to step into a situation so patently made to order for him, he most assuredly would have created one, less remunerative though it might have been. As a matter of fact, it could have resulted in considerably less opulence for him without in the least detracting from his business methods, when the rather limited financial resources of the territory in which he operated are taken into consideration.

After the war the most pressing problem of Raht's, other than that of getting the mines and smelters at Ducktown back in operation, was that of restocking the shelves of his commissaries at the mines. Every wagon that could be begged, borrowed, or hired was pressed into service. Not only was the refined copper hidden at the mines to be hauled out to the railroad and materials and supplies for the operation to be moved into Ducktown, but food and clothing had to be made available for the growing number of employees at the works. These latter items were no less important to Raht's personal interest than they were to the copper industry and the workers. Four years of war had left Ducktown wholly inadequate to furnish flour, meal, meat, lard, green coffee, sugar, salt, molasses, soda, soap, brogans, shoes, shoe-leather, domestics, prints, jeans, thread, and various other articles, in quantities that would be necessary for the returning miners and their families. Other merchants in the district were confronted with the same problem of securing new stocks of merchandise, and those who could do this first would profit most. In this race, Raht was by no means at a disadvantage as he had the whole caravan of copper haulers at his disposal.

Not only was it a difficult task to secure equipment and materials needed at the mines and furnaces, but it was equally difficult to secure the merchandise needed for his commissaries. Wholesale and jobbing houses, with ample stocks of goods were, of course, scarce in nearby southern cities at that time. As a result of this he made many of his purchases at Cincinnati, Pittsburgh, New York, and other northern cities. The fact that he was doing all he could to build up his stocks with little solace to his store managers at the mines who were being called upon constantly for brands of goods they did not have. A letter by Raht to William Speck in December, 1865, furnishes an example of this. Speck had written the Captain a rather discouraging letter about his problems to which Raht replied: "If you have not just the article your customers want, please only state it to me and give me your opinion what kind of goods I ought to buy—but do not complain; we are getting old enough even without complaining. Be cheerful and make the best of it. It is always well to have several brands of tobacco, and why should the Hughes tobacco not be one of them.... Leave these [other] matters until I shall have the pleasure of seeing you, that is to say, if you remain in an ill humor, I will delay seeing you."

When he re-established his store business after the war, Raht had consolidated his former stores at the Mary's, Tennessee, Isabella, Hiwassee, and East Tennessee mines into two large commissaries: one at Isabella and one, the Burra Burra store, at MacPherson Mine. In 1870 he built the Isabella store, the first brick building erected at Ducktown. A visitor to Ducktown, writing in the Cleveland *Banner* of April 27, 1871, said that the brick store recently built by Captain Raht at Isabella had all the conveniences of a city store. In his financial statement of December 31, 1870, Raht valued the building at $7,000. After his split with the Union Consolidated Mining Company, he sold the building to the company for $8,000. The Isabella store is, in a figurative sense, the lone living reminder today of copper mining at Ducktown in the era once referred to as "back in Raht's time." The building is symbolic of the rugged permanence of its builder's character. It is entering its eighth decade under its original name. With additions that have in more modern times been added to the rear of the building, it stands today in sombre dignity as the Tennessee Copper Company's Isabella Store.

It should be interesting to learn of the efficiency of some of Raht's clerks at the Isabella store. In giving the Captain a brief appraisal of some members of the force at the store, A. S. Hoffman, the store manager, said:

"There is not enough harmony, presence of mind, and interest in the business manifested by three of our body.

"Mr. J. B. W. seems willing, but his mind does not seem to keep up with his work.

"Mr. F. M. is well qualified for business, but—well you know him.

"Mr. A. A. P. is still very hard to keep from selling goods on time to come."

J. B. W., with the vacillating mind, was James B. Witt, who was just entering upon a long career behind the counters of mercantile establishments. The young man was even then probably envisioning himself as head of a store where customers vied with each other for the privilege of buying his goods. Following the shut-down in 1878, Witt moved into the Dahlonega gold district, struck it lucky there, returned to Ducktown after the mines were reopened in 1890, and operated a store of his own at Copperhill for several years.

The Burra Burra store was a large, two-story frame building, situated in order to serve employees at the MacPherson and East Tennessee mines. The building was the property of the Burra Burra Copper Company. Jacob Lang managed the store until he and Livingston Shugart purchased the stock of goods from Raht in 1877. The sale of the Burra Burra store marked the end of Raht's activities on a large scale at Ducktown. Lang and Shugart continued to operate the store until the mines closed. Soon thereafter Lang moved to Cleveland, but Shugart remained at Ducktown as agent of the mine owners throughout the shut-down period.

One of the principal accusations of the Union Consolidated Mining Company against Raht's conduct of his commissaries was that the prices charged by him were higher than those charged by other merchants at Ducktown. Raht made no attempt to disprove this charge. As a rebuttal, however, he offered evidence that the class and quality of his merchandise were invariably superior to those of his competitors. While it is true that he handled the quality of goods that was in demand at Ducktown, yet he was proud of his stores and insisted upon receiving the best in the class of merchandise he ordered. Much of the corn, flour, and meal sold at the Isabella and Burra Burra stores came from his own farms and mills. Especially was he careful to handle only the best grades of meats and groceries. Established as he was at Ducktown, there was nothing that could have prevented his charging exorbitant prices for inferior grades of merchandise. Instead, however, his profits were apparently no greater on the class of goods he sold than they should have been had he preferred to buy and sell only the cheaper grades. The man seemed simply to apply in selling the same principles that he used in buying—and that was that the cheapest was always the dearest.

Total sales at both the Isabella and Burra Burra stores amounted to between $150,000 and $200,000 a year. The only year for which complete figures were available was that of 1872. In that year, the total gross sales at the Isabella store was $106,755.39, while at the Burra Burra store the total was $71,704.23, making a grand total of $178,459.62. It was estimated that from 1865 until he disposed of his stores, Raht sold a total of two million dollars' worth of goods at Ducktown. His total net profit during this time was probably close to half a million dollars.

The Union Consolidated Mining Company sued to recover from Raht all his store profits in excess of 10 per cent. They made a belated revelation that he had agreed to restrict his net profits to that figure, but no one took them seriously on this point. The company estimated that his profits over and above 10 per cent had amounted to $1,000,000, which sum they said he should turn over to them for the so-called store privileges. This figure was, of course, somewhat exaggerated and they failed to collect any part of it, but they were correct when they asserted that the store business had, as everyone knew, made a rich man of their superintendent.

In addition to his commissaries at Ducktown, Raht also operated a general store at Cleveland, which he had opened immediately upon his return to Cleveland in 1865. He opened the store principally, it seems, as a warehouse to serve the mines and his stores at Ducktown. It was his intention at that time to handle chiefly mine and mill supplies, either on his own account or on commission. Within a few years, however, the business had grown into one of the largest retail stores in Cleveland. It operated under the name of Raht and Walker. This firm knew the value of a little off-hand advertising, as will be noted from the following item which appeared in the Cleveland *Banner* of May 16, 1873:

THANKS

While strolling around the other evening, the junior of the Banner "shebang" was called into the store of Raht and Walker and presented by Mr. Walker with a nice pair of shoes—for which they will accept our thanks. In this connection we would remark that the trading public will do well to call and see their large stock of drygoods, boots, shoes, hats, ladies' dress goods, notions, groceries, etc. They are running a big thing; sell on short profits; in fact, are doing a genuine live and let-live business, but don't take our word for it, but go and see. Pryor, the chief of the establishment, has the peculiar knack of knowing how to treat his customers.

The junior partner of this firm, P. H. Walker, had come to Ducktown from England when a young man and had been employed by Raht at the Isabella store. Raht was struck by Walker's ability and took him to Cleveland and made him a partner in the business there. The Raht and Walker partnership was dissolved in August, 1873, and the stock of goods was sold to W. L. Sharp. However, Raht continued as principal owner of the store after Walker's withdrawal.

With the Civil War marking the end of the Ocoee Bank, the only institution of its kind at Cleveland, Captain Raht was handicapped for want of convenient banking facilities for over a year after his return to Tennessee. In the latter part of 1866 he initiated a movement to have a bank established at Cleveland. On November 19 he wrote to John C. Gaut at Nashville: "I had a conversation with Colonel D. C. McMillin yesterday about a bank, and we have concluded to request you to draw up a bank charter, which is most favorable, and at the same time certain to pass at the present session of the Legislature. The name may be 'Bank of Discount and Deposit' at Cleveland. We do wish a National Bank charter, and will write you about this at another time. Meanwhile as we cannot get such one at present, would like to procure a State charter. I will write to Colonel Parks about this and ask his good service to pass the same. Colonel McMillin will write to the member from Hamilton County. We beg you to use your influence to have it passed."

On the same day that he wrote to Gaut, Raht also wrote to Representative James Parks and apprised him of the plans for the bank. In this letter he said: "Since starting operations again at the mines, I have worked under great disadvantage for want of banking facilities... a bank at this place will facilitate the mining operations very much and, I think, we are entitled to the same. The charter to be granted to D. C. McMillin, J. E. Raht, and associates. If more names are required, please add John Tonkin and Jacob Lang."

In the meantime, while Gaut and Parks were proceeding with

their efforts to secure a state charter for the bank, Raht was continuing his efforts in behalf of a national bank charter. Presumably his success in this respect was more immediate than he had anticipated, for December 15 he wrote the Honorable T. Clarke, Comptroller of the Currency, Washington, D. C., as follows:

SIR:
I beg to acknowledge receipt of the blanks and pamphlets in reference to starting a National Bank at this place, and will only add that we will lose no time to organize and comply with the requirements forthwith.

I have the honor to remain, Sir,
Very Respectfully
your
Obedient Servant,
J. E. RAHT, for
Self, D. C. MCMILLIN, W. B. REYNOLDS,
M. W. LEGG, and Associates.

Assisting Raht at Washington was Congressman W. B. Campbell, of Lebanon, Tennessee. On December 15 he wrote to Campbell, too, and informed him that the necessary documents for establishing the bank at Cleveland had been received and thanked him for his assistance in the matter. With this gratifying turn of events, the question of a state charter was dropped at Nashville.

No time was lost by Raht in executing and returning to Washington the documents that the Treasury Department had forwarded to him, for the organization of the Cleveland National Bank took place on December 26, 1866. The capital stock of the bank was fixed at $100,000. This was subscribed for as follows: J. E. Raht, $30,000; W. B. Reynolds, $30,000; M. W. Legg, $20,000; D. C. McMillin, $10,000; John Tonkin, $10,000. These five men being the owners of the entire capital stock of the bank, they proceeded to select the president and board of directors from among themselves. W. B. Reynolds was made president; J. E. Raht, vice-president; D. C. McMillin, cashier; and M. W. Legg and John Tonkin, directors. Captain Raht induced W. B. Reynolds, a native of Benton, Tennessee, to participate in the formation of the bank, not only because of his financial success, but because Raht was anxious that Reynolds serve as head of the institution on account of his executive and business ability. Raht himself declined to serve as president of the bank, as he was just then swinging into his stride at Ducktown. He needed the bank's services and facilities, but he had neither the time nor the intention to involve himself in its routine affairs to the neglect of his other and more profitable interests.

Before turning to local citizens to assist in financing the bank, Raht had endeavored to interest his associates in the Union Consolidated Mining Company in the matter. He said in a letter to Samuel Congdon at that time that he had discussed the question at New York, but that neither John Thomas, George S. Cameron, nor anybody else there seemed inclined to take stock in such an institution. And, strange as it may seem, twelve years later, when the Cleveland National Bank was going along in a serenely healthy condition and the copper industry at Ducktown was definitely coming to a close, the Union Consolidated Mining Company was giving serious consideration to establishing a bank at Ducktown.

That the Cleveland National Bank was anything but Raht's bank, there was never any question. He gradually added to his holdings in the stock of the bank until, on January 1, 1875, his accounts showed that he owned 614 shares, valued at $70,000. He at last assumed active management of the bank when he was elected president on January 25, 1877, to succeed W. B. Reynolds, who had retired the previous year because of ill health. By this time Raht had all but finished his mining and merchandising career at Ducktown and was turning his attention to real estate, farming and farming lands, milling, investments, and money lending.

Few indeed are the business institutions in the South that can match the Cleveland National Bank's record of three-quarters of a century of unbroken service to the public. And since 1872 when the present building, designed by Edward Raht, was erected, the business has been carried on at the same location. The bank has continued through the years to follow unswervingly the course charted for it by its founder, Julius E. Raht.

One of the many items on Captain Raht's agenda after his return to Cleveland was that of acquiring title to James Giddings' interest in the London Mine. Litigation to this end had been instituted in 1861 because of Giddings' failure to comply with the terms of his agreement with Raht, but the coming of the war had forced a postponement of the case. The case was revived by Raht in the fall of 1865, and at the session of the chancery court at

Benton in December of that year a one-third interest in the mine, representing that portion of the interest acquired by Raht, Giddings, and Samuel T. Waters in 1861, was decreed to the Captain.

The remaining two-thirds interest in the London property was held by William A. Bartlett, administrator of the estate of William H. Peet, and by Augustus Bohn and Madam S. K. Boughlinval. But there still hung over the property the lien on it held by the Baltimore Copper Smelting Company. Having decided, it seems, to acquire full possession of the mine, Raht first turned his attention to the clearing up of the lien. In this connection he made a trip to Baltimore in July, 1866, for the purpose of conferring with Galloway Cheston, president of the Baltimore Copper Smelting Company. But about all he accomplished at this conference was to have his figurative fur rubbed in the wrong direction. In telling Bartlett by letter of his talk with Galloway Cheston, Raht said: "The old Quaker President of the late Baltimore Copper Smelting Company does not demand any money of us at all; he is content to own the London mine in behalf of his company. I told the old gentleman that he might prepare for war if he could not arrive at a better conclusion."

Several months later Raht wrote to Samuel Congdon about his meeting with Cheston, and in this letter he was more lucid in his analysis of Quaker presidents. Said he:

I considered myself under great obligations to you when you had the kindness to give me a letter of introduction to Galloway Cheston, Esq., at Baltimore. I know you intended the letter to be of assistance to me, and I had great expectations of a favorable settlement, thinking that, Mr. Cheston being a Quaker, he would act on the principle of fairness and equity. But, lo! was I a disappointed man when the old gentleman, as soon as I had hardly seated myself, commenced speaking of *their* mine, the London Mine. I asked him what mine he meant; he said the London mine. I got up from my chair very quick, and said that I had come in a spirit of compromise and peace, but that we could not converse on the subject if the Baltimore Copper Smelting Company really thought themselves the owners of *my* copper mine. I told Mr. Cheston he could prepare for war. We had a very pleasant conversation, but pointed. Mr. Cheston had been so generous to you he wanted to make it up again. If all Quakers are like Mr. Cheston, I shall beware to have any more dealings with Quakers.

Negotiations between Raht and Cheston were continued following the "pleasant but pointed" conversation at Baltimore. By

October they were making and rejecting definite proposals. However, the lure of ready cash soon had its effect, for November 12, 1866, Raht informed William A. Bartlett that "I have settled with Judge Van Dyke, attorney for the Baltimore Copper Smelting Company, and paid him $16,203.17 in full for the interest the said company had in the London mine, for which they will send me a quit claim deed...."

It was not until February, 1868, that Raht returned to the question of the London mine. At that time he wrote to Bartlett and inquired of him if he thought their silent partner, Augustus Bohn, would consent to a division of sale of the mine. "I cannot afford," said Raht, "to have my investment lying dead any longer." A year passed before he was able to revive the question. Finally, on April 28, 1869, he succeeded in purchasing the one-third interest in the London Mine held jointly by Madam S. K. Boughlinval and Augustus Bohn, by paying each $9,000. The remaining one-third interest in the London Mine, held in the estate of William H. Peet, was acquired by Captain Raht by decree of the chancery court at Benton, on February 23, 1872.

Sometime prior to the time of coming into full possession of the London Mine, Raht had the opportunity of acquiring a second of the more important mines at Ducktown, the Eureka Mine. Financial difficulties had forced a suspension of operations by the Eureka Mining Company just prior to the Civil War and the company was never able to resume satisfactory operations following the close of the war. Litigation followed upon the heels of these difficulties, and, as was often the case within the sphere of his influence, when such difficulties were of a financial nature Captain Raht was soon upon the scene.

Doomed to be the grounds of a lawsuit and put upon the auction block, as were many of the most valuable mines at Ducktown during that era, the Eureka Mine was sold to satisfy a judgment against the trustees of the defunct Eureka Mining Company. The certificate of sale as issued by R. N. Fleming, clerk and master, read: "I do hereby certify that J. E. Raht, being the highest and best bidder, this day became the purchaser at public sale of the Eureka Mining Company land, appurtenances and improvements thereon, sold for the debt of Oates, Wadlaw and Company according to the attested printed notice of sale and has complied with the terms and conditions of said sale. This the 6th day of December 1870."

Whereas the London Mine had cost Raht a total of nearly

$35,000, he bought the Eureka Mine, under forced sale, for $4,500.

Worked to a small extent during the early days of mining at Ducktown, but never since that time, the Culchote property was also sold soon after the war to satisfy an old and lingering debt. In May, 1867, the property was attached pursuant to a judgment secured by William H. Brown against Robert C. Gist, Benjamin Y. Coleman and others of the old Culchote Mining Company. On March 17, 1868, the clerk and master sold the mine at public outcry. The buyer was William H. Brown. Captain Raht then moved in on the scene, and on June 8 Brown transferred and conveyed to Raht all rights and interest in the property acquired by him in the purchase. Brown still held an interest in the mine that he had presumably owned since before the war. In July, 1869, he sold one-half of this interest to Erby Boyd and C. L. Hardwick, and in May, 1872, his remaining interest he sold to Raht. The mine-buying Captain completed acquisition of the Culchote property when he purchased the interest in it held by Boyd and Hardwick on September 2, 1873.

The conditions were never propitious for Captain Raht to operate his own mines on a large scale. He did take relatively small tonnages of ore from both the London and Eureka mines soon after their acquisition, but this he sold to the Union Consolidated Mining Company. His chief operations at his own properties consisted in recovering copper through the precipitation process.

Immediately following the court decision in his favor in June, 1877, Raht wrote several letters in which he told of the efforts lately made by him to furnish employment at Ducktown and revealed his feelings regarding his future obligations to the district. He said that throughout the time of the trial he had worked the Eureka and London mine waters at an outlay of $22,000 and that this work had been done because he had to provide employment for Edward Mueller, Thomas Osborne, Jacob Lang, Livingston Shugart, and others. But he admitted that these expenses could not go on indefinitely.

Again, he said that while he might not be called patriotic, yet he was in favor of helping the district and was willing to do so, even at a sacrifice. Out of his long years of service at Ducktown he had formed, as he said, an attachment for the place that extended beyond a mere interest in the properties there.

It might be revealing to learn that the tremendous loss of sulphur that occurred at Ducktown "back in Raht's time" seems to have been more fully realized and appreciated at that time than was the same loss which occurred here for nearly two decades in the beginning of the present era. With regard to the loss of sulphur in Raht's day, witness the following excerpts from a letter by Raht to Dr. George M. Burdett, Lenoirs, Tennessee: "In the various processes of making copper at Ducktown, millions of pounds of sulphur have been expelled from the copper ores and copper matte during the past twenty years and driven into the atmosphere as a waste, which could have been utilized with great profit, provided always we had had railroad facilities...." He continued by stating that bluestone, copperas, and other chemical products could have been manufactured at Ducktown and that these latter products would have helped to reduce the cost of ingot copper. But without a railroad, "... nothing can be done at Ducktown until the Resurrection takes place."

The two principal purchases of real estate by Captain Raht prior to the war were those of the Turtletown farm in Polk County, and the Callaway home and farm at Cleveland. However, between 1866 and 1869 he added several other valuable pieces of Polk County property to his growing empire. In May, 1866, he purchased the Half-Way House and adjoining lands on Greasy Creek and the large farm on Silco Creek of Abraham McKissick. In February, 1868, he purchased the lands and mill of Samuel Parks and several months later he bought the properties of D. C. Haskins and Jesse Rymer located on and near Greasy Creek. In February, 1869, he acquired the farm and ferry of Isaac N. Greer. This farm lay south of the Ocoee River, opposite George Barnes' farm. Later that year he also bought what was known as the Hannah farm, situated near the Parksville mill. Thus, from Ducktown to Parksville Captain Raht owned practically all of the more valuable lands.

The mill at Parksville played an important part in Raht's merchandising flow-sheet. Wheat, corn, and rye, grown on his own farms, were ground at the mill and disposed of at his stores and commissaries at Cleveland and Ducktown. Until he retired from the commissary business at Ducktown, grains, vegetables, meats, sorghum, flour, and meal, produced at his farms and mills, furnished much of the "back-hauling" for copper haulers on their return trips to the mines.

In addition to the properties mentioned, Raht from time to time purchased other lands in the Ducktown and Turtletown districts. In October, 1876, he purchased an interest in the 888-acre tract of land lying on both sides of the Ocoee River, known as the United States Mining Company property. He did this, he said, that he might have a voice in the question of landing wood on the banks of the river and in the proposed plans of the Union Consolidated Mining Company to extend their railroad to the woodyard at the pontoon bridge. He was deep in his lawsuit with the Union Consolidated at that time, and it seems that he did not intend that the company should acquire any new rights and privileges at Ducktown without paying for them, if he could have anything to do with the negotiations.

By the time Raht had ceased purchasing lands at Ducktown he had acquired some seven thousand acres. His total investment here he estimated to be nearly $100,000.

With the end of mining at Ducktown in sight, Raht began turning his attention to other lines of endeavor. He was firmly entrenched in the fields of agriculture, real estate, and finance in lower East Tennessee, and it was here that he intended to remain. When he withdrew from Ducktown, he was still vigorous and active and the possessor of a tremendous fortune. How and where to employ himself and his means, now that his copper mining days were over, was, of course, not an easy question to decide. It is true that he was serving as president of the Cleveland National Bank and was actively engaged with his own loans and real estate, yet these were non-productive pursuits and his capacity far exceeded their demands. He was concerned, too, with his lawsuit with the Union Consolidated Mining Company that was being dragged out in the courts. While he was confident of the outcome of the case, yet it was, as he said, ruinous and disagreeable mentally to have to wait so long for a decision, because "...it is so disagreeable to me to keep any one thing so long on my mind; you know how I am constituted—I can't help it." Nevertheless, his inactivity was not to be permanent.

Raht made his initial re-entry into industry when he erected and put into operation a large flour mill at Athens, Tennessee, in March, 1878. This was not to be a mill of local proportions. He expected his biggest markets to be in Baltimore and New York until such time as his product became more widely known. He opened the business on a strictly cash basis, but soon retreated to some extent from this stand for the sake of a wider distribution.

From his letters to J. C. Mansfield, manager of the mill at Athens, it is evident that Mansfield had never before worked for a man like Raht. In his reports on operations the miller soon learned that terms such as "nearly," "almost," and "about" had little meaning for his employer. Even after the mill had been in operation for over a year Raht had to write Mansfield the following: "I regret that you have not conducted the business in such a way that you could have given me the statement desired about custom work. I request you to give orders and arrange that every grist is recorded, after receipt of these lines. I want all business conducted, that we can see through it." And as he had just recently acquired the Matthews mill at Athens and had hired H. K. Brown as manager there, he continued in the same letter to say: "Please think of the above and instruct Mr. Brown from the beginning of grinding at the Matthews mill."

It is obvious that but for his untimely passing, Captain Raht would have turned to milling as one of his principal lines of business.

Like his real estate transactions, Raht's loans and investments were many and varied. For several years his principal loans were to the copper companies, as well as to copper haulers and others of more modest means. As his income increased, and more particularly after 1875, he grew into virtually a loan and investment institution in his own right. His position, whether as head of the copper industry at Ducktown, as president of the Cleveland National Bank, or as an individual businessman in his own private office at Cleveland, was a magnetized force that drew to it those who had money, real estate, or other possessions which they desired to dispose of at bargain prices—and Raht never passed up a bargain.

Although he kept a bookkeeper employed at his Cleveland office, his final yearly recapitulations of his own accounts he compiled himself. In these reports he displayed a thorough familiarity with the single-entry system of bookkeeping. His "Bills Receivable" account, under which he carried the notes due him, revealed the extent of his loans. The total of this account was invariably in excess of $100,000.

It was one of Raht's fixed policies never to retract or change the form of a contract once it had been entered into. If, as it sometimes happened, a party to a contract was unable to fulfill his agreement, and Raht desired to make the terms less stringent in order that the contract might be completed, whatever terms or concessions to that effect he made were strictly off-the-record and in nowise affected the original document. For instance, the Reverend T. Sullins, of Athens, Tennessee, had borrowed $3,000 from him in 1874. Some three years later Raht wrote to Sullins, insisting that he take steps to repay the loan, and said: "The interest which you have contracted to pay me is high and is more than you can afford to pay, taking into consideration the use you make of the money. A good trader can use money at such rate of interest frequently and do well with it. The interest ought to be paid up by all means. If you will pay the interest due till date, and one thousand dollars of the principal within the next thirty days, I will carry the balance of the loan, viz: two thousand dollars, for twelve months at six percent. If you will pay one thousand dollars at the expiration of the twelve months, and the interest then due, I will carry the last one thousand dollars another twelve months at six percent. I don't propose to change our contract, but I will make a rebatement as stated if payments are made prompt to the day as indicated."

Sullins was unable to take advantage of the offer, and a year later Raht wrote to Mrs. Sullins: "I am sorry to learn from your statement that you have been deceived and disappointed. The only thing I have to regret in my dealings with Mr. Sullins is that my indulgence has not been of any benefit to you, and will likely prove injurious to myself. Had I as the money-lender insisted upon the prompt payment of the interest three years ago, and in default thereof caused the sale of the properties, it would have been to the advantage of all of us because real estate has since declined and the debt has increased. Mr. Sullins' real estate investment has proven to be a very unfortunate one which, in your condition, is to be deplored, but it is no fault of mine. I don't wish to inconvenience anyone, but there seems to be no alternative left to me in this instance." Soon thereafter he foreclosed on the mortgaged property.

Another instance is cited of Raht's willingness to mitigate the stipulations of a loan agreement. In 1872 he loaned Colonel J. L. Divine a total of $20,000 on four notes of $5,000 each. As the loan had not been repaid, he wrote Divine early in 1879: "As our mutual understanding and wish is that I shall not become the owner of your farm opposite the city of Chattanooga, let us plan how to avoid this. You know that I do not place such a high value upon the farm as you do, and as you have a good deal of other real estate unincumbered, I would be willing to take a deed of trust for all the past due interest to this date at the rate of six percent per annum for twelve months, and continuing the notes for the principal also for twelve months at the rate of interest as heretofore. If this meets your approval, I wish this agreement closed within the next ten days." The outcome of this proposition unfortunately is not clear as Raht's death occurred not long afterwards.

Raht was, of course, a keen analyst of human nature and when a debtor acted in good faith with him he never pressed for payment so long as there was hope of a satisfactory settlement. But a contract was a contract to him, a thing to which he was bound no more by legal statutes than by his own sense of honor. Between the party of the first part to a contract and the party of the second part there was no inequality; neither was there high nor low, rich nor poor, smart nor stupid. If either party failed the other, the injured party was justified for any recourse he might legally take to secure relief. A man signed a contract, Raht reasoned, for some expressed or implied benefit or advantage he hoped to realize therefrom. But if, instead, only disappointment and a heavy burden resulted, that was simply a risk that had to be assumed.

In manipulating his loans, Raht played them "close to his chest." But despite the care which it was necessary that he use, he often found that many borrowers were more sincere in their efforts at securing loans than they proved to be ever thereafter. For instance, in December, 1876, he wrote to D. C. McMillin, who was then in the banking business at Chattanooga, and said: "I intend to visit your city sometime this month, and I shall not fail to call upon you. I have loaned some of your neighbors some money and, as one good turn deserves another, I will come now to pay their taxes and fire insurance upon their dwellings and business houses."

No doubt there were times when it looked as though the Captain had been left holding the bag, yet more often than not the bag was later found to contain collateral of greater value than that expended by him in coming into possession of it. Especially was it true after he retired from Ducktown in 1875 that Raht's income was derived principally from his loans and investments. There was often no way of recouping a lost loan. Hence his policy of lending money only when collateral could be furnished that was ample to cover the principal, plus several years' interest, and taxes and insurance that it might be necessary for him to look after before a loan was repaid.

It was the client's place to furnish proof of the soundness of his proposition. Sometimes a client unwittingly did just the opposite. E. F. Sevier did the latter when he applied to Raht for an additional loan, probably thinking that the real estate of his on which Raht already held a mortgage was sufficient security. In declining to make a further loan on such terms, the Captain said: "The insurance companies are very good guides for prudent business dealings. I notice in the printed statement on the back of your letter that the Continental Insurance Company has loaned only $540,500.00 upon real estate worth $1,512,350.00." Sevier lost a golden opportunity here of coining an axiom for posterity to the effect that the borrower and the lender seldom laugh at the same thing at the same time.

Among Raht's other customers who at different times secured loans of substantial sums were Thomas Webster, A. and T. Cleage, L. M. and J. W. James, J. H. Magill, A. Bohn, William Crutchfield, R. M. Hooke, Montague Wheeler, William Lenoir, and General John T. Wilder. The clients of the Cleveland capitalist were drawn principally from those of the so-called higher income bracket. He left to his and other banks the detailed business of handling smaller loans of the character type. Character, to him, was a noble thing, but in big money deals there was nothing like value for value.

It was only natural that the Captain should receive many communications of doubtful significance. No doubt the very simplicity and frankness of some of these had a wholesomely deflating effect upon his own generously proportioned ego. If they did nothing else, they proved to him that there were at least a few people in his own community who considered him not invulnerable. Two instances of this will be cited. Raht had loaned A. C. Joseph $1,000, and about this he received the following letter:

> 4 MILE BRANCH, MONROE CO.,
> December 27, 1872.
>
> *Capt. J. E. Raht,*
>   *Cleveland, Tenn.*
>   DEAR SIR:
>   This is to notify you that you must collect the note which I am security for A. C. Joseph within fifteen days, and if it is not collected on that time you can consider me no longer on the same. Please write me saying when you have collected the note so that I may know that it is settled up.
>
>   Yours truly
>   L. L. CALLAWAY

Raht's reply, if any, to the letter is not known. But if Callaway was exercising a prerogative of that day, whereby an endorser of a note could disclaim any further liability if the note should not be paid when due, then truly it is to be regretted that this prerogative does not still exist.

The second instance to be cited concerns a proposition made Raht by F. F. Neel, a hardware merchant of Cleveland. After calling at Raht's office one morning and finding him absent, Neel wrote him a letter and explained the proposition about which he had called. He said:

I am going west in a few days, and my proposition is this: if you will furnish money I will select the best locality I am capable of and invest the money and attend to all the buying and disposing of the land and divide profits.

My experience in western lands has not been great but have realized more than 100% on my investments. Your good judgment will enable you to see this whole subject and needs no argument of mine to call your attention to details. If you think favorable of the plan let me know; if not please keep this strictly confidential as I do not want a blowing horn made of my trip out west.

Neither was Raht's reply to this letter available. He probably disdained answering it, for if there was anything of which he felt wholly capable, it was trusting his own ability to do his own investing. Neel was agreeable to dividing any profits he might realize from his investments with Raht's money, but he said nothing about sharing any losses that he might incur. In all likelihood Raht was as anxious to have Neel's questionable opinion of him kept secret as Neel was to have the nature of his trip west kept quiet. The whole matter undoubtedly blew over without a single horn being tooted by either.

It was in his investment policy that Raht revealed the distinction he adherred to between tangible and intangible values. By this is meant that so far as stocks and bonds are concerned, he loaded his investment portfolio with bonds to the almost total exclusion of stocks. Bonds represent real estate, buildings, machinery; things that are in themselves of value and can be seen and appraised. On the other hand, stocks are simply engraved parchment that bespeak faith, or hope, in management, products, service; intangibles that might or might not produce dividends. Be that as it may, when he laid his cash on the line for investment purposes, Raht invariably walked away with gold embossed bonds on his hip. But it was a different matter with bank stocks. A study of his investments after the year 1870 showed that Raht's larger holdings were divided into three groups, bank stocks, government and state bonds, and railroad bonds. A typical year was that of 1875 when he owned, in addition to the $70,000 worth of stock in the Cleveland National Bank, $40,000 in stocks of other banks; $85,000 in state and government bonds; and $43,000 in railroad bonds.

Anything to the contrary notwithstanding, there have been such things as "good old days" in Tennessee; especially was this true when the legal rate of interest in the state was 10 per cent, and one had, as Raht did, large sums of money to lend. Because references have been made to the important part interest rates played in Captain Raht's affairs, it should be of interest to discover how he greeted the proposal to amend the interest law in Tennessee when the subject was being debated by the Legislature in 1877.

To establish a uniform interest rate in the state, the writers of the 1834 Constitution of Tennessee provided in Section 6 of Article 11: "The legislature shall fix the rate of interest, and the rate so established shall be equal and uniform throughout the State." Pursuant thereto the Legislature of 1835-36 passed an act which provided a general legal rate of interest of 6 per cent. This rate remained in effect until 1870, except for a brief period of about a year when, according to the acts of 1859-60 the legal rate of interest was increased to 10 per cent. This law, however, was repealed on January 31, 1861, and the old rate of 6 per cent was re-established.

When the writers of the 1870 constitution took up the question of the uniform interest rate, they merely restated, under Section 7 of Article 11, the provisions of the 1834 constitution, but they paved the way for a higher rate when to the section they added the following clause: "... but the legislature may provide for a conventional rate of interest, not to exceed ten per cent per annum." The Legislature of 1869-70 took prompt advantage of the additional clause and passed a conventional rate of interest of 10 per cent. For several years following, trying to borrow money in Tennessee at less than 10 per cent interest was as futile as trying to induce a home-town umpire to change his decision.

The question of lowering the interest rate to 6 per cent came up, however, at the 1877 session of the Legislature, and it was at this time that Raht and all other moneyed interests in the state threw off their wraps and entered the contest. This meddling with the interest rate as the Legislature was doing was getting too close home for Raht's own peace of mind. Prior to the outcome of the struggle he predicted the most dire results should the interest law be changed. He said that it would be a suicidal act, that legitimate banking in Tennessee would be at an end, and that lending money would cease. The earnings would be too small, he said, to induce good and competent businessmen to give their attention to financial pursuits, and money would become even more scarce. "I for my part," he wrote to R. C. Jackson, "shall prefer to invest my money in United States 4% Bonds, instead of loaning it on real estate security in Tennessee at 6%."

In the letter to Jackson, who was president of the East Tennessee National Bank, Raht offered to relinquish the $10,000 stock he held in the bank, because he said, "I think that we outside stockholders ought to retire entirely and let you gentlemen, who do the business, own the entire stock, which you can employ profitably, because it will not justify you to attend to the business unless you can have the entire profits when the capital is reduced." Jackson evidently prevailed upon him to retain a portion of his stock, and probably convinced him that there would still be considerable banking business despite the lowering of the interest rate, for shortly thereafter Raht again wrote to Jackson, saying: "I shall be glad to retain $5,000 of my stock, and whenever the business improves again I will take more stock, if it is desired."

But for better or for worse the interest law was amended on March 20, 1877.* Raht went down fighting with the powerful minority who believed that business in the state was doomed to disintegration at a rate much greater than that of 6 per cent per annum. That there might be more borrowing at the lower rate than there had been at the 10 per cent rate was beside the point. Borrowers were simply so accustomed to paying the higher rate that they knew nothing better. After the law was passed, however, Raht had little further to say about it. He was soon back in the market with money to lend at 6 per cent.

It will be in order at this point to show some figures which will reveal Raht's uninterrupted climb to financial independence. From these will be seen how his wealth increased from the time when he was but an ambitious young mine captain, with a small

---

* See Shannon's *Annotated Constitution of Tennessee* (1916), pp. 525-26, for a review of the interest laws discussed here.

store on Copper Hill which he tended in his spare time in 1856, until late in the 1870's when he bore the somewhat odious title of the Richest Man in Tennessee. Another thing that the statements bring out is the fact that had he lived his life in Yucatan, Wiesbaden, or New York, he would most asuredly have been, as he was in Tennessee, among the richest men in his district. He possessed every attribute commonly deemed necessary to the attainment of wordly opulence. Physically, mentally, and termpermentally he was capable of thriving under tremendous weights of work and responsibility. He had courage, self-discipline, and was endowed with a mental acuteness that filtered out the personality of every individual who stood before him in business matters. He was as impersonal as the inanimate things in which he traded. He had neither friend nor foe when a business proposition was under consideration. Under given circumstances, a friend could be as expensive as an unfriendly person could be profitable.

These were some of the characteristics, undeveloped and unpolished though some of them might have been at the time, that led young Raht to take a piece of blue paper and laboriously list thereon in legible English script his financial status in 1856. And it was these same characteristics that led him year after year thereafter to list in his own handwriting the things he was liable for and those he owned. When he instituted this record-keeping of his own affairs, the future was as unpredictable for him as it was for those with whom he was associated. Ducktown was still a wooded region in which several mines were being worked, but for how long the operations might continue was anybody's guess. That Raht, himself, had faith in the future of the district is evident; that he had faith in himself was proven.

In his first years of record-keeping the energetic young merchant-miner was concerned with the value of such things as steers, fattening hogs, a few bushels of wheat and corn, and other items of but nominal value. But if wheat was worth a dollar a bushel and pork six cents a pound to others, they were worth that much to him. Although he later came to deal in larger terms, he never lost sight of the value of units, however small. From a net worth of some $3,000 in 1856, he had increased the value to $20,000 by January 1, 1860. But this was the last time that he listed his horses, mules, steers, and bulls by name and value of each. At the end of the year 1861 his assets had climbed to $80,000. It was in this year that the Union Consolidated first turned to their superintendent for financial assistance.

On January 1, 1863, after the Civil War had been in progress for over a year, Raht showed a credit of $108,000. But before he again resumed this intriguing chore of charting his path to wealth, Ducktown had suffered a long period of virtual desertion; he and his family had followed the refugee trail to strange places; a once proud Dixie had bowed to a stronger foe; and both politics and government in the South had passed into strange hands. In 1867, however, with the copper industry at Ducktown fairly well re-established and his own affairs re-organized on an apparently solid basis, Captain Raht was able once more to make his annual summary of his personal accounts. His resources for the year totaled $185,000.

A comparison of the statement of 1856 with the last one in 1879 revealed the tremendous distance Raht had traveled in a financial way over that period. Whereas his first report dealt in worldly possessions in terms of a few bushels of wheat, yokes of steers, and a few hundred pounds of pork, his last report included only items worth thousands of dollars and totaled well over $600,000. Potentially, he was immeasurably richer than his own estimate of his wealth indicated. For instance, he put a value of $23,000 on all his holdings in and around Ducktown. Included in this figure were the London and Eureka mines, which later proved to be among the more valuable mines in Tennessee's copper and chemical empire. He could just as well have listed their value at nothing, or at $1,000,000 each.

The source of practically every dollar of Raht's wealth was humble, remote Ducktown. That this was true, and that there was nothing strange to him about his amassing a fortune there, he told J. T. Newberry in a letter written during April, 1876. He said, "I couldn't help to make money, receiving salary from three different companies, having store privileges, and the selling of copper at a high commission."

Long after the old organization that had piloted the Union Consolidated Mining Company through years of valiant effort had been broken up, Raht maintained contact with Samuel Congdon and John Thomas, two of his former associates in copper mining at Ducktown. But it was not in every instance a pleasant matter for the Captain. Especially was this so insofar as Thomas was concerned. He still owed Raht the $12,500 he had borrowed in 1872, but this did not deter him from making repeated requests for additional loans. The former president of the Union Consolidated developed into an irritating problem for his erstwhile subordinate. On the other hand, Raht's relations with Congdon were always cordial. At least on one occasion when Congdon's luck was running out, Raht made a loan of $2,000 to him. In his letter to the man who over a quarter of a century previously had pioneered the mining industry at Ducktown, Raht said: "You have been like a father to me when I was sick, and you have acted in the same manner to me for many years, while we were connected in business. My wife sends her best regards to you. She also remembers the days of 1857, and will remain ever grateful to you." Always did Raht retain a feeling of deep respect for the man who was instrumental in placing him on the high road to success at Ducktown in the days before the Civil War.

Thomas' chief virtue was his persistence. A year after his resignation as president of the Union Consolidated he was hot on the trail of some mining properties in the west. He endeavored to interest Raht in these, but was unsuccessful. Soon thereafter he applied to his former superintendent for a loan. He received, instead, a reply which read, in part, "I have considered your request well, but I can't see how I can continue to make these loans to you...." But with Thomas it was, in golfing parlance, "never up, never in," for within a short time he wrote again, this time endeavoring to enlist Raht's co-operation in a mining venture in Ontario. "In making your proposition," Raht replied, "you are looking only on the winning side. You state that you did not wish me to make an individual venture in mining, but to assist you. Supposing the Ontarion does not succeed, isn't there a good chance for me to lose the $12,500 entirely? Isn't it, therefore, a personal venture?"

And thus it went, with misfortune relentlessly dogging the footsteps of Thomas. He had entered suit against the Union Consolidated for libel growing out of the charges made jointly against him and Raht by the company in 1875. The suit was still pending in Tennessee when circumstances forced him into bankruptcy in 1877. In what was probably Raht's last letter to Thomas, in 1878, he said: "Your conclusion drawn from my last letter was entirely correct. I do think that I have done even more than my part towards you. I regret only that the various advances or loans didn't serve a better purpose...."

CHAPTER 17

RAHT, FRIEND AND CITIZEN

Captain Raht's life, however, was not confined to a circumscribed orbit within which moved only those with whom his relations were reduced to a dollars and cents basis. Moving in an arc with him on his long swing from the low road to the high road were divers interests, movements, and individuals—all drawn to him by the very force of his unswerving journey. All these were simply by-products of the power he symbolized. They offered opportunities and entailed obligations. The way in which he responded to them revealed Raht, the man, just as vividly as did his balance sheet reveal Raht, the capitalist. And it is to him as friend, counselor, and citizen that this chapter will be devoted.

Insofar as participation in local politics was concerned, Raht was discreet to the point of bland neutrality. He had little to fear from either party that might be in control in the counties where he was the principal business figure. He was, however, a faithful follower of the Republican banner in national politics. But he was more interested in politics as a science of attaining desired ends than in politics as the term is more commonly understood. Only once was he threatened with poltics which would involve himself. That was when an attempt was made to send him to the state legislature, as is shown by the following letter:

Capt. J. E. Raht   Cleveland Aug. 20, 1872
Dear Sir,
At the request of a number of your friends of the Republican party I tonight drop you a line to ask you if you will serve us in the next legislature if we elect you. We are satisfied that all parties will vote for you and we do not believe any other candidate would run.

We would be glad—if you are not coming down soon, that you would give us a word by return mail.
Yours Truly
John W. Ramsey.

Among the reasons that caused Raht to decline this opportunity to add law-making to his already varied accomplishments was that of the length of time it would take him away from his duties at Ducktown.

Only rarely did Captain Raht find his own interests at stake to the extent that he appeared in the background of legislative action. One rare instance of this was the unsuccessful attempt by him to have the law court at Ducktown abolished in 1875, the details of which were related in an earlier chapter. He was, however, kept informed by friendly representatives at Nashville of the progress of legislation in which he was interested, such as that of laws affecting mining, railroads, banking, and taxes. But he shied away from involvement in the grape-vine method of legislation as he did from everything else that might produce repercussions out of proportion to the ends sought.

No attempt will be made here to shed new light on the presidential election of 1876. The outcome of that election in which Samuel J. Tilden, Democrat, won about everything over Rutherford B. Hayes, Republican, except the right to succeed Ulysses S. Grant as President, is well enough known. The election of that year came while the closed season on Democrats in several southern states was still in continuance, and as a result the majorities in three of these states, South Carolina, Florida, and Louisiana, were as a matter of absolute necessity turned to Hayes's column. So great was the confusion and turmoil that followed this election that for a time it was feared there would be no Inauguration Day, and, worse still, that Grant might continue as President. Before fatigue had brought to a close the balloting on election night of that year, Tilden had been conceded 184 of the 369 electoral votes. He needed only a single vote to win, with the returns from South Carolina, Florida, Louisiana, and Oregon still to be allotted. These four states represented a total of 22 electoral votes, and how every one of them was finally turned to Hayes, giving him a total of 185 to Tilden's 184 electoral votes, has long since been written into the records.

It was not until after Inauguration Day had come and gone in March of the following year that the more hopeful skeptics were satisfied that Hayes was actually to be President. Raht, himself, was among those who had feared for the worst. Several days after the election he had written to Carl Raht: "I fear Tilden will be the coming man. Wouldn't it be glorious if it was the other way!" And again, on the very eve of Inauguration Day, he write to S. P. Gaut, "Grant is still President, but report says that he is packing up to leave." The very thought of Grant was undiluted poison to Raht. The Chattanooga *Daily Times* of February 28, 1877, stated that the question of who was to be President was still about as uncertain as it had been for the past six months, but that the uncertainty no longer lay between Tilden and Hayes. Tilden's chances were gone, but rumors around Washington were that Levi P. Morton was to be elected as President of the Senate. In this capacity, Morton, "that mass of human villainy," would be elevated to the presidency of the United States should the special election commission be unable to agree on Hayes. But Rutherford B. Hayes, who was soon to fall into disrepute with his own party because of his lack of political partisanship, was inaugurated March 5.

When it became apparent that Hayes was to be the next President, Captain Raht set the wheels in motion in behalf of an honored friend. This friend was David M. Key, and it was to Jacob M. Thornburgh, Congressman from the Second District in Tennessee, that Raht addressed his recommendation for a job for Key. Thornburgh had served like a stevedore in man-handling Florida into the Republican column, and Raht was confident that in recognition of this, the Tennessee congressman's voice would not go unheeded in future caucuses of his party.

It will be remembered that David M. Key had been on Raht's staff of attorneys in the early days of the Captain's trial with the Union Consolidated Mining Company. Previous to this time Key had served as chancellor of the Third Division (Tennessee) from 1870 until 1875, and following this had served a portion of a term as United States Senator. It was shortly after James M. Bailey had been elected by the Legislature to succeed Key as United States Senator that Hayes was inaugurated as President, and the quadrennial turn-over at Washington got under way. Being the kind of politician he was, Raht was not inconsistent in desiring that Hayes, a Republican, be elected, and then in turn that Key, a Democrat, be given a place in the administration that befitted his character and ability. Key had served in the Confederate Army and had labored diligently and impartially in all efforts that were made to bring about political and social stability in Tennessee during the reconstruction period. Raht could see the wisdom of the new administration's recognizing such southern men as Key, and to this effect he addressed the following letter to Congressman Thornburgh:

CLEVELAND, TENNESSEE
March 2, 1877

Hon. J. M. Thornburgh,
Washington
DEAR SIR,

As the victory is ours at last I take the liberty to suggest a matter to you and see if it coincides with your views.

Would it not be a good policy to secure a suitable position for ex-Senator Key? My opinion is, that it would be a good policy and very proper; I know it would have a good effect among the people.

I know you have a great influence and this deservedly, too; your services in Florida were very important. I considered Florida the most dangerous case for our success.

I have a very high opinion of Senator Key; as you have had an opportunity to know him also, I hope that you agree with me.

I would consider it a handsome deed on the part of the new Administration.

Please excuse my suggestion.

Yours
very truly
J. E. RAHT

P.S. Gold below 105; General Grant can well afford to retire now.

Whether or not the foregoing letter was the beginning of the movement that led to David M. Key's appointment sometime later as Postmaster General this author is unable definitely to say. Evidently Raht had no particular position in view for Key, but left to Thornburgh the question as to whether Key should be recommended, and for what duties. Coming from Raht as it did, the congressman apparently received the suggestion in the spirit in which it was conceived, and followed it through. It was easy enough to approach the President on this subject, for Hayes had announced that his policy was to be one of uniting the country and bringing about harmony and stability on a national instead of a sectional basis. The fact remains that David M. Key, a Confederate, was appointed as Postmaster General in 1877, and served in that position until 1880.

The boys out in the sticks began lining up at the patronage counter as soon as the Tilden menace was past. As usual the more alert ones were first on the streets and turnpikes with hastily prepared petitions setting out their claims for consideration. And as usual many of the petitioners later found themselves in embarrassing positions when called upon, by the more dilatory aspirants, for signatures that had already been affixed to previous documents of the same nature. But such was not the case with Captain Raht, as we shall see.

It seems that a new postmaster was to be appointed at Cleveland. Dr. William Hunt was among those who aspired to this position. And being one who knew the advantage to be gained by "getting there fustest with the mostest names," the Doctor promptly circulated a petition in his own behalf. Captain Raht signed Hunt's petition, only to be later presented a similar paper by W. L. Tipton. Having little reason to choose between the two and not wishing to appear unduly partisan in the matter, Raht extricated himself from this predicament by again writing to Congressman Thornburgh, as follows:

CLEVELAND, TENNESSEE
March 5, 1877.

Hon. J. M. Thornburgh
Washington
DEAR SIR,

Mr. W. L. Tipton, who has been Assistant Postmaster here for a number of years is an applicant for the office as Postmaster here.

It gives me pleasure to certify that he has been a very efficient and good officer and that he would fill the office as Postmaster well.

Mr. Tipton called upon me this morning to sign my name to a petition to obtain for him the above named office, but, as I have already signed the petition of Dr. Wm. Hunt for the office, I take this method to certify to Mr. Tipton's efficiency and character.

I remain, Sir, with high regard.

Yours
very truly
J. E. RAHT

No fond mother ever took more pride in showing off her first born than Captain Raht took in advertising the copper industry at Ducktown. His pride in the mines and their products found expression in the many displays he furnished for fairs and expositions. To the State fairs at Nashville, the Eastern Division fairs at Knoxville, the Centennial Exposition at Philadelphia, and the Smithsonian Institute, he sent samples of ores and copper products that all might see what was being done at Ducktown. At the State Fair at Nashville in the fall of 1868, he had on display, in addition to specimens of ores and copper, a hearth set consisting of a shovel, tongs, and poker. The set was made of Ducktown copper, highly polished. In preparation for entering the implements to compete with others for awards that were to be made for excellence of design and workmanship, Raht had three of his more skilled blacksmiths each to design and manufacture a hearth set. He selected the set made by James Nankivell, Sr., and forwarded it to Nashville. Nankivell's efforts were rewarded when several months later, in March, 1869, S. D. Morgan, an official of the Tennessee Agricultural and Mechanical Association, sent to Raht for delivery to the winner a silver medal engraved, "Awarded to James Nankivell, Ducktown, 1869."

In reporting on the Ducktown display at the State Fair in 1869, the Knoxville *Daily Press and Herald* of October 31 quoted S. D. Morgan as saying: "Here we have exhibited what is known to copper smelters as 'first matt,' 'second matt,' 'concentrated matt,' 'black copper,' 'pig copper,' and lastly the refined and pure 'ingot' in its finished state,—those being the different names given to the metal in its various stages of transition from the crude ore to the refined metal."

On March 11, 1872, James M. Safford wrote at length to Raht about plans that were being made for the exposition to be held at Nashville in May. Said he, in part: "Ducktown this time must be fairly presented, and I am glad to know that the material— most of it at least—is already on hand.... Last Friday night, in speaking of Tennessee minerals before the Board of Managers, I said something of the Ducktown series presented by you to the State, etc. The newspaper reporters botched it up—got 200 lbs. in the place of 2000, and made other mistakes.... The Board of Managers have taken the liberty to elect you an honorary member, and I trust you may find it consistent with your feelings to accept and give us your sympathy...."

Visitors at the Eastern Division fairs at Knoxville were also treated to the spectacle of the evolution that takes place in a lump of copper ore from the time it is mined until it appears as an ingot of copper. On one occasion C. W. Charlton, secretary of the Eastern Division Fair, wrote to Raht in regard to the spring exposition in 1871. The letter said in part: "I send you our programme of Industrial Exhibition the 25th of May. I am desirous that you should have a large and imposing collection of your copper on the occasion. I will set apart a special place for you in our building. Be on hand by all means...."

There were large fairs and small fairs, but the Ducktown exhibits took them all in stride. Before Raht left Ducktown in 1875 he had prepared an elaborate display of copper products to be used in Tennessee's exhibit at the Philadelphia Centennial the following year. So effective was this display that a certificate of merit was awarded the Union Consolidated Mining Company by the Centennial Commission. The Centennial was to celebrate a hundred years of peace, progress, and plenty in America. But as the definition of some of these terms was open to discussion, the South looked upon the coming exposition with divided enthusiasm. But not so in hybrid Tennessee. This state began early to make preparations for participation in the event. The Nashville *Bulletin* of March 20, 1873, reported a speech made before the Legislature by Colonel Bailie Peyton in which he urged that Tennessee take advantage of the Centennial to advertise her resources and opportunities to all the world. The same paper also listed the Centennial committees that had been named for the three grand divisions of the state. These gentlemen, among whom was Captain J. E. Raht, thus had over three years in which to prepare for the big event—or to prepare their expressions of sorrow at not being able to serve.

Many of those selected on the committees probably accepted their appointments, as did Raht, in a passive way, as they might have done in endorsing a long-term note. The effective date was too far off to worry about. But when, early in 1875, it came time to get down to business, the Centennial took on an ominous meaning. In May of that year John H. Crozier, of Knoxville, wrote to Raht that he had been appointed a member of the Executive Committee for East Tennessee, and that the committee was to begin functioning at once. Thereupon Raht sought to be excused from serving. Crozier then informed him that "... I have no power to excuse you from serving on the Committee. And if I had the power, excuse me for saying, I would not grant your request. The State of Tennessee, and particularly East Tennessee, requires the services of just such men as you are to make preparations for the grand peace contest with the world that is to come off at Philadelphia next year...." Whether Raht succeeded in withdrawing entirely from the Centennial Committee is not known. He did, however, as previously stated, contribute to the success of Tennessee's part in the exposition by furnishing a display of Ducktown products.

Mention has already been made of the effective way in which Raht protected the law-abiding element at Ducktown by refusing employment to rowdies and troublemakers. Although he never returned to Ducktown to live after the war, this did not tend to lessen his interest in the moral and social welfare of the district.

He visited the mines at least once each quarter when he accompanied the wagon which hauled the heavy safe containing the money for pay-day. He was otherwise kept informed of conditions there through the commuting copper haulers.

It was told of Captain Raht that on his trips to Ducktown with the pay-roll he would often place the money in a sack, throw it into his buggy, and follow the wagon that was hauling the heavily guarded, empty safe. It seems that this ruse was no secret at all, but it was never known, at the time, just which vehicle was transporting the money. The sack would often be thrown into the buggy, empty. However, no attempt was ever made to rob the convoy.

Current reading matter was scarce at Ducktown for sometime following the war. To help as best he could to overcome this condition, Raht subscribed for the weekly issue of the New York *Tribune* for several of his friends and employees at the mines in 1866. Included in the list of those for whom he secured subscriptions were B. I. Lowe, James Phillips, A. S. Hoffman, D. M. Collins, Jacob Lang, James Jory, John Tonkin, Henry Jory, William Humphrey, Henry Falls, M. Douthit, John Baugh, E. B. Freeman, and A. Matthews.

Not all could read, but all had to eat. For this reason Raht wrote to John Tonkin in the spring of 1866 to see that the few families of darkies living at Ducktown be allowed to have gardens, just as the white population had.

Throughout the tremendous number of letters penned by Raht himself, there were lines heavy with bluntness, satire, and reproach, and lines light with wit, humor, and metaphors. No better example of the latter could be cited than a letter written by him to Mrs. J. E. Rudizinski at a time when he was laboring day and night to re-establish his own affairs and the affairs of the copper companies at Ducktown. But the woman was relying on him to assist her in disposing of a house at Ducktown. How he proposed to do this is shown in the letter which follows:

Cleveland, Tennessee
June 9, 1866

Mrs. J. E. Rudizinski,
  Dandridge.
  Madam;
Although Miss Katinka answers my letters addressed to you in her own name, I keep writing to the Old Lady (beg to be excused). Young folks know a good deal, of course, but still old folks know

best. I am getting old myself, and I know this to be a fact, even if Young America will not admit it.

Before I go any further, I request you to give your daughter a warning for me. I know she will not think hard of it. Miss Katinka may take a notion some of these days and want an husband; I do not know that she will, still she may; her own mother took an husband. I wanted to warn her if such should ever be the case, not to be quite so sharp in the negotiations as she is in this house trade, otherwise she will not get the right one.

Now about the house; I recommend to you and Miss Kantinka to sign the deed, acknowledge the same, affix the U. S. Revenue Stamp, and forward to me with your instructions, I think I understand to be $1000.00 cash in hand....

I am no friend of slow trades. You know, Madam, I went to Europe in 1854, entered into a lifetime contract, married and returned to America in less time than it will take Miss Katinka to sell the house. You also know that I made a good trade that time, therefore please tell Miss Katinka not to be slow....

With kind regards to you and Miss Katinka from Mrs. Raht and myself, and the request to excuse my superfluous remarks, I remain,
>Yours
>very truly,
>J. E. RAHT.

It was during the months immediately following the close of the war that the predicament in which he found himself reminded Raht of a frantic woman at Ducktown. He was hard pressed for money with which to pay expenses at the mines until the copper companies could come to his assistance. In a letter to his brother, in which he was telling of his straitened circumstances, he said: "'What shall I do for currants?' a lady called out at Ducktown during the late war. 'What shall I do for money?' I now call out!"

In an effort by the author to learn what the men and women of this region who lived back in Raht's time actually thought of him, a set of fixed questions bearing on Raht's character was asked each of the older residents who were interviewed. Except in rare instances the older citizens were, and are, one generation removed from Raht's day. Their parents were the ones who knew the Captain personally. But each was well acquainted with him through first-hand, word-of-mouth accounts. To each was asked: "What did the people back then think of Raht? Was he fair and honest with everyone? Was he kind and charitable, or overbearing and stingy?" These were questions that written records of the man, however complete they might prove to be, would not reveal in the sense that they were desired. For this reason a sincere effort was made to learn whether or not Raht's character, as it was appraised at Ducktown, was in keeping with his legendary reputation.

Answers to these question were, without exception, favorable to the memory of Raht. The answer given by Joe Waters was a summation of those given by all to whom the questions were put. He said that his people all liked Raht, for "he was the cleverest man to the poor that they ever knew." The word clever as here used meant kindly, charitable, and helpful. Another common answer was, "He must have been all right; I never heard anything against him."

Knowledge of how Raht was accepted by the natives of this region was, it must be admitted, of immeasurable benefit to the author in his study of the trouble and consequent litigation between Raht and the Union Consolidated Mining Company. It is true, of course, that a great deal of evidence unfavorable to their former superintendent was beaten out of the coves and knobs around Ducktown by the company. But certainly the preponderance of evidence was in his favor. And what was equally important, or more so, public sentiment was overwhelmingly on his side. While public sentiment probably played no part in the decision handed down by Chancellor Cooper at Benton, yet it can be doubted that had the decision been otherwise the Little Chancellor would have received the favorable publicity he did for the way in which the trial was conducted. Certainly Raht should not have had the moral backing of the citizens of this region had he for twenty years been speaking with the voice of Jacob but dealing with the hand of Esau.

Too many years have passed since Raht's time, and too few of those who personally knew and remember him remain, for it to be possible to recount many specific incidents out of which grew the high respect in which he was held. What is left to us of this day is but an unintelligible murmur of a chorus of admiration that once welled through this district for the man who grew above but never away from it. But Mrs. Sally Ketron, who was born in 1855, remembers having seen Captain Raht many times. Her father came to Ducktown from Murphy before the Civil War and worked here as a blacksmith for several years, and her mother ran a boarding house at Isabella after the war. Mrs. Ketron said of Raht that he was the most charitable man she ever knew. She recalled an incident that was, she said, typical of his character. A miner was injured and his family was soon reduced to dire straits. Raht learned of this on one of his visits to the mines and forthwith sent a stove, a month's supply of provisions, and cloth to make clothes for the family to the miner's home.

The following letter tells its own story. It was from the secretary of the Eastern Division Fair. The premium money referred to was awarded Raht for displays which he furnished for the fair of 1872:

KNOXVILLE, TENN. Oct. 31, 1872

J. E. Raht, Esq.
Cleveland, Tenn.
DR. SIR:
I am in receipt of your esteemed favor of the 29th inst. Allow me to say that the disposition you propose to make of your premium money is worthy of your heart. Let me make the following suggestion: That you authorize me in proper legal form to find some worthy poor boy and invest the amount in his behalf, taking the note of a responsible party to be renewed every six months including the interest. By the time he is 21 years of age he will have a snug sum to start life upon. What say you to this suggestion? Answer.
Yrs. & C
C. W. CHARLTON

What Raht's answer was is not known. Copies of his letters of that period were not available.

It is not always easy to distinguish between charity, philanthropy, and chivalry. Sometimes this can be done only if the motive or spirit that prompts a deed or an act is known. In the absence of this knowledge, then, the nature of the deed itself often furnishes its own clearest definition. But, on the other hand, no distinction might be possible, because charity, philanthropy, and chivalry might all be involved. For instance, Raht came into possession of a house at Athens, Tennessee, in 1878, in which lived a widow with several children. He wrote the woman, Mrs. Hattie Cleage, that it was, as she knew, through unfortunate circumstances that the house fell to him and that at that time he contemplated deeding the little cottage to her provided she decided to make Athens her permanent home. As that was still his intention he requested that she let him know her plans and tell him the names of her children for inclusion in the deed. Shortly thereafter the deed was registered in her name and delivered to her.

There are times, too, when it is difficult to label an act as one of philanthropy, nobility, or expediency. A case in which all these elements seemed to be present, however, was Captain Raht's sending young James B. Witt to school to study bookkeeping and penmanship. Raht had difficulty in keeping a dependable bookkeeper at his Isabella store. He saw in the youth, who lived near the store, an opportunity to relieve himself of this uncertainty. The offer made by Raht to send him to school, after which he would be employed at the store, was accepted by the young man. This experiment worked to their mutual advantage, and Witt, although dubbed the clerk with the wandering mind, remained in Raht's employ until the Captain left Ducktown.

Captain Raht's generosity was a cloak of many colors. His gifts and donations were poured down endless channels that irrigate the whole field of human indigence and adversity. That a great many of these proved to be but vanishing rivulets that feed the insatiable river of charity there is no doubt. But some, at least, might have trickled down through the years, exerting their beneficent influences in ways not readily discernible. Especially might this have been true insofar as his interest in schools was concerned. The inadequacy of the school system of this region was a matter of constant concern to Raht. There was, of course, little he could do to increase the number of schools. Neither could he extend the length of their terms nor improve upon either the courses of study or the teaching methods. But the one way in which he could be of help he was a source of invaluable aid. This was in respect to equipment, or more particularly lack of equipment, at practically all the one-room schools from Cleveland to Ducktown.

Raht's own children were tutored by private teachers during their early years. At appropriate ages they were sent to the subscription school in Cleveland. This school, naturally enough, was an object of interest to Raht. In October, 1871, he made the following offer to the Rev. R. D. Black: "If you can accomplish by subscription the building of a public school house of the size and description, and at the location of which we have spoken, you may call upon me for one thousand dollars, provided a sufficient subscription is secured during this month." The offer was extended to December 31, but in the following January the Reverend Black had to report his inability to secure the needed help. He said that many who favored public schools were even opposed to the issuance of bonds for the purpose, as they considered this plan too expensive. For this reason he felt that the bond election to be held on January 6 would go against those who favored issuing bonds for public school purposes. There is every reason to believe that had Raht's fellow citizens of Cleveland shown a lively enough interest in the promotion of the proposed school he would have increased his contribution to whatever extent necessary for construction of the building. But the public school in this region was still pretty much of an untried experiment. For the day and region illiteracy was too common to be a noticeable handicap. Raht could not change this either.

It seems that by 1875 Raht had taken the school situation at Cleveland more firmly in hand. This is indicated by a letter to him from John J. Harvey which said in part: "From a letter just received from Cleveland, I learn that the Cleveland High School has changed hands, and that you are now the controller of the entire school. Such being the case, I would be willing to accept any position in the same at a fair salary. . . ." This was the Masonic Institute, which had an enrollment of about ninety pupils at that time. On one occasion, in November of that year, the principal, William Chalmers, sent Raht by one of the Captain's sons a note telling him that with his approbation, he, Chalmers, would get up a subscription for new furniture that was needed at the school. There is not much doubt about the principal's motive in mentioning to Raht the need of new equipment. It was about the same as telling the only man in the county who had a plow that you would cultivate your field if someone would lend you a plow.

Throughout this region were small schools that save for the self-sacrificing spirit of the teachers and the co-operation of a few of the more far-seeing and intelligent citizens had little reason for existence. It was to these schools, even more so than to the school at Cleveland, that Captain Raht made some of his largest and most useful contributions. "He was liberal in his aid to schools and churches," was a frequent expression of those to whom Captain Raht was a symbol of magnanimity of an era long past. Books, stoves, maps, repairs to buildings, bells, and financial aid to underpaid teachers were some of the ways in which he encouraged these embryonic educational adventures.

Fortunately there appeared in the Cleveland *Banner* of March 19, 1875, a tribute to Captain Raht which lends credence to the somewhat disconnected legends and accounts of his interest in rural education. The article is reproduced here:

JUSTICE TO THE DONOR

Believing that the recipient of favors should by some means show an appreciation of the same, we desire to make this statement:

When Cookston's Creek Seminary was built, Capt. J. E. Raht, presented it with an excellent bell, and furnished the rooms with first-class desks for both teachers and pupils. Recently he has given the school two latest improved artificial globes, which are admirably adapted to the use of the schoolroom.

This school is one of the many that have shared liberally in valuable donations from this gentleman. We have been told that the Captain in his accustomed liberality usually helps those who try to help themselves, and this we believe a good motto.

Believing that a statement of these facts is due the donor, we in behalf of the patrons of the school, submit the same to the public.

PARKSVILLE, TENNESSEE
March 13, 1875   (signed) F. M. CONES
                                                G. E. CURRY

Requests for aid were received by Captain Raht from some who knew more about his assistance to others than they knew about his policy of helping only those who helped themselves. This was true in the case of Cane Creek Academy at Cog Hill, McMinn County. A letter written to Raht by J. H. Brunner, principal of the Academy, in March, 1873, said, "Your favor of the 10th was received on my return today. It was bold in me to ask what I did. And in declining my offer you very generously propose to favor us if certain conditions be met. Thank you for this kindness. As soon as I can look around a little I can be able to tell what these people propose to do."

To the orthodox religionist there could have been all the difference in the world between Captain J. E. Raht's actions and his motives. His life as he lived it was unavoidably a succession of events that marked him at times as a relentless Shylock and at others as a modern Good Samaritan. Weighed in the balance of pious observance, he could well have been just another rich man on the velvety road to perdition. And even judged by his many manifestations of compassion for the less fortunate, he might still have been but another rich young ruler who would hesitate to sell his worldly possessions for more lasting treasures in heaven. Beyond a doubt Raht was religious in the noblest sense of the term. But his philosophy of religion stood out in bold relief against a regional religion that was religion sans philosophy. There was nothing about religion to him that shut out honor, integrity, and thrift; nothing about it that glorified dullness, superstition, and unbridled passion. Religion to him was character, a way of life—hard, disciplined conduct. To him some were capable of achieving this standard, others undoubtedly were not. A lazy saint would have been to him one of the wonders of creation.

Captain Raht was what he was because of his own spiritual intellect. He was what he should have been had he, in a material way, been wealthy or poor. He was reared in an atmosphere of dignity and refinement, was educated at two of the leading universities in Europe, and rose to a position of power and influence. Despite all this he was neither a fatalist nor an agnostic. "Life is uncertain," he would say. Once when lightning struck his barn and killed a mare and a moment later ripped through a trellis in his yard, he thankfully remarked on how lucky he was after all. And in a letter of condolence to J. H. Gaut, written in July, 1864, upon the death of Gaut's wife, while the Civil War was still raging, he said that there was so much trouble in the world that a person might wish never to have been born, "if it was not injustice to our Maker." Nor was atheism a by-product of his education or his financial success. That man had learned how to mine and smelt ores; that there were chemical elements in every animate and inanimate thing; that steam had power; that some objects were heavier than others; that silica was plentiful and gold scarce; that man could see, hear, and talk—these were things that intrigued his own reasoning powers. But their riddles were not sufficiently important to Raht to induce him to attempt to analyze God away.

Half his life-time was spent in a region where the fervor of the individual's religion was manifested by his attendance at church services. All who attended church services, camp meetings, and all-day singings were by no means devout, but all the devout ones were usually to be found at these gatherings. But here Captain Raht was unorthodox in that he was not a church-goer. Furthermore he felt no qualms of conscience for his apparent lack of interest in public worship. His philosophy in this respect, expressed in his own words, was, "It will not do to judge religion by churchgoing. Some sheep will do well without a shepherd, while others won't do well even with a shepherd." This was not said in defense of his own lack of religious manifestations, but was written to a minister who was deploring his flock's indifference to their religious vows.

The Captain could view the preacher's dilemma with sincere compassion. The greater part of his own time was spent in seeing that men kept their promises to him in such mundane matters as loans, contracts, and agreements. Vows, after all, were relative. Too often they were made under conditions and impulses radically different from those under which it would be necessary that they be kept and fulfilled.

Raht's defense of those who were lax in their church obligations was by no means an affront to the church and its principles and objectives. Just as he was a champion of schools and a benefactor to teachers, so was he liberal in his aid to churches of all denominations. He was himself a member of the Lutheran Church, and when the German population of Knoxville was endeavoring to establish a church of their own, he came to their aid in a most effective way, as will be seen by the following letter which was written to him by Peter Kern, Knoxville's foremost baker and confectioner for many years:

KNOXVILLE, TENN. Dec. 23, 1869

Mr. J. E. Raht, Cleveland, Tenn.

Your letter of the 22nd inst, came to hand with a enclosed draft for $300.00 for which please accept my heartfelt thanks in the name of the German Lutheran Church Congreation, it came unexpected and at a time most needed and I feel proud of you although I am not acquainted with you personally but from what I learned I know that you are a German and your heart is still with us with this great and good undertaken, may God reward you tenfold for what you done for us Germans here, and every one in Knoxville will appreciate your deed highly. You will hear from the Congregation next week after they have a meeting, I am Yours

Respectfully,
PETER KERN

(P.S.) Our Pastor has come last week and the work will go on a great deal better henceforth, his name is Johannes Heckel and is a good Preacher.

P. KERN

And here is another letter that tells its own story:

CLEVELAND, TENN.
DELANO HOUSE NO. 3
Dec. 3rd, 1875

Capt. J. E. Raht

DEAR SIR:

I regret that I am not able to comply with your request in furnishing you a copy of the prayer offered at the Funeral of our mutual friend and Bro. Harry Jory. The prayer was inspired by the occasion, and was strictly original and impromptu. You can appreciate the circumstances that surrounded me, the intense feeling, and universal sorrow of that grief stricken community, you being present to witness the sad rites.

Dear Sir, I assure you, it is not for want of respect for you, or inclination to comply with your request, but a want of ability to reproduce the prayer. Wishing you a speedy and successful issue out of your present trouble, and that when we meet, it may be on a far less afflictive occasion than when we last met, I am yours

Most Respectfully
J. Albert Hyden

Raht's present trouble referred to in the letter was the lawsuit between him and the Union Consolidated Mining Company, which was just then beginning.

On the face of it the good Reverend must have prayed a masterful prayer—which he undoubtedly did. On the other hand it had probably been so long since Tennessee's industrial and financial tycoon had heard a prayer of any kind that the one delivered by the Reverend Hyden bore all the earmarks of long and careful preparation. The sad occasion upon which Captain Raht heard the earnest supplication contributed to its appeal to him. Harry Jory, it will be remembered, had served Raht in an important capacity for many years. To the devout minister who had lifted him up by a prayer Raht responded by sending him fifty dollars.

A son, Adolphus Washington, was born to Captain Raht a year after he returned to Ducktown with his bride. Babies appeared in the Raht household at regular intervals thereafter until a total of twelve had been born. Six sons and two daughters grew to maturity.

From the school at Cleveland, Raht sent his sons to Roanoke College, Virginia Military Institute, and to the Moravian School at Nazareth, Pennsylvania. His eldest son, Adolphus, later attended Rensselaer Polytechnic Institute, while his second son, William, went to Sheffield Scientific School.

Mathematics was, to Captain Raht, the basis of education. "Mathematics," he said, "will develop the mind more than all other studies."

The Captain allowed his sons a certain amount of spending money, but, alas, it was sometimes necessary to increase this in order that mysteriously accumulated debts might be paid. About matters of this kind he once wrote to Roanoke College: "I hope for the honor of the boys and the honor of Roanoke College, that the boys will be kept under better control this next year than the past year, in regard to the finances as well as the attendance of the lessons. Unexcused absences require punishment." At Christmas time that year (1876) Raht wrote the Reverend William B. Yonce, treasurer of the college, "In reference to an extra allowance of money on account of Christmas, I don't know what to say, as the boys have no doubt received presents from home and should make out with their regular monthly allowance of $5.00 each. Still, if you approve it and consider it necessary, you may give each $5.00 extra for Christmas—but I don't advocate it."

It is only when looking back upon certain common-sense remarks on otherwise commonplace subjects, made in the light of things as they were, that it can be realized just how tragically ironic the remarks sometimes prove to be. Such was lamentably true, in part, in respect to an exchange of correspondence between Captain Raht and his brother Carl, and events that followed, in the summer of 1879. The letters concerned the health of Captain Raht and his brothers, Carl and August.

Good health had always been one Captain Raht's prime assets. He had disciplined himself to rigid temperance except in matters of food and work. Beer was the strongest alcoholic beverage of which he partook. A fine table wine was an accepted part of the Raht menu. The Old-World custom of a substantial breakfast, followed by lunch, four o'clock tea, and a heavy dinner, was followed in his home. The Captain did not live to eat, but hearty and bountiful eating was a prelude to enjoyable living for him. He dined in a dining room that was accoutered in heavy furniture, heavy silver, exquisite china, heavy carpets, and lighted by a massive gold-plated chandelier that sparkled brilliantly in the reflection of its myriad candles.

Added years and a voracious appetite transformed his stocky and powerful figure into one of commanding rotundity. He went clean-shaven, dressed with austerity that befitted his physical and financial stature, and wore a watch chain that was but a miniature gold trace chain. Other than for an occasional cold, he was rarely incapacitated. Once, in the spring of 1876, he had to drink lemonade before breakfast for several days because of a sticky tongue. He remarked then on his obesity, but his health was good, nevertheless.

Thus the letters that passed between Captain Raht and his brother in the summer of 1879 contained only perfunctory remarks on the good health of each. But they were both very much concerned over their brother August's health. August Raht, it will be remembered, had left Ducktown and gone to the West after the shut-down. In 1879 he was in Utah and was in very poor health. After commenting on what they should do to assist in restoring the health of their brother, Carl Raht said to the Captain in a letter of June 11, 1879: "I am glad to hear that you are enjoying good health. It is a blessing beyond all others, and yet seldom valued until lost.... I have myself had very fair health for some time." The irony of this, in part at least, was that in a little over two months from that time Captain Raht was dead—and August Raht died thirty-eight years later, in 1917. A business visitor who called at Captain Raht's office at Cleveland on Friday morning, August 15, 1879, found him hale and hearty. But before the conference had ended the Captain had died, a victim of heart failure.

In reviewing his life, and his sudden passing at the age of fifty-three, certain observations tend to bring out both the fallibility and the infallibility of his life's conduct. They bring out, too, just how far advanced for his day were Raht's business methods. His besetting weakness was his own tireless energy and boundless capacity for work, plus a gnawing impatience at delay and uncertainty. In fact it seems probable that it was the rasping tread of slow-motion legal procedure incident to his lawsuit with the Union Consolidated Mining Company, more so than it was his business activity in his later years, that sapped his physical vitality. He conducted the mining operations at Ducktown, his farms, mills, stores, and banks largely through subordinates. But in addition to these chores, he transacted a tremendous volume of more personal business over his own desk. Especially did he assume personal control over his financial affairs and the off-stage maneuvers of the trial.

By no means the least of his tasks was his correspondence. He wrote thousands of letters. All were written by his own hand, as were his financial and other reports and accounts. He made copies of all his letters by means of a hand-press which forced an imprint of the letters onto tissue sheets in specially bound books for this purpose. The energy he put into these personal tasks was immense. The typewriter had not come into general use in Raht's time. It was not perfected to the point where it could be put on the market until 1874 and even then the machine was little more than a novelty for several years. The typewriter, as well as a great many other labor- and time-saving devices that were later developed, did not appear until after Captain Raht had demonstrated just how much one individual could accomplish with his own head and hands, if these personal tools were guided by an intelligent and unflagging purpose. But the man was often tired, physically and spiritually—probably more so than he would admit, even to himself.

There were times during the long years of the trial when, if the officials of the Union Consolidated Mining Company had shown any conciliatory attitude whatever, Raht would undoubtedly have ended the litigation by cancelling the entire debt owed to him. He realized that irresponsible officials were leading the company to disaster and were at the same time doing their best to discredit and weaken him. But his determination was equal to theirs; his resources were far greater; and he felt that his was the just cause. Two years before his death he expressed the hope that he might be spared to see the end of the trial. So long as the trial continued he could not embark wholeheartedly upon new business ventures. The strain finally told when he collapsed, only a few months before the final decision was rendered in his favor. He had learned to live and thrive under pressure; he could never adjust his plans and energies to the creeping tempo of court proceedings.

Placed beside balance sheets of the gigantic corporations of the 1940's, Raht's balance sheets of the 1870's would not be impressive. But what is impressive is the fact that industrialists of the present day have amassed their huge holdings on theories and methods not unlike those followed by Captain Raht. For instance, he mined the ore and sold the copper. He owned a portion of the wood that was used by the mining companies. He owned or controlled the teams that transported the copper to the railroad. He owned the mine commissaries. He owned farms from whence came much of the grains and meats sold at these commissaries, and he owned the mills that ground the grains into flour and meal. He owned strategic ferries and stretches of roads and owned or directed the principal financial institutions in his territory. In other words, he did not attempt to strum a harmonious tune on the industrial harp while outside fingers were plucking at the strings.

The passing of Raht marked the end of an era at Ducktown. With his going went all hope of a resumption of mining there. But it does not seem likely that he should again have attempted operations in this isolated region without railroad facilities. He once remarked that the resurrection of Ducktown would never take place until a railroad was built into the district. In this, of course, he was correct. The railroad came and mining on a large scale was resumed—ten years after his death.

And so we have seen that the designation "back in Raht's time," heard so frequently in the early days of the present era at Ducktown, had a significance that probably never again will be matched here. No page in the phantom history of Ducktown reflects greater brilliance than that on which is inscribed the individual achievements of Captain Raht. No man ever worked harder to make of Ducktown a district of moral and industrial strength or assumed greater responsibility for its well-being. And, in turn, no man ever reaped greater rewards for his efforts than did Julius Eckhardt Raht.

APPENDIX

A NOTE ON SOURCES

INDEX

APPENDIX

IRON MANUFACTURE AT DUCKTOWN

Preliminary to and contemporaneous with the early copper industry in the Ducktown district was the manufacture of limited quantities of iron products at several different forges located in and adjacent to Ducktown. While these small iron works never exerted any permanent influence on the history of the region, it should, nevertheless, be interesting to learn of the locations of some of them and of the extent to which they were worked.

The iron works in this region were what were known as bloomery forges. A bloomery was similar to, but larger than, the ordinary blacksmith forge. The large crucible, or furnace, was heated by a fire which was kept at a high temperature by means of a bellows which was pumped by an arm-like contrivance attached to a water wheel. Broken ore was placed in the crucible, or furnace, where it was heated into a semi-molten state. This spongy mass was stirred constantly with an iron bar and at the proper time the fiery ball, called a "bloom," was lifted out of the furnace and placed under a heavy hammer, also operated by the water wheel, where it was worked, or shaped. Smaller implements of iron could be made by re-heating and cutting the larger piece as desired. The skill required here was in the manipulation of the iron under the steady pounding of the heavy hammer.

Few impurities in the ore could be removed in a bloomery. Consequently only a very high-grade iron ore could be used, and the presence of copper in an otherwise good grade of iron ore proved costly to the original iron master of Ducktown.

In the year 1847 Benjamin C. Duggar, "an enterprising iron master from Johnson County," Tennessee, came into the little-known district of Ducktown, purchased eighty acres of land on Potato Creek in March of that year and erected a single forge and tilt hammer which came to be known as the Zion Iron Works. The land cost Duggar $20 and two hundred pounds of iron, which was to be delivered when the forge was put in operation. An additional sum of about $700 was spent on the forge and on a dam that was built across the creek for power purposes. The Zion Iron Works was located on Potato Creek near its junction with the Ocoee River and on what was later the property of the Cherokee Mining Company. Duggar had his forge ready for operation in April, 1848.

There was a ready market for iron, at prices of from eight to nine cents a pound, throughout this mountainous section. The supply of ore was seemingly unlimited and Duggar's enterprise gave promise of being a lucrative one. But it proved to be otherwise. "The product looked to be of a good grade of iron, welded in the loop readily, and drew well—until cooled to a cherry red, then it would break across and into pieces. When heated to a white heat, then immersed in water until cooled it showed a thin copper precipitate on the surface." The outcome was that the high copper content of the ore rendered the iron useless, and tests of other iron outcroppings in the vicinity showed them to be likewise unfit for iron manufacture.

Just as Lemmon's "gold" five years previously had suddenly turned to copper. Duggar's iron had now just as disastrously turned to the same disappointing metal. But whereas Lemmon's experience had cost him nothing but a sad awakening following a night of revelry, Duggar had a heavy financial investment to protect. To do this a supply of ore suitable for iron manufacture had to be found. Such a supply was discovered, but it lay fourteen miles away, near the present site of Blue Ridge at what was later known as the Buchanan ore banks. It cost $5.00 a ton to haul this ore to Duggar's forge and the cost of charcoal was twenty-three cents a bushel. But despite these costly handicaps the forge was operated for about two years. During this time there was turned out some five hundred tons of iron, which was sold to points as far away as Ellijay and Dahlonega. The Tennessee markets were not open to Duggar's products as the copper road to Cleveland was not completed until some three years after the closing of Zion Iron Works.

Another iron forge, operated by John and Frank Waters, was located on Fightingtown Creek near the present site of Epworth. This forge was in operation prior to and during a part of the Civil War. The works consisted of a forge and trip-hammer and an undershot water wheel which operated the hammer and furnished the blast for the forge. The ore was hauled by ox wagons from the Buchanan ore banks. Before the war much of the manufactured iron was hauled to Rome, Georgia, and Cleveland, Tennessee, but during the war the entire output was taken by the Confederacy.

The Hemptown Iron Works, owned principally by Johnson Wilson, was located on Hemptown Creek about two miles up the creek from the present site of Mineral Bluff, Georgia. The forge was established in 1851 and was worked more or less regularly for about twenty-five or thirty years. Iron products from here were hauled by wagon to Dalton, Marietta, and Atlanta. A grist mill was later erected at the site of the Hemptown forge and came to be known as the Forge Mill.

Two other iron works in proximity to Ducktown were in operation during the 1850's. One of these, the Persimmon Creek Bloomery Forge, was located on Persimmon Creek about twelve miles west of Murphy. About forty-five tons of bar iron was made at this place in 1855. The other, known as the Shoal Creek Bloomery Forge was on Shoal Creek about five miles west of the Persimmon Creek Forge. The Shoal Creek forge was near the old Turtletown, North Carolina, post office, about half a mile south of the present Oak Park post office, and was owned by John Jones, who was granted three thousand acres of land, called the "forge donation," in consideration of his erecting the forge and manufacturing iron. With possibly one or two exceptions, the Civil War marked the end of the era of iron forges in the vicinity of Ducktown.

BEN DUGGAR
IRON MASTER AND MASTER POLITICIAN

Benjamin C. (Ben) Duggar, born December 7, 1813, was a member of the Duggar family that early worked the famous Cranberry Iron Works on the Watauga River in Carter County, Tennessee. Julius Caesar Duggar, Ben's grandfather, was among the first adventurous pioneers to settle in the Watauga country. In fact, Andrew Greer and Julius C. Duggar were said to have been the first settlers on the Tennessee side of the Virginia-Tennessee boundary line about the year 1766. Duggar was assocoated with Daniel Boone on the Watauga. While some doubt exists as to who first worked the Cranberry forges, it is conceded ·that "the Duggar family had been the first to build forges and hammer iron in Tennessee...." William, Abe, and John Duggar, sons of Julius C. Duggar, were operating the Cranberry forge in the 1830's or 1840's. Benjamin, a son of John Duggar, was connected with the Cranberry Forge until coming to Ducktown.

When Ben Duggar let the fire in his iron forge on Potato Creek die out "... he traded his entire stock holdings for a yoke of oxen and a carriage, hitched his oxen to the carriage and moved to Fannin County and went into politics." And it is an accepted fact that Fannin County has produced a no more astute politician than the good Ben Duggar proved to be, nor one who was more popular generally.

From 1873 to 1879 he represented Fannin County in the Georgia Legislature. In 1880-81 he represented the Forty-first District, comprising Fannin, Gilmer, and Pickens counties, in the state Senate. He took time out in 1882-83 and made an unsuccessful bid for Congress. Coming back to state politics, Duggar served as representative in 1884-85, was defeated for the state Senate by Samuel Higdon in 1886, and served again as representative in 1888-89.

Not only did Duggar seek votes for the election at hand, but he laid the groundwork for votes years ahead. For instance, he once met a group of boys in the road, on their way to Sunday school at Cherry Log. Ben was wearing his faithful linen duster, in the pockets of which he had some candy and chestnuts. Stopping the boys, and reaching into his pockets, he gave each of them a piece of candy and some chestnuts, saying, "Remember to vote for Ben Duggar when you get old enough."

At another time Duggar visited at Morganton while court was in session. He was ill, and went to the home of Thomas Trammel. This news was spread around, and the result was that so many of the people went to see Ben that the judge was forced to adjourn court temporarily. Overconfidence, however, almost lost an election for Duggar once. So lightly did he regard the chances of his opponent that he disdained campaigning against him. But much to his amazement, and to the remorse of many of his followers who had let attendance at protracted meetings keep them from the voting places, the election ended in a tie. Before the run-off Duggar donned his long linen duster, filled the pockets with candy, toured the county slowly and methodically, and swamped his rival on election day. Benjamin C. Duggar lived for several years at Pierceville, where he died on July 30, 1891.

PRECIPITATION OF COPPER AT DUCKTOWN

Mention was made several times in this volume of the recovery of copper from mine water at Ducktown, and in Chapter 10 is a description by a visiting committee of the Union Consolidated

Mining Company in May, 1860, telling how this was accomplished. Neither the chemistry nor the method of recovery by this process was discovered at Ducktown. For instance, the *Mining Magazine* of September, 1854, contained an article on cupreous water by a correspondent of the *London Mining Journal*. In this article it is stated that the metallic copper in water adheres to iron, if the iron is not rusty, and that to prevent the copper water from injuring mining machinery that comes into contact with the water, sheets or scraps of iron should be placed in the cisterns and bottoms of the shafts. The article further revealed that during the working of the Ovoca Mines in Ireland nearly sixteen thousand pounds of copper was obtained by the method in the short space of seven years. (There was obviously a typographical error somewhere in this "obtained" figure or in the length of time it took to recover the sixteen thousand pounds.)

In his report on the Ducktown Copper Region in 1859, Professor Charles Upham Shepard said: "In addition to the above resource for copper [the abundance of low-grade ore], attention is now being turned to the preservation of the blue vitriol waters of the mines and roasting heaps, which heretofore were suffered to run waste. This water is now detained in extensive tanks and reservoirs and made to precipitate its copper, through the addition of scrap iron, thereby materially adding to the returns of the mines."

Although the precipitation process was an old story even before the Ducktown mines were discovered and was then practised here for nearly a quarter of a century after the mines were opened, the method was apparently not generally known among copper miners in some of our western states at late as the 1880's. For instance, a Ducktown miner, W. L. Ledford, known locally as "Mug" and "Fate," migrated westward after the shut-down in 1878 and through his knowledge of the precipitation process was able to make a fortune. Ledford noticed one day that water from the Butte, Montana, mines where he was employed was depositing a heavy coating of metallic copper on a pile of tin cans over which the water was running. Realizing at once what was taking place, the crafty miner from Tennessee moved into action. With all the blandness of a man buying the Rocky Mountains, Ledford requested and received for a nominal sum the right to utilize for two years the mine waters that were running merrily down the hill. He then began erecting and placing scrap iron in a system of long, crude troughs. With these preparations completed he diverted the water into the troughs and waited.

In due course the water was drained off and the queer fellow was seen to get down in the troughs and begin sweeping the iron with a stiff broom. He was not scrubbing the iron as some probably thought. The full significance of what was taking place became apparent when Ledford began shoveling up huge quantities of sludge containing finely grained metallic copper. When this most pleasant chore was finished, the water was again turned into the troughs. This routine went on for over a year, despite the fact that the mining company made vigorous but vain attempts to have the lease declared null and void. Upon expiration of the lease the company took up the process while "Mug" Ledford retraced his steps to Tennessee with some $90,000 to $100,000 which he had cleared on his unique enterprise.

The foregoing is another old story, one that was and still is familiar to older native citizens of both Bradley and Polk counties. But what makes it unusual is in that credit seems to be given in certain circles to Ledford for discovering the precipitation process, and to Butte for being the place where it was first practised.*

For some additional information on W. L. Ledford, witness the following excerpts taken from a Special Illustrated Trade Edition of the Cleveland (Tennessee) *Journal,* published in December, 1900: "Capt. W. L. Ledford, the subject of this sketch, was born in Cherokee County, North Carolina, and is 55 years of age....

"Mr. Ledford was an employee in the copper mines at Ducktown, Tenn., where he commenced work at seven years of age, working there until 33 years old....

"About this time he became imbued with the spirt of the great throng who were treking westward in the hopes of bettering their fortunes, and in accordance, in a two horse wagon, set 'sails' for Colorado in 1878, finally landing in Montana in 1885.

"While in the west Mr. Ledford discovered how to mine copper by a precipitation process, and mines that were considered worthless were made profitable, and thus Mr. Ledford was enabled in a short time to make a considerable fortune from his valuable discovery.

---

* See C. B. Glasscock, *The War of the Copper Kings* (1935), p. 145, in which (Jim) Ledford's experience at Butte is dramatized, and he is acclaimed for a metallurgical "discovery" that had up to that time remained "hidden" from copper miners.

"He returned to Bradley County in 1896, buying a farm of nearly 2,000 acres on the Hiwassee river, which he has improved and it now contains all the improvements of any farm in any agricultural locality.

"Mr. Ledford is the richest man in Bradley County and owns the finest farm in the state. Although very wealthy, yet he is of a social disposition, and has a good word for every one. To know him is to like him.

"Although a republican in politics, he is one of Senator Clark's warmest friends. Mr. Clark is the democratic senator from Montana."

It will be noticed in the foreging article, too, that W. L. Ledford was credited with discovering the precipitation process. When the author inquired of certain older citizens who knew Ledford about why he permitted himself to be given credit for the discovery, they only smiled and replied by saying that "he probably did not think it important."

As a matter of fact "Fate," or "Mug," Ledford was for some twenty-five years in and around the mines at Ducktown before migrating westward. And during practically all these years there were systems of troughs filled with scrap iron at several mines where copper was being recovered by keeping the iron immersed in water pumped from under ground. It was his foreknowledge of this chemical action that enabled him later to "work" the Anaconda interests for a huge sum of money. The precipitation process was, obviously enough, not first practised at Butte, and neither Captain W. L. Ledford nor his brother Jim discovered its secret. Jim Ledford's name is associated by some with the Anaconda episode. Even as early as 1860, long before Butte was born into the copper kingdom, Eugene Gaussoin, in writing rather caustically of men who did not know all they should about copper mining, said: "... because I believe every man engaged in copper business knows, or ought to know, that in some localities this process [the old and well-known process of cementation by iron] is the only way of collecting the copper." This method has long since been abandoned at Ducktown.

BESSEMERIZING COPPER MATTE

While the subject will not be of widespread interest, it will, nevertheless, be interesting to some to learn of the controversy that followed the discovery of the process of bessemerizing copper matte. This will not, of course, be gone into at great length, but only in sufficient detail to bring out that, as in the precipitation of copper, metallurgical practices and improvements at Ducktown following the Civil War were probably more advanced than they were advertised. For instance, it is evident that August Raht's invention of bessemerizing copper matte in 1866 was never generally known. It was not until 1879 that credit for discovering this process was publicly claimed by him. In that year James Douglas called the attention of the editor of the *Engineering and Mining Journal* to a paper read by John Hollway before the Society of Arts, London, in which Hollway explained his method of smelting cupreous pyrites. This then brought to light the claim of H. M. Howe of a simultaneous invention with that of Hollway's of passing air through molten sulphides. August Raht read these articles in the pages of the *Engineering and Mining Journal* and thereupon sent to this publication a copy of his patent upon the same subject. The copy was published, but as there were no other claims or statements made by Raht in defense of his patent, very little attention was paid it. The controversy ceased after discussion of Hollway's process by the editor of the *Engineering and Mining Journal*, but it broke out anew in 1883, four years later.

In that year the subject of bessemerizing copper matte came up again and was heatedly discussed in the issues of the *Engineering and Mining Journal*. This time the controversy was between Paul Johnsson and H. M. Howe, and Johnsson claimed to have been in on the ground-floor of this process. Howe, of course, attached little credence to Johnsson's claims, but their controversy was traced no further than that of the May 5, 1883, number of the *Journal*. The last two articles on the subject, in the May issue, are given below, principally to show other references to the process as mentioned by Johnsson, and to include August Raht's opinion of the claims of others. It will be seen that Raht's patent predated all other such claims.

"EDITOR ENGINEERING AND MINING JOURNAL:

"SIR: In reply to Mr. Howe, in your issue of April 21st, allow me to mention only the following: The first attempts to Bessemerize copper matte were made in Russia in 1867 by Jossa and Laletin, by forcing either air or steam, or a mixture of both, through molten copper matte in a converter described in the *Oesterreichische Zeitschrift für Berg- und Hüttenwesen*, 1868, No. 50; in *Berggeist*, 1868, No. 50; and *Jernkontorets Annaler*,

1882, Vol. II. Experiments were made in 1868 at Vestanfors, in Sweden, by Stridsberg and Kollberg, to Bessemerize iron pyrites rich in copper, in a converter, mentioned in *Jernkontorets Annaler,* 1882, Vol. II. Rittinger proposed in the *Oesterreichische Zeitschrift,* 1871, No. 35, to blow compressed air in copper matte in a reverberatory furnace, and to put in silica to take care of the oxidized iron.

"I did not mention any thing about Mr. Howe's experiments, for the natural reason that I did not know any thing about the nature and quality of his experiments. When I read Dr. Tamm's description of the process in France to the superintendent at Bergen Point, I was told that the company had made experiments in a similar way before; but these experiments had not been successful. When I told my ideas of Bessemerizing copper matte to Mr. J. L. Thomson and Mr. W. C. E. Eustis, just before I left Bergen Point, these gentlemen did not mention any thing about their having made such experiments before.   PAUL JOHNSSON.

"ISHPEMING, MICH., April 27."

"EDITOR ENGINEERING AND MINING JOURNAL:

"SIR: I have followed with much interest the controversy about Bessemerizing copper matte between Messrs. H. M. Howe and Paul Johnsson in your valuable paper. I have just now received the copy of April 21st, in which Mr. Howe ascribes the priority of the Bessemerizing to Mr. Hollway, and the use of tuyeres in reverberatories for the same purpose to himself. Permit me space enough to correct this. I patented the Bessemerizing of matte in 1866; and a few years ago, when Mr. Hollway's process was much talked about, I sent you a copy of my patent, which you were kind enough to publish. I began the use of tuyeres in reverberatories for oxidizing matte in 1867, at the Ducktown copper-mines, and continued it with much success until 1875, when I left that place. Mr. Howe, no doubt, was not aware of these facts; nor do I consider them great inventions, and I think that any rational copper-smelter would invent them if placed in my position.

"A. RAHT.

"FRANCKLYN FURNACES,
"NEAR SALT LAKE CITY, UTAH, April 28."

Comparing Raht's statement that he employed his process of passing air through the liquid mass at Ducktown until 1875 with the description of smelting methods here in 1876, wherein was shown that the blast was directed over the surface of the charge and not through it, would indicate that Raht's process was discontinued here after he left Ducktown.

The mechanical features of the bessemerizing of copper matte have evolved into the method employed today which introduces air into converters through tuyeres that are kept open by constant "punching." Recessed steel balls drop into place when the long punching rod is withdrawn to prevent the escape of matte through the tuyere ports. Previous to the invention of passing air through the liquid bath, impurities in the matte were partially eliminated through "poling" or " splashing" the charge with a long rod or rabble. This was done by hand, and the practice was followed at some smelting works until well into the present century.

The process of forcing air through molten (iron) oxides is said to have been invented by Sir Henry Bessemer, a British engineer, in 1855, and the process thereafter bore his name. It is, therefore, a term more common to the iron and steel industry than it is to the copper industry.

THE FUEL PROBLEM

With each passing year the securing of wood and charcoal at Ducktown became more difficult. The Union Consolidated Mining Company consumed annually between 15,000 and 20,000 cords of wood and about 500,000 bushels of charcoal. As it required about one cord of wood to produce forty bushels of charcoal, the wood used for this purpose amounted to 12,500 cords a year. Therefore, estimating the company's annual wood consumption at between 25,000 and 30,000 cords, cut from lands that produced about 20 cords of wood to the acre, there was an area of some 1,200 to 1,500 acres being stripped of its trees each year. Estimating further that the Union Consolidated stripped some 18,000 acres of land of its trees; that the Burra Burra Copper Company and Polk County Copper Company took the trees from 6,000 additional acres; and that domestic and other uses required wood from 6,000 acres, it is found that an area of 30,000 acres, or nearly 47 square miles in this region was stripped of its merchantable timber between 1865 and 1878.

To secure adequate quantities of cordwood it became necessary in 1876 for the Union Consolidated to go far afield for its requirements. In that year the company leased three acres of land of Harbert T. McCay on the Ocoee River, where later grew the town of Copperhill, and built a pontoon bridge to recover wood

APPENDIX 263

that was being floated down the river from as far away as Morganton. It was here that the fashionable element of Hiwassee often spent their Sunday afternoons.

Three principal wood contractors in Fannin County were Michael McKinney, J. B. Dickey, and L. B. Crawford. These influential citizens leased state convicts for this work, which practice drew considerable criticism. An item by a Morganton correspondent, "Wood Chopper," in the Ellijay *Courier* of May 19, 1877, told of an injunction that had been secured to prevent J. B. Dickey and L. B. Crawford from cutting wood in Fannin County and floating it down the Toccoa River and to forestall the use of convicts in this service. The convicts, said "Wood Chopper," were supposed to be grading the Marietta and North Georgia Railroad, and their employment for the benefit of the "monied monopoly" of the Ducktown copper mines was resented by him. This worthy writer advised the mining company to build a railroad of its own, which was somewhat like telling a man to start a weather system of his own if he did not like the weather he was getting.

Opposition to using the river for floating wood seems to have developed early, but this was circumvented by a bill introduced in the Georgia Legislature by Representative B. C. Duggar. The bill, which was passed February 26, 1876, made it unlawful to obstruct by the erection of fish traps or otherwise the main current of the Toccoa River in Fannin County to a width of thirty feet, so as to interfere with rafting or floating timber. Wood continued to be floated down the river until the mines closed.

COPPER HAULERS

As the murmuring copper heart at Ducktown rose and fell it poured through the artery-like Ocoee forge a pulsating stream of wagons loaded with ingots and bars of copper to the railhead at Cleveland and drew insatiably back to it these same wagons loaded with provisions and materials for consumption at the mines. And plodding tirelessly with the wagons, or snatching rides on stubborn spring seats when the drag on the sturdy draft animals was not too great, were the conductors of Ducktown's early transportation system—the copper haulers. Forming as they did the life-line between the remote mining district and Cleveland, the copper haulers played a vital part in early mining at Ducktown. In winter and summer, in sunshine and rain, they pushed their teams over the old copper road with a faithfulness and dependability that recompensed to some extent their lack of speed and carrying capacity. Inseparably a part of the copper industry, but, nevertheless, by the very nature of their function and occupation somewhat apart and aloof from the actual mining operations, the copper haulers were of a truth the aristocrats of labor at Ducktown. They were inured to hardships, accustomed to responsibilities, and were "mule-skinners" of a high order.

Copper haulers had to spend at least one night of each trip to and from Cleveland in camp by the roadside. From both starting points they could usually reach Greasy Creek in one day, where they camped in the vicinity of the Half-Way House. Enough food for themselves and the animals was carried for the two-day trip each way. Because of the constant down-grade between Ducktown and Greasy Creek, it required nearly half a day longer to make the up-trip than it did the down-trip.

Down-loads, from Ducktown to Cleveland, were limited to 500 pounds of copper for each animal in the team. In the early days of mining, horses, mules, and oxen were used in this service, but by the 1870's mules were used almost exclusively. Four-mule teams were standard, although six- and eight-mule teams were not uncommon. In fair weather a large four-mule team could handle some 2,500 pounds, but in rainy, rough weather, 2,000 pounds for such a team was the limit. The load limit was determined at the copper-loading house. This rule was followed in order to prevent over-ambitious teamsters from loading their wagons to excess and suffering break-downs and delays en route.

Following are the names of the copper haulers in the month of October, 1875, showing the revenue earned by each on a single round trip between Ducktown and Cleveland:

Name	DUCKTOWN TO CLEVELAND		CLEVELAND TO DUCKTOWN	
	Weight (in pounds) of Copper	Amount	Weight (in pounds) of Supplies	Amount
G. B. Barnes	2,438	$12.19	3,257	$19.54
I. A. Gassaway	1,618	8.09	7,311	36.55
Jas. Rymer	3,447	17.23	5,626	28.13
W. C. Barnes	2,522	12.61	1,734	10.40
R. Boyd	2,155	10.77	2,627	13.13
W. P. Barker	2,209	11.04	2,500	12.50
A. J. Cloud	2,160	10.80	1,650	8.25

J. H. Williams	5,203	26.01	4,898	24.49
R. M. Cole	1,601	8.00	1,650	8.25
Jas. Lingerfelt	2,802	14.01	3,042	15.21
John Lowry	1,455	7.27	1,443	7.21
Wm. Center	3,005	15.02	3,000	18.00
W. A. Center	2,830	14.15	2,850	17.10

THE FIDDLE-PLAYING COPPER HAULER

The road through the Ocoee Gorge was lonely but never quiet. The roar of the river was as eternal as the waters and mountains themselves. The only discord was the muffled rumble of wagons, and an occasional lusty yell of command by a driver at his struggling team. Strangely enough, an exotic harmony welled up at times along this melancholy stretch of road. The harmony came from the violin of George Barnes who capitalized on his mules' weakness, their love of music, to soothe them with long, piteous strains when their strength and spirits lagged. The saga of Barnes's fiddle playing to put new life into his fatigued teams goes on. But time has a way of producing new angles to old stories. For instance, it has come to light that Barnes's mules became so thoroughly familiar with his repertoire that they tired of its sameness. In fact they strove harder and harder to make it unnecessary for their kindly master to resort to the fiddle for their delectation. But one day the wagon became hopelessly bogged down and was immovable. One of the mules, glancing back over its shoulder, saw Barnes reaching for his music box. Setting himself firmly in his collar he said to his dejected mates, "Come on, boys, let's get going, there comes that damned old fiddle again."

George Barnes is credited with having hauled the last wagon load of copper from Ducktown.

THE COPPER HAULER'S GRAVE

The shuttling back and forth between Ducktown and Cleveland; the roaring of the Ocoee en route; the swapping of yarns over nightly camp fires; the bantering over the weight of loads to be hauled with employees at the copper-loading house; the spending of days and nights in the bustling village of Cleveland —these composed the varied routine of copper hauling. All of those engaged in this service felt a singular attachment to it. This is illustrated most poignantly by the copper hauler's grave. On a high hill just west of the place where Grassy Creek empties into the Ocoee River is the burial place of a Greer boy who died while employed as a driver of a copper wagon. Before he died he requested that he be buried on this hill so that he could "see" the copper haulers as they passed over the road just across the river. The lad chose an ideal spot from which his spirit could watch the passing of his earthly companions. From his grave an unobstructed view of the copper road could be had for nearly a mile. This section of the road, at the eastern limits of the old George Barnes's farm, is now covered by waters held by Ocoee Dam Number 3

A NOTE ON SOURCES

The principal sources for this history of Ducktown were the letters and papers of J. E. Raht, together with records and reports of the mining companies he served, and the reminiscences of older citizens of the district and of descendants of early settlers. These sources provided not only facts but a great deal of local color—and local prejudices, ideas, and attitudes. Raht's correspondence in itself was almost a complete commentary on the first era of consolidated mining attempts at Ducktown. His letters also gave a vivid picture of the conditions (both financial and social) at Ducktown during the Civil War and following the war. The records of the three principal mining companies were available to piece together many loose ends left by the correspondence.

Primary sources used to establish facts dealing with the early history, the settling, and growth of the Ducktown district included abstracts of land grants, county deeds, old court records, and legislative acts of the dates mentioned in the text. These documents helped to determine the names of original settlers and the organization and development of the district. An abstract of the Polk County Register of Deeds' books rendered information about the numerous transfers of mining properties in the 1850's. The original property records were destroyed in the court house fire at Benton in 1894.

The Post Office Department in Washington furnished the names of early post offices and their dates of establishment. The Department also provided information about the establishment of mail routes and about postal service conditions.

Much of the material about the lawsuit over the Tennessee Mine was taken from a Memorial to the State Legislature, Session of 1866, by R. M. Edwards, attorney for the school commissioners.

Old reports on the geology of the Ducktown district provided adequate information on copper deposits and their exploration. These reports, some of which were published, are the following:

Ansted, D. T., "Report on the Ducktown Mining Region," *Quarterly Journal of the Geological Society of London*, Vol. 13 (1857).

Currey, Richard O., and Maury, M. F., "The Polk County Copper Company, Its Mineral Resources and Mining Prospects" (1859).

Gaussoin, Eugene, "The Ducktown Copper Mines of Tennessee, Their Value, Present Management, and Future" (1860).

Report of the American Bureau of Mines, on the Property and Works of the Union Consolidated Mining Company (October 10, 1866).

Shepard, Charles Upham, The Ducktown Copper Region and Mines of the Union Consolidated Mining Company of Tennessee (1859).

Tuomey, M., "On a Copper Mine in Tennessee," *American Journal of Science,* 2nd Series (May, 1855), pp. 181-82.

J. B. Killebrew, *Resources of Tennessee* (1874), pp. 246-52.

Other sources of information about the geology of the district and the copper mines and mining companies were reports of the mining companies themselves. Most valuable among these reports were the following:

Burra Burra Copper Company: Minutes of First Meeting of Board of Directors (April 10, 1860).

Polk County Copper Company: First Annual Report of Board of Directors to the Stockholders (April 4, 1860).

Union Consolidated Mining Company: Report on the Union Consolidated Mining Company of Tennessee (1857 and 1860).

The following papers and documents relating to *J. E. Raht* vs. *The Union Consolidated Mining Company of Tennessee* and *The Union Consolidated Mining Company of Tennessee* vs. *J. E. Raht* were available: much of Raht's correspondence; several newspapers containing accounts of the two trials; copies of practically all depositions, judgments, and decrees; copies of the pleadings of P. B. Mayfield, S. P. Gaut, A. S. Colyar, and John Baxter before the Supreme Court, State of Tennessee; a copy of the Supreme Court's decision as rendered by the Honorable Jordan Stokes.

The financial plight of the Union Consolidated Mining Company in its last years was readily determinable from reports and records of the company, as well as from Raht's correspondence.

A NOTE ON SOURCES

The discussions of the financial difficulties of the other companies were also based upon their own reports and records.

Local newspapers of the period covered by the book not only gave facts about the early history of the region but provided much information about social events and small business activities. The papers most frequently referred to were the Ellijay *Courier* and the Cleveland (Tennessee) *Banner*. The *Courier* of January 25, 1878, described the death of Colonel Fannin.

The Fannin County *Times* contained in its January 25, 1936, issue "A Condensed History of Fannin County," by Colonel William Butt, in which was discussed the naming of Morganton. The *Historical and Pictorial Review*, Cleveland and Bradley County (1932), offered information about the naming of Cleveland. The account of the guerrilla bandit, Gatewood, was taken largely from the Cincinnati *Commercial* (June 30, 1873).

The *Mining Magazine* published many articles about different aspects of the Ducktown district in volumes 1-7 and 10 (1853-56, 1858). *The Engineering and Mining Journal* offered information on the Monier Process (March 11, 1873) and on the mining and smelting methods of the Union Consolidated Mining Company (July 1, 1876). The subject of bessemerizing copper matte was also treated in the *Journal* (Vol. 27 [1879], pp. 201-2, 218, 260-61, 273-74; Vol. 35 [1883], pp. 118-19, 144-45, 192-93, 219, 250).

Information about the Cherokee Indians was for the most part obtained from *The Cherokee Nation of Indians* (Fifth Annual Report, Bureau of American Ethnology, 1883-84), by Charles C. Royce. Countless pages of history have, of course, been written about the Cherokees. For the lay reader, however, reference is made to *The Story of the Cherokees*, by Dr. W. R. L. Smith.

Other publications containing pertinent historical data were John Preston Arthur's *Western North Carolina* (1914), which discussed iron manufacture and the Western Turnpike; the Goodspeed Publishing Company's *History of Tennessee* (1884), which contained detailed information about the Ocoee District and the formation of counties in East Tennessee; and Philip M. Hamer's three-volume *History of Tennessee* (1933), which furnished information about the contributions of Archibald Deboe Murphey (I, 364-67).

Publications dealing with the geology of the Ducktown region and the region's possibilities are *A Sketch of the Geology of Tennessee* (1857), by Richard O. Currey, and *A Geological Reconnais-*

sance of Tennessee (1856), by James M. Safford. Both authors wrote at length about the Ducktown mines in the fifties.

Dr. Augustin Gattinger added to the store of information about early Ducktown by telling of his arrival at and flight from Ducktown in his *The Flora of Tennessee* (1901).

For a satirical treatise on Ducktown, as it appeared to a humorist who visited the district in the 1850's, see *Carolina Humor* (1938), published by the Dietz Press.

Thomas P. Janes's *Handbook of the State of Georgia* (1876) furnished the facts about the burning of the Mobile works. Further information about the Mobile Mine, and information about the Sally Jane Mine, is contained in S. W. McCallie, H. K. Shearer, and J. P. D. Hull, *Bulletin No. 33, Geological Survey of Georgia, and the Pyrites Deposits of Georgia* (1918).

Private A. J. Williams' *Confederate History of Polk County, 1860-1866* (1923) provided much of the material regarding Polk County companies in the Civil War.

INDEX

Aaron, James P., mail carrier, 112-13; courtship of, 112-13
Abstract of Information, on mines and rolling mill, 91-92
Academy, The, at Hiwassee, 104-5, 126
Adams, Henry, 70
Adams, L. L., 38
Addington, Joab, store of, 16
Ainesworth, James, 26, 27
Alexander, James A., director, Union Consolidated Mining Company, 80, 91, 143, 162; and misplaced memorandum, 171-72
Amburn, John, 174
American Bureau of Mines, report of, 55-56
American Smelting and Refining Company, 154
Anderson, Thomas, 28
Angellico Gap, 3, 19, 29, 32
Animals, draft, 41; whim, 147
Ansted, D. T., report on copper deposits cited, 54; mentioned, 78
Armstrong, Allen, 23
Armstrong, Louis, 24
Arnold, D. H., 51
Arp, A. M., 174
Athens, Tennessee, 24
Athens Mining Company, incorporated, 51
Aubright, Dr. Sylvester, as company physician, 113; treats Raht's children, 204-5
Ault, S. B., 90

Bacon, E. H., 158
Bailey, James, as juror, 27; as mine captain, 148

Bailey, James M., 231
Baltimore Copper Smelting Co., and London Mine, 72, 214-15; and tariff on copper, 140-41
Barker, Elizabeth, 39, 188
Barker, W. P., 264
Barker family, 28
Barnes, George, ferry of, 27; shot by guerrillas, 101; deposition of, 174; as copper hauler, 264-65; mentioned, 103
Barnes, W. C., 264
Bartlett, P. M., 169
Bartlett, William A., associate of Peet, 96; announces Peet's death, 200; mentioned, 176, 214, 215
Baugh, John, 236
Baxter, John, chief counsel of Union Consolidated Co., 174, 176-78
Baxter, William, 177
Baymiller Street, Cincinnati, Raht's residence on, 193
Bean's Ridge, 43
Beckler family, 27
Becknell, Mr., 156
Bell, J. C., 33, 34, 50
Benton, naming of, 22; seat of Polk County, 22; first session of court at, 23; postoffice established, 23
Benton, Thomas Hart, 22
Benton, Thomas Hart, Chapter, United States Daughters of 1812, 22n
Benton Mining Company, incorporated, 51
Bentonville, Tenn., 22
Berry, W. D., 158
Bessemerizing copper matte, patented, 149; copy of patent, illus-

INDEX

Bessemerizing copper matte *(cont'd)* trated, 150; controversy over discovery of, 259-62
Bessemer, Sir Henry, 262
Big Frog Mountain, 1
Biggs, John M., and wife, 104
Biggs Mine, 73-74
Bilbo, William N., 50
Black, A. G., president, Union Consolidated Mining Co., 168 ff.
Black, Reverend R. D., 240
Blairsville, Ga., seat of Union County, 17
Blakely, Professor, 104
Blalock girl, 76
Bledsoe, Yancey S., 63
Blizard, A., 116
Blue Ridge, Ga., settlement, 17; postoffice, 18
Blue Ridge Mining Company, incorporated, 75
Bluestone, 94, 217
Boardtown Creek, 17 ff.
Boardtown Road, *See* Roads
Bogert, G. C., 142
Bohn, Augustus, 214-15, 222
Bonn University, 186
Bostwick, Leonard, 50
Boughlinval, Madam S. K., 214-15
Boyd, Erby, 23, 34, 121, 174, 216
Boyd, Hugh, 105
Boyd, R., 264
Boyd, S. B., 90
Bradford, Chancellor, 171
Bradley County, organized, 15; size reduced, 21
Braine, George T., and London Mine, 71-73
Bransford, M. H., 158
Bray, Mr., mining engineer, 54
Bridge, pontoon, 125, 262
Brooks, Dr. Adolphus, 114
Brown, H. K., 219
Brown, N. H., 158
Brown, William H., 216
Brownlow, William G., and Radicals, 103; paper of, 193
Brunner, J. H., 242
Brush Creek, 3
Buchanan Ore Banks, 254
Buildings, erected by Hiwassee Mining Co., 61; erected by Tennessee Mining Co., 65; at Cherokee Mine, 67; at Eureka Mine, 68-69; at East Tennessee Mine, 69; at Isabella Mine, 70-71; at Mary's and Callaway mines, 73; at Polk County Mine, 84
Bunter, William, 74
Burdett, Dr. George M., 217
Bureau of American Ethnology, report of, and roll of Cherokee annuities, 5
Burgess, Benjamin, 28
Burgess, N. G., 52
Burnett, Enoch, 27
Bush Head Mountain, 29
Butte, Montana, 257-58n
Burra Burra Copper Company of Tennessee, incorporated, 51; purchases Hiwassee Mining Co., 62; reorganization of, 81; origin of name, 82; property of sequestered, 91; conditions after war, 129-33; operations resumed and discontinued, 135-36; properties sold, 142
Burra Burra Store, 208-9

Caldwell, John, quoted on taxes, 40; on first mining at Ducktown and building of copper road, 46-47; and Polk County Mine, 49, 66; and Ocoee Mining Company, 51; and Ocoee Turnpike, 57; and Tennessee Mine, 62, 63; mentioned, 10, 20, 26, 50, 56, 81, 134
Caldwell, Robert, 80
Calhoun, Georgia, 8
Callaway, L. L., 222-23
Callaway, Thomas H., surveys Ocoee District, 11; sells Callaway and Eureka mines, 49, 67; and Ocoee Turnpike, 57; and Tennessee Mine, 63; interest in Callaway Mine, 73; mentioned, 45, 48, 50, 81, 144
Callaway farm and home, purchased by Raht, 204
Callaway Mine, transactions concerning, 49, 73; operations at, 73
Callaway Mining Co., incorporated, 51; mentioned, 73

INDEX 273

Camerden, F., 137
Cameron, George S., visits Ducktown, 83; assists Raht, 95; flees Dixie, 201; mentioned, 80, 88, 143, 162, 213
Cammack, Addison, 162; deposition of, 174
Camp, J. C., 52
Campbell, A. A., 104, 174
Campbell, W. B., 212
Camp Ground, 106
Camp meetings, held, 33; Methodist, 47; annual, 109-10
Cane Creek Academy, 242
Cannon, Will, 157
Carding and weaving, mentioned, 41; machine for, 121
Carroll, Governor William, Indian Commissioner, 9
Carruth, Walter, 27
Carson, W. C., 115
Cartersville, Ga., 24
Cass County, Ga., 8
Castings, for copper molds, 133
Cave Springs, 35
Cawoneh, 5
Center, W. A., 265
Center, William, 265
Chable, A., on mineral wealth of townships, 10
Chalmers, William, 241
Champe, T. C., 90
Chancey, Joseph, family of, 98; mentioned, 35
Charcoal, 68, 132, 173-74
Charles, James, 117-18
Charleston, Tenn., 35
Charlton, C. W., 234-39
Chastain, Benjamin, 17
Chastain family, 27
Chatata Mining Company, 52
Chattanooga *Daily Times*, 231
Chattanooga *Dispatch*, 175
Cherokee County, Ga., 8
Cherokee County, N. C., organized and settled, 18-20; disposal of lands, 19; early roads of, 20; mentioned, 15
Cherokee Indians, dominion and boundaries, 7; treaties, 7-9; dominion capital, 8; lands in Ga. surveyed, 8; population, 8; deportation of, 9; lost silver mine of, 10
Cherokee Iron Co., 174
Cherokee Mine, 67
Cherokee Mining Co., incorporated, 51; sells mine, 67
Chestnut Gap, Ga., 29, 119, 121
Cheston, Galloway, 214
Churches, Pleasant Hill, 1; State Line, 29; Methodist, at Ducktown, 34; Baptist, at Hiwassee, 34, 105-6; Zion Hill, 36, 38; Bethlehem Baptist, 38; Damascus, 38; Grassy Creek, 38; Lebanon, 38; Macedonia, 38; Mt. Moriah, 38; Sugar Creek, 38; United Baptist, 38; Hopewell, 38, 105-6; Flint Hill, 38, 105-6; Northern and Southern Methodist, 104, 106-7; Hipp's Chapel, 106; Mine City Baptist, 106; Croft's Chapel, 107; Union Church, at Isabella, 107
Cincinnati, Ohio, Raht's war-time residence, 193 ff.
Civil War, effect of on Ducktown, 87-101
Clarke, Honorable T., 212
Clay, Henry, 22
Cleveland, Colonel Benjamin, name honored, 15; and "Cleveland's Bulldogs," 15
Cleveland, J. F., 11
Cleveland, Tenn., as frontier village, 13; postoffice, 15; seat of Bradley County, 15; growth of, 15-16
Cleveland (Tenn.) *Banner*, 104, 115, 118, 210, 241
Cleveland and Ducktown Railway Co., 153
Cleveland (Tenn.) *Journal*, 258
Cleveland National Bank, 212-13
Cleage, A., 222
Cleage, Mrs. Hattie, 239
Cleage, T., 222
Cloud, A. J., 264
Cobb County, Ga., 8
Cocheco Mine, 62
Cocheco Mining Co., incorporated, 50; mentioned, 62, 73

INDEX

Cochran family, 28
Cochran, Ferdinand C., 127
Cochran, Pink, 28
Cog Hill, 242
Cohutta Mining Co., incorporated, 75
Coker Creek, gold region, 4
Cold Springs, 10
Cole, R. M., 265
Coleman, Benjamin Y., 216
Coleman, William, 27
Coleta, Texas, 17
Collins, D. M., 174, 236
Colton, Henry E., 24
Columbus, settlement of, 22; first seat of Polk County, 23
Colyar, A. S., argument of, 170n; and Raht's lawsuit, 175 ff.
Companies, Mining, first organized, 49. *See* names of individual companies
Conasauga Mining Co., incorporated, 75
Cones, F. M., 242
Confederate government, sequesters mining properties, 88-93; titles faded away, 142
Congdon, Charles, and Mary's Mine, 49, 73; and Tennessee Mining Co., 51; works Tennessee Mine, 62; as director, 80; mentioned, 50, 91
Congdon, Samuel, buys school section, 48; and East Tennessee Mine, 49; and Mary's Mine, 49, 73; and Tennessee Mining Co., 51; and Ocoee Mining Co., 51; and Ocoee Turnpike, 57; and Tennessee Mine, 62-63; and Cherokee Mine, 67; position with Union Consolidated Co., 80; leaves Ducktown, 81; deposition of, 174; and Raht, 227-28; mentioned, 46, 50, 91, 142, 162
Congdon, Walter, 46, 80
Congdon corporation, 62, 64, 67
Congdon Mining Company, 62
Conner, John, 27
Continental Insurance Company, 222
Cooke, Daniel, 27, 28, 30
Cooke, Talitha Frances, 28

Cookston's Creek Seminary, 242
Cooper, W. F., Chancellor, and Raht's lawsuit, 175-76; succeeds to Supreme Court, 176-77
Copper, production of, 65, 69, 92, 155; price of, 68, 86, 92, 94, 138-39; precipitation of, 83, 133, 149, 216, 256-59; refined, first produced, 85; hidden at Cleveland during Civil War, 95, 197; stored at Ducktown, 130-31, 137, 193-95; tariff on, 138-41; loss of in smelting process, 165. *See also* Ore, Smelting Works, Mining
Copperas, 94, 217
Copper Basin, referred to as, 1; population of, 4
Copper haulers, 263-66
Copperhill, town of, 1, 4, 106, 262
Copper Hill, site of Polk County mine, 53, 66; Raht's residence at, 188
Copper Mines Postoffice, 36
"Copper Mines of Ducktown, The," report, 31
Cordwood, 125, 154, 262-63
Cornish engine, 72
Cornish miners, monopolistic position of, 72; mentioned, 6, 14, 35, 60, 71
Cornwall and Stevens, 156
Cotter, James M., 34
Cotton rock, 20, 84-85, 130, 151
Couves, Gabriel W., 81, 82
Cowanee Club, Copperhill, 5
Cowpen Mountain, 1
Cragnon, Mrs. Harvey A., Jr., 22n
Craigmiles, P. M., 50
Cranberry Iron Works, 255
Crawford, L. B., 263
Credner, Dr. H., 56
Creevy, William, 137
Croft, W. M., 107
Crossville *Standard*, 74
Crozier, John H., 235
Crutchfield, William, 222
Culberson, N. C., 20
Culchote Postoffice, first at Ducktown, 30; name changed, 36
Culchote Mine, history of, 73-74; bought by Raht, 216

INDEX 275

Culchote Mining Co., incorporated, 50
Currey, Richard O., description of Ducktown cited, 31-32; on discovery of copper at Ducktown, 44; reports on mines cited, 53, 55; mentioned, 43, 46, 58
Curry, G. E., 242
Cut Cane Creek, 17

Dalton, Ga., terminus of railroad, 35; ore transported to, 45, 57
Davidson, John, 34, 98
Davidson, Samuel W., 34, 98
Davidson's Store Postoffice, 36
Davis, Daniel, 118
Davis, Elias, sells Isabella Mine, 49; wife of, and naming of mine, 71; mentioned, 50
Davis, Isabella, wife of Elias D., 71
Davis, John, 25, 27, 40, 50
Davis, Young, 27
Davis Copper Co., incorporated, 51; and Isabella Copper Co., 70; mentioned, 189
Davis Mill Creek, 3, 25
Davis Mine, 70
Dawson, A. M., 104
Day, Isaac, 52
Deadrick, Chief Justice, 177
Deaver, Gabriel, 27
Deby, Professor Julian, examines Number 20 Mine, 75
Delano, Franklin H., 136, 142
Delano, Warren, and London mine, 49, 72-73; and Ocoee Turnpike, 57; bonds held by, 137; buys Burra Burra properties, 142
Delano House, 244
Denegre, James D., 81
Denison, Lyman, 50
Denton, Samuel, school commissioner, 63
Denton family, 27
Dickey, B. K., deposition of, 174
Dickey, J. B., 263
Dietz, August, 194n
Dilbeck, David, 27
Dillenburg, Duchy of Nassau, 186
Dividends, 61, 69, 83
Divine, Colonel J. L., 220

Dodson, Elisha, 56
Dombois, Mathilde, marriage to Raht and arrival at Ducktown, 187-88
Donaldson, Mr., killed, 97
Douglass, A. E., 57
Douthit, M., 236
Dow, John M., and Callaway Mine, 49, 73; opens Eureka Mine, 67; interest in London Mine, 71; bonds held by, 137; mentioned, 50
Dow, Nathan T., 50
Drill, diamond, 136; machine, 146; pneumatic, 147
Duck, Indian chief, 5, 101
Ducktown (Basin), location and area of, 1; physical features of, 1-4; origin of name, 5; first settlers of, 25-28; early settlements at, 28, 33; principal routes to, 29; postoffice at, 29, 36; social conditions at, 30, 38-39, 123-26; development of in 1850's, 31-42; first school, 37; population of, 40; effect of mining industry on land values at, 40-41; on other industries, 41; copper discovered at, 44-45; evidence of financial faith in, 47-48; first mining companies at, 49; geological reports on, 52-55; road system developed, 56-57; mining at, 58 ff.; economic conditions, 78, 121-23, 127; reorganization of industry at, 79-82; effect of Civil War on, 86, 87-101; mines closed at, 96; companies organized at, 96; exodus from, 98; following Civil War, 102-5; qualified voters at, 103; post-war schools, the Academy, 104-5; religious practices, 105-10; mail routes and service, 110-17; private enterprises at, 119-23; inaccessibility of, 122; without a railroad, 217; as source of Raht's wealth, 227; end of an era at, 249; mentioned, 162, 163
Ducktown, town of, 4. See also Hiwassee
Ducktown *Eagle*, 34
Ducktown Mining Co., incorporated, 51

276 INDEX

Duggar, Abe, 255
Duggar, Benjamin C., iron forge of, 45-46; as school commissioner, 63; as iron master, 253-54; as politician, 255-56; mentioned, 263
Duggar, John, 255
Duggar, Julius C., 255
Duggar, William, 255
Dunn, James, ferry of, 29; farm, 35
Dunn, Edward, 132
Dury, Miss Josephine, 35
Duvall, E. G., succeeds Raht, 152, 167; referred to as "Cotton Broker Miner" and "Moses," 154; leaves Ducktown, 156-57; report of cited, 166-67; company property deeded to, 169; and Raht's lawsuit, 176
Dyer, John H., 34
Dynamite, 146

Eager, Jennison, as sales agent, 160; mentioned, 142, 162
East Tennessee and Georgia Railroad. See Railroads
East Tennessee and Maryland Mining and Smelting Co., incorporated, 51
East Tennessee Mine, transactions concerning, 49, 69; first operated, 69
East Tennessee Mining and Smelting Co., incorporated, 51; operations of, 69
East Tennessee National Bank, 225
East Tennessee's Great Lawsuit, 175. See Raht
Echota (and New Echota), Cherokee capital, 8-9
Edom, negro slave, 190
Edwards, Isaac H., 35
Edwards, P. J. R., 12
Edwards, R. M., 64
Edwards' Ferry, 106, 125
Election, presidential, of 1876, 230-32
Ellijay, Ga., 17, 29, 36
Ellijay *Courier*, 114, 155, 263
Ellijay Seminary, 107
Elliot, Henry, clerk, 91
Elrod family, 28

Employment at copper mines, 83, 84, 86, 92, 135, 152
Engineering and Mining Journal, 150, 260-61
Epworth, Georgia, town of, 4, 105
Esterbrook, T. J., 67
Etowah Iron Works, 195
Eureka Mine, transactions concerning, 49, 67; opened and worked, 67-69; operated after war, 145-48; bought by Raht, 215-16
Eureka Mining Co., purchases Eureka Mine, 49, 67; incorporated, 51; operations of, 67-69; becomes insolvent, 69
Eustis, W. C. E., 261
Excelsior and Ocoee Mining Co., incorporated, 51

Fain, Clayton, 100
Fain, Dr., 114
Fair, Tennessee State, 233-34
Falls, Harvey, 76
Falls, Henry, 236
Falls, John, frozen feet of, 114
Fannin, James Walker, 17
Fannin County, Ga., organized, 16-17; settlers of, 17; first roads in, 17; mines in, 74-76; mentioned, 15
Farmers Loan and Trust Co., 165, 169
Fightingtown Camp Ground, 29, 33
Fightingtown Creek, 3, 17
Fillmore Mining Co., incorporated, 51
Flat Top, 1
Fleming, Robert N., 145, 215
Flint Hill, Ga., 106
Flora of Tennessee, The, 99
Floyd County, Ga., 8
Forge Mill, 255
Forges, bloomery, 253-55
Forsyth County, Ga., 8
Fort Butler, 9, 18
Fort Cass, 9
Fort Glimer, 9
Fowler, Senator Joseph H., 140
Franklin Mountain, 2, 19
Freeland, Howell, 27
Freeman, Alexander H., 50
Freeman, E. B., 236

INDEX

Fuel, problem of, 262-63. See also Charcoal
Furnaces. See Smelting Works

Gaines, John G., 81, 82, 201
Galloway, Ga., 2
Galloway family, 28
Gassaway, I. A., 264
Gaston, P. C., 96
Gatewood, Captain, guerrilla leader, 100, 101, 103
Gattinger, Dr. Augustin, biographical data, 34-35, 99; flees Ducktown, 99; and Williams boy, 99
Gaussoin, Eugene, report on mines cited, 31; and Raht, 84; mentioned, 61, 259
Gaut, Jesse H., 50, 243
Gaut, John C., 211
Gaut, S. P., and Raht's lawsuit, 173 ff.
Generes, L. F., 134-35
Geologists, report of on Ducktown, 52-55
Gibson, Elias, and wife, 118
Giddings, James, 73, 212-13
Gilbert, Lyman W., on draft animals at mines, 41; and Isabella Mine, 49; president, Isabella Copper Co., 70; visits England, 78; and Polk County Co., 81; and debt of Burra Burra Co., 137; mentioned, 50, 82, 91
Gilliam, Jasper, 28
Gilmer County, Ga., 8, 16
Gist, Robert C., 216
Glasscock, C. B., 258n
Goliad, Texas, 17
Goodman, John, 63
Goodman, Dr. John, 96
Goodman's Mill, 117
Goodner, John, 52
Grange Iron Works, 174
Grant, Ulysses S., Raht on, 230-32
Grassy Creek, 3, 38
Greasy Creek, 117-18
Great Consolidated Company of Tennessee, 78
Great Copper Basin, referred to as, 1
Greene, R. C., 51
Greer, Andrew, 255

Greer boy, grave of, 266
Greer, Isaac N., operates ferry, 27; mentioned, 217
Guerrillas, raids of during Civil War, 96-100, 131-32
Guilford, N. C., 187
Gunter's Landing, 9

Half-Way House, described, 117-19; mentioned, 217, 264
Hamilton, Alexander, 70, 189
Hamilton County, Tenn., 8
Hammell, D. C., 90
Hancock, William W., 27, 71
Hancock Mine, 71
Hancock Mining Co., 71
Hannah, J. H., 96
Hannah, John F., 11, 23
Hannah farm, 217
Hardwick, C. L., deposition of, 174; sells Culchote property, 216
Haren, Alexander, 106
Haren, James, 112
Harmon, I., 90
Harper, Thomas, 23
Harper, William, 28
Harper's Ferry, Va., 187
Harris, Benjamin C., 51
Harris, John, mine captain, 60
Harris lad, stabbed, 99
Harvey, John J., 241
Haskins, D. C., 217
Hats, stock of, 118; Christmas sale of, 190
Hawkins, James, 23
Hayes, Rutherford B., election discussed, 230-32; mentioned, 175
Haynes, Landon C., report to confederate judge cited, 88-90
Heckel, Johannes, 244
Hemp, settlement of, 17
Hemp Top, 1
Hemptown Creek, 17
Hemptown Iron Works, 255
Henegar, H. B., and Union Consolidated's debt, 144-45; mentioned, 50
Henshaw, Professor, 104
Hickok, William, and East Tennessee Mine, 49; and Mary's Mine, 49, 73; mentioned, 70, 81, 83, 91

Hick's Mill, 120
Higdon, M., 108
Higdon, T., 108
Higdon's Store, 75
Hipp, Mountville, 106
Hiwassee (or Hiwassee Town), Ducktown known as, 6; first village in the Copper Basin, 33; assumes regional leadership, 34; schools at, 37, 104; effect of the Civil War on, 97, 101; social conditions at, 124-27; brass band at, 124; morality of, 125-26; elite society of, 125-26; effect of closing of mines on, 126-27; mentioned, 82, 102
Hiwassee Copper Mines Postoffice, 36
Hiwassee District, 8
Hiwassee Mine, 58, 62
Hiwassee Mining Co., incorporated, 50; and Hiwassee Mine, 58; second annual report, quoted, 59-60; operations of, 58, 61-62; property sold, 62; mentioned, 34, 51
Hiwassee River, 3, 4, 8
Hoffman, A. S., 196, 208, 236
Hollway, John, 260-61
Holmes, Dr., 96
Hooke, R. M., 222
Hooper family, 27
Hot House Creek, 2
Hot House Postoffice, 19
Howe, H. M., and bessemerizing copper matte, 260-61
Hoyle, James, 23
Humphrey, William, 236
Humphreys, Judge West H., 89-90
Hunt, Dr. William, 233
Hunt and Douglas copper process, 150
Hunter, A. C., 174
Hunter, Archibald R. S., 18
Hunter, Dr. S. M., 144
Hunter, Thomas A., 119-20
Hunter House, 119, 124
Huntingdon Postoffice, 18
Hutsell, Will, 157
Hutton, William, 126
Hyatt, J. R., 174
Hyden, J. Albert, 245

Indians. *See* Cherokee
Indian trail, 24
Indian villages, 2, 9, 10
Interest, dispute over legal rate of, 224-25
Iron forge, at Ducktown, 45. *See also* names of individual forges
"Iron Hat," 55
Iron works, 253-55
Isabella, town of, 4; school at, 37; Union church and school at, 107
Isabella Copper Co., incorporated, 51; operations of, 69-70
Isabella Mine, transactions concerning, 49, 70, 144-45; opened and worked, 69-70; origin of name, 71; production of, before and after Civil War, 148-49
Isabella Store, 154-56, 208

Jackson, Andrew, 22-23
Jackson, R. C., 225
James, Colonel John H., 204
James, J. W., 222
James, L. M., 222
Jarnagin, A. S., and Raht's lawsuit, 173 ff.
Jenkins, David, 27
Johnson, Andrew, 141, 175
Johnson, Ebenezer, 45, 48
Johnson, John, 28
Johnson, Joseph, 73
Johnson, Samuel M., 33, 45, 48, 50, 63
Johnson family, 28
Johnsson, Paul, and bessemerizing copper matte, 260-61
Joint Stock Companies Act, 78
Jones, Alonzo, 100
Jones, John, 255
Jones, Pendleton, 10, 119, 174
Jones, Stephen, 190
Jory, Harry (Henry), letter from Raht quoted, 116-17; death of, 245; mentioned, 104, 133, 236
Jory, James, mine captain, 73, 74, 236
Jory, James, Jr., 174
Jory family, 98
Joseph, A. C., 222
Justices of the peace, 26-27

INDEX

Keener, D. C., 57
Keith, Alexander H., and purchase of Polk County Mine, 134-35; mentioned, 49, 66, 81
Kell, Kem, 112
Kendall, S. A., and Raht's lawsuit, 173, 175-76
Kennedy, John C., 11
Kern, Peter, 244
Ketcherside, Dr. J. D., 34, 104, 113-14
Ketcherside, Dr. J. N., 104, 108
Ketron, Mrs. Sally, 238
Key, David M., appointed Postmaster General, 231-32; mentioned, 175
Kilpatrick, E. M., 34, 36, 174
Kilpatrick, Elias W., 19
Kilpatrick, Florence, 36
Kilpatrick, Lucie, 36
Kilpatrick and Ketcherside, 119
Kilpatrick and Mosley, 119
Kimber, Alfred, 162, 172, 180
Kimsey, Dr. Fred M., 105
Kimsey, Humphrey, 157
Kimsey, Dr. Lucius E., 105
Kimsey, William, 27
Kimsey's Store and Postoffice, 36
Kincaid, James, 18
Kincheloe, J. F., 104
Kinser, William, slain by guerrillas, 100
Kirtland, F. A., 143
Knoxville *Daily Press and Herald*, 234
Knoxville Whig and Rebel Ventilator, 193

Laflin and Rand Powder Co., 147
La Grange, Ga., 160
Land Boom, at Ducktown, 49
Lang, Jacob, 209, 211, 216, 236
Lamson, C. E., 69
Law Court, Common, established at Ducktown, 115-17
Lea, Luke, 12
Ledford, Jim, 157, 258n, 259
Ledford, W. L. (Mug), the Butte episode, 257-59; mentioned, 157, 174
Lee, A. L., copper consigned to, 94
Leesburg, Va., 187

Legg, M. W., 212
Legriel, Lewis, 51
Lemmon, Jesse, 27
Lemmon, James, school commissioner, 63
Lemmons, Mr., discovered copper at Ducktown, 44
Lenoir, William, 222
Leslie, Professor, 59
Lewis, George T., 174
Lewis, Isaac, 90
Lillard, Abraham, 56
Lincoln, Abraham, Raht quoted on, 202
Lindsey, G. W., 174
Lingerfelt, James, 265
Literary Society, at Hiwassee, 125-26
Little Frog Mountain, 1
Little Gassaway Creek, 3
Little Tennessee River, 8, 11
Locomotive, saddle-tank, 147
Lonas, John L., 90
London Mine, transactions concerning, 49, 71; opened and worked, 71-72; litigation over, 72-73; bought by Raht, 213-15
London *Mining Journal*, 257
Long, Bud, mail carrier, 112
Low, Andrew, 80
Lowe, B. I., 173, 236
Lowry, John, 265
Lumpkin County, Ga., 8
Luttrell, Mr., killed, 97
Lyon, T. C., 45, 48, 63

Macaulay, Andrew J., 169
Macaulay, John L., 162, 180
Macon County, N. C., 18
MacPherson, E., president, Polk County Copper Co., 134; visits Ducktown, 134; report of visit, 136; president, Burra Burra Copper Co., 137; tribute to, 142; mentioned, 82, 105
MacPherson Mine, operations at after war, 135-36
Macy, Josiah H., 67, 69
Madisonville, Tennessee, 24
Madola, settlement, 29
Magill, J. H., 222
Mail routes, 19, 30, 36, 110-11

Mail service, at Ducktown after war, 112; in South during war, 111, 194
Mansfield, J. C., 218-19
Marshall, John K. P., 105, 108
Marshall, Dr. W. R., 114
Mary's Copper Co., 51, 73
Mary's Mine, transactions concerning, 49, 73; operations at, 73, 148
Maryville College, 168
Masonic Lodge, at Hiwassee, 34
Mastin, heirs of Thomas W., 49, 66, 81, 134
Mastin, Thomas W., 81
Mastin, T. M., 50
Mathews, Aaron, 174, 236
Mathews, Miss, 104
Mathews family, 28
Matthew's Mill, 219
Maughan family, 35
Maury, M. F., report of cited, 52-53
Mayfield, P. B., and Raht's lawsuit, 175 ff.
Maynard, Congressman, 140
McAdoo, William G., 90
McCampbell, Robert, 47
McCay, Archibald, 28
McCay, Harbert T., 28, 174, 262
McCay, Thomas, 28
McCay and Marshall, merchants, 119
McCaysville, Georgia, 4
McClary, Joel, 26
McClellan, General George B., 202
McClure, Enos, 18
McCulloch and Glenn Copper Co., 51
McDonnel, Russell, 27
McFarland, R. J., 177
McGee, E. P., 35
McGinnis, E. W., 142
McGonigal, J. M., 51
McJunkin, John, 27
McKamy's Farm, site of Benton, 23
McKinney, Michael M., 121, 174, 263
McKinney and Keller, merchants, 121
McKinney's Mill and Store, 119-21
McKissick, Abraham, 217
McLeod, Sydney, slain by guerrillas, 100
McMillin, D. C., 211-12, 221
McMinn County, Tenn., 8, 21-22

McNabb, A., 51
McNutt, W. B., 90
Mechanicsburg, Ga., 17
"Memorial Upon the Free Admission of Foreign Copper Ores," 138
Menko, Joseph, 121
Menko, Martin, 73, 121
Meroney, A. D., 27
Middlecoff, G. W., 52
Middlecoff's Store, 52
Military headquarters, of Federal Army, 131
Mill Creek, 3, 25
Mills, grist, 28, 41, 120-21; saw, 41; powder, 202; flour, 218
Mills, William, 56
Millsaps family, 28
Mine City University (Institute), 104
Mineral Bluff, Ga., 17
Mining, copper, methods in vogue, 66, 145-49; equipment used, 85, 131, 133, 146-47. See also Copper, names of individual mining companies, Ore
Mining Magazine, 48, 72, 74, 78, 79, 257
Mobile and Atlanta Mining Co., 158
Mobile Mine, accident at, 76; mentioned, 75, 158
Monier process, 150
Monroe County, Tenn., 8
Moore, A. H., 158
Moore, R. H., 75
Morgan, S. D., 234
Morganton, Ga., history of, 16-17; postoffice, 18; jail at, 114
Morton, Levi P., 231
Mountain House, 119
Mt. Pisgah Mine, 75
Mueller, Edward, as mine captain, 148; as receiver, 154; and Raht's lawsuit, 173-74; mentioned, 196, 216
Mule Top, 1
Mullins, Mrs. Matilda, 118
Murphey, Archibald Deboe, 18
Murphy, N. C., 18
Murray County, Ga., 8

Nance, G. P., 90
Nankivell, Annie, 35

INDEX

Nankivell, James, wife of, 35; leaves Ducktown, 98; prize awarded to, 234; mentioned, 36, 121, 157
Nankivell, James R., Jr., 35, 105, 114
Nankivell, John, 36
Nankivell, Octavus, 36
Nash, Patrick, 39
Nashville *Bulletin*, 235
Nashville *Daily Press and Times*, 40
Nautlee River, 4
Nautlee Town, 4, 29
Neel, F. F., 223
Neptune's cartridge, 147
Newberry, J. T., 227
New Jersey Copper Co. of Tennessee, 51
New Orleans *Daily Crescent*, on southern enterprises, 93-94
New York and London Mining Co., incorporated, 51; and London Mine, 71-72
New York Stock Board, 62, 67, 70
New York *Tribune*, 236
New York University, 104-5
Nicholson, Governor, 7
Nicholson, A. O. P., 50
Nichols Height, N. Y., 45
Nigger Creek, 36
Nobel, Alfred, 146
Nobel, Samuel, 174
Norridgewock, Maine, 200
Nottely River, 3
Number 20 Mine, 75, 158

Oak Park, N. C., postoffice, 19, 255
Oates, Wadlaw and Co., 215
Ocoee Bank, 211
Ocoee Dam Number 3, 3, 266
Ocoee District, visited by Troost, 4; established, 11-12; disposal of lands, 12-13; mentioned, 19, 21
Ocoee Gorge, 3, 56
Ocoee Leather Company, 121
Ocoee Mine, 74
Ocoee Mining Company, 51, 74
Ocoee River, described, 2
Ocoee Town, 121
Ocoee Turnpike and Plank Road Co., 57, 59, 60, 130, 189
Officials, public, 26-27

Old Fort, 24
Oothout, William, 80
Oram, Francis, 69-70
Ore, copper, samples sent to England, 48; analyses and grades of, 55, 61, 66, 67, 69, 135, 148, 163; freight on, 57, 59; production of, 62, 65, 66, 67, 69, 70, 72, 92, 148; sold in England, 67, 70
Orr, Jack and Simon, slain by guerrillas, 100
Osborne, Thomas, 216
Otis, Isaac, 70
Ovoca Mines, in Ireland, 257

Pack, Jerry, 27
Pack Mountain, 1
Padleford, Edward, 80
Panic of 1857, 68, 86
Panter, William, 28
Parks, Dr., 114
Parks, George C., 174
Parks, Colonel James, 211
Parks, Paul, 174
Parks, Samuel, 217
Parksville, Tenn., 242
Parksville Mill, 217
Passmore, F. F., 174
Patterson, Jeptha, 33, 49
Paulding County, Ga., 8
Paydays, quarterly, 122
Payne, C. B., 143
Payne family, 27
Payroll, Raht's ruse with, 236; mentioned, 135, 152
Peck, Jacob, 118
Peet, William H., and Burra Burra Co., 81-82; cited as owner of mining properties, 89; buys Ducktown mines, 91; loyal to associates, 95, 199; and blockade running, 96; death of, 96, 200; tribute to, 200-1; mentioned, 50, 88, 134, 142, 144, 196, 214, 215
Peet, Mrs. Sarah H., 200
Perkins, Edmund, 80, 83
Persimmon Creek Bloomery Forge, 255
Persimmon Creek postoffice, 19-20
Peyton, Colonel Bailie, 235

Philadelphia Centennial Exposition, Ducktown's contribution to, 233-35
Philips, William A., 19
Phillips, James, and Number 20 Mine, 158; deposition of, 174; mentioned, 35, 76, 236
Pierce, Joseph, 28, 33
Pierceville, Ga., settlement, 28, 29, 33; postoffice, 33
Pierson, Henry L., 142
Pill, Captain J. R., and London Mine, 71
Pill, Thomas, 76
Pill, William, 98
Pleasant Hill, first settlement at Ducktown, 28
Polk, James K., 22
Polk County, Tenn., organized, 21-23; first roads, 23-24; a "Rebel" county, 103; mentioned, 1
Polk County Copper Co., purchases Polk County Mine, 49, 66; incorporated, 51; reorganized, 81; property sequestered, 91; conditions after Civil War, 129-33; operations and sale of mine, 133-35
Polk County Mine, transactions concerning, 49, 135; first operated, 66; operations at after the Civil War, 133
Postmaster General, report of the, 111
Potato Creek, 3
Potomac Copper Company, 70
Powell, Dr., 76
Powell, Mr., miner, 146
Powerhouses, at Caney Creek, 3; at Little Gassaway Creek, 3
Precipitation of copper. *See* Copper
Prince, Cooper, 27
Prince, Ephriam, 52
Prince, Frederick O., 50
Prince, Jackson, 27
Prince, W. L., 174
Printup, Daniel S., 142
Proctor, C. A., 57, 70, 73

Quinn, Julius, 35
Quintrell, John, 35
Quintrell family, 98

Radical Party, the, 103
Ragsdale, L. F., 90
Raht, Adolphus Washington, 245
Raht, August, and smelting operations, 149; retirement and death of, 154; death of wife, 152; report on copper loss, 165; immigration to America, 186; and bessemerizing copper matte, 149-50, 260-62
Raht, Carl (Charles), as secretary of Union Consolidated Mining Co. on copper tariff, 140-42; resignation of, 162; and brother's lawsuit, 171; arrival in America, 186; and Captain Raht, 205 ff.
Raht, Edward, 186, 213
Raht, Julius Eckhardt, personal papers of, v; as mine captain, 66, 73; secures equity in London Mine, 73; as superintendent of copper companies, 81-82; revives industry, 82-86; mining policies during Civil War, 88-95; residence at Cincinnati, 98, 192-203; and churches, 105-7, 145; and establishment of law court at Ducktown, 115-17; acquires Half-Way House, 118; deals in mules, 120; and commissaries, 81, 123, 213-16; restraining influence of, 124; mining policies after Civil War, 129-33, 206-8; levies on Burra Burra Co., 137; and tariff on copper, 138-41; transactions with Union Consolidated Co., 152, 160-61; letter of, quoted, 164; loan to Thomas, 168; lawsuit of with Union Consolidated Co., 170 ff.; court's decision in favor of, 180 ff.; biographical data, 185-92; receipt of, illustrated, 203; has eye operation, 203; return of to Cleveland, 203-6; establishes Cleveland National Bank, 211-13; real-estate dealings of, 213-18; other business endeavors, 218-19; loans and investments of, 219-24; and dispute over interest rate, 224-25; summary of financial growth of, 225-27; and Congdon and Thomas, 227-28; political activities of, 228-33; advertises Ducktown, 233-35; philan-

INDEX

Raht, Julius Eckhardt *(cont'd)*
thropies of, 235-42; contemporaries of opinions of, 237-38; religion of, 242-45; family of, 245-46; death of, 247; summary of life accomplishments of, 247-49; mentioned, 16, 50, 64, 98, 119, 142
Raht, William, 245
Raht, William L., patent of, 150-51; mentioned, 186
Railroads, Louisville and Nashville, 4; East Tennessee and Georgia, 15, 16, 56, 194; Georgia and South Carolina, 35; East Tennessee and Virginia, 131; "Air Line," 146; "Crooked Line," 146; narrow-gauge, connecting mines and smelters, 147-48; Nashville and Chattanooga, 194; Marietta and North Georgia, 263
Ramey, H. P. (Hard), 157, 174
Ramsey, John W., 229
Red Clay, Cherokee capital, 8
Revere Copper Co., 138
Revere Smelting Works, 45
Reynolds, W. B., 212
Ridge, Major, Cherokee chief, 9
Roads, Georgia Highway No. 5, 4; Kimsey Highway, 4, 10; Boardtown Road, 17, 29 ff.; Western Turnpike, 20, 29, 57; first in Polk County, 23-24; Old Federal Road, 23, 24; Stock Road, 23-24; Armstrong Ferry Road, 24; Copper Road, built by Caldwell, 46-47, 101-2, 130; development of in preparation for mining, 56-57; Ocoee Turnpike Co. and, 57, 59, 60
Robb, R. H., 105-6
Rochereau, Albin, 137
Rogers, Dr. H. A., 105, 114
Rogers, John, 25, 27
Rogers, Seburn, 27
Rogers' Ferry, 17, 25
Rolling Mill, for copper, 88, 96
Ross, John, Cherokee chief, 9
Ross's Landing, 9, 13
Rudizinski, Mrs. J. E., letter of Raht to, quoted, 236-37
Rudizinski, Katinka, 236, 237

Rymer, James, 264
Rymer, Jesse, 217

Safford, J. M., 69, 234
Sally Jane Mine, 75
Santa Lucah, Ga., 36
Sassafras Knob, 1
Savannah Farm, 22
Schermerhorn, J. S., 9
Schofield, General, 195
Schools, first established, 36-37; following Civil War, 104-5; Raht's aid to, 240-42
School Property Mine. *See* Tennessee Mine
Scott, General Winfield, 9
Seaton, Dr., 149
Section sixteen, Ducktown township, property of citizens, 12; source of school revenue, 37, 63; lawsuit over, 63-64
Sevier, E. F., 222
Sewanee Mining Co., 58
Shannon's *Annotated Constitution of Tennessee*, 225n
Sharp, W. L., 211
Shepard, Charles Upham, 82, 257
Sherman, General William T., 197-98
Shoal Creek, 20
Shoal Creek Bloomery Forge, 255
Shugart, Livingston, 209, 216
Shumake, John, 90
Simmons, J. L., 52
Sims, J. M., 96
Sketch of the Geology of Tennessee, A, 46
Slate, William, guerrilla leader, 100
Slaves, 28
Slick Rock Creek, 13
Sloan, J., 57
Smelting process, described, 84-85, 149-52
Smelting works (smelters), Hiwassee, 61; first erected, 64-65; Eureka, 67-68; furnaces for, 64-65, 67-68, 151; at Mobile, 76; Burra Burra, 84, 147; at Polk County Mine, 133; at Isabella, 143, 147, 150-52
Smith, G. W., 27
Smith, Henderson, 27

Smith, William G., 75, 162, 180
Smithsonian Institute, 233
Sneed, John L. T., 177
Snow, S. T., 138
Soapstone. *See* cotton rock
Society of Arts, London, 260
South Carolina, secession of, 86
Spargo, James, 35
Spargo, John, 148
Spargo family, 98
Speck, William, 208
Spring, Nicholas, 15
Spring Place Mining Co., 75, 158
Staffordtown, 5
Stamper, I. J., 106, 119, 126-27, 174
Stansbury, Solomon, 27, 100
Stansbury Mountain, 1
Stanley, H. H., 137
Stanton, John, 57, 67, 70
Steatite. *See* Cotton rock
Steedman, Major General James B., 132, 204
Steele, Robert I., 34
Stevenson, Andrew, 23
Stewart, Elam, slain by guerrillas, 100
Stewart County, Tennessee, 174
Stiles, Benjamin, 19
Stone, James S., 51
Stone, William, 105
Stokes, Jordan, and Raht's lawsuit, 170 ff.; renders decision, 180
Stores, at Hiwassee, named and discussed, 119; at Isabella, 154, 156, 208; Burra Burra store, 208-9
Strike, at Eureka Mine, 68
Strother, W. W., 158
Stuart, Jacob S., 90
Stuart, Joe, 157
Stuarttown Creek, 121
Sturges, W. C., 69
Styles, Albert, 27
Styles, Carey W., 158
Sugar Creek, 2, 17
Sullins, T., 220
Sulphur, loss of, 216-17
Summerour, Mr., 75
Sunday School, picnics held by, 107-9, 126; mentioned, 106
Sutherland, family, 27
Sweet, George O., 81-2

Symons, J. V., 50, 62-63
Tacoah, Ga., 17, 18
Taliaferro, Benjamin, 41
Taliaferro, Charles, 96
Tallassee, 11
Tatham, Charles B., 80, 91, 142, 162
Tatham, Tyra A., 19
Tecumseh Iron Co., 174
Tellico River, 11
Tennessee Consolidated Copper Mining Co., Ltd., 78
Tennessee Copper Co., 4
Tennessee Mine, operations at, 62-65; lawsuit over, 63-64; first furnace at Ducktown erected at, 64-65
Tennessee Mining Co., 51, 62-65
Tennessee River, 8, 11
Tennessee Rolling Works Co., 88
Tennessee Smelting Co., 51, 64, 65
Tennesese Valley Authority, 3
"Theseus," newspaper correspondent, quoted, 112, 124-25
Thies, A., 150
Thomas, Major General George H., and Raht, 193; mentioned, 196, 198
Thomas, John, president, Union Consolidated Mining Co., 142, 162 ff.; resignation of, 167; and Raht, 168, 227, 228; and Raht's lawsuit, 171-74; baukruptcy of, 228; mentioned, 50, 81, 82, 88, 91, 92, 160
Thomas, Mattie, and J. P. Aaron, 113
Thomas, W. F., 113
Thomson, J. L., 261
Thornburgh, J. M., Raht's letters to, quoted, 231-33
Threewitt, L. L., 26, 27, 189
Threewitt Mountain, 1
Tift, William P., 51
Tilden, Samuel T., 230
Tipton, John B., 11, 45, 48, 63
Tipton, J. C., 11
Tipton, W. L., 233
Toccoa River, origin of name, 2
Toccooee Mining Co., incorporated, 51
Tocoah Mining Co., incorporated, 75

INDEX

Tonkin, John, and East Tennessee Mine, 69; and mines during Civil War, 98-100; deposition of, 174; mentioned, 133, 145, 157, 236
Tonkin, John, Jr., 96, 97
Towns, John, 23
Tracy, Samuel F., organizes Ocoee Turnpike, 57; president, Hiwassee Mining Co., 58; bonds held by, 137; mentioned, 50, 79
Tracy shaft, 60
Trammel, Thomas, 256
Transportation, hack line operated, 120. See also roads, railroads, copper haulers
Travena, Charles, 37
Travers, William, 162
Trenewith, Captain, 67
Trewhitt, William R., 116
Tripple, Dr. Alexander H., and American Bureau of Mines report, 56; and Eureka smelters, 66-68; mentioned, 174
Troost, Dr. Gerard P., reports on Ducktown, 4, 43-44; mentioned, 29
Tuckahoe Postoffice, 17
Tucker, St. George, 22n
Tumbling Creek, 3
Tuomey, M., report on mines cited, 55
Turner, Peter, 174
Turner, Prestly, 27
Turtle, Indian chief, 5
Turtletown, district, location, 5; postoffice and mail route, 19; mentioned, 36
Turtletown Mining Co., incorporated, 51
Tuthill, George A., 158
Tyree, T. T., 158

Union County, Ga., 8, 17
Union Mining Co., 52
Union Consolidated Mining Company of Tennessee, incorporated, 51; organized, 78-80; properties of, 80, 145; map of properties purchased by, 80; property of sequestered, 91; conditions after Civil War, 129-33, 142-57; reorganization of, 142, 162-63; report on, 143-44, 153; smelting works of, 149-52; and Raht's store, 154; operations ceased, 154, 169; financial history of, 159-69; Raht's lawsuit with, 170 ff.
United Refining Works, 85,143
United States Copper (or Mining) Company of Tennessee, 51, 218
United States Highway Number 64, 3
United States Mine, 73-74
United States Mining Journal, The, 70
United States Patent Office, 150
University of Berlin, 186
University of North Carolina, 18
University of Pennsylvania, 113
Urrea, General, 17

Vanderbilt University, 105
Vestal, David, 28
Vestal family, 28

Walker, John W., 30
Walker, P. H., 211
Walker Valley Co., 52
Wallis, D., Raht's substitute, 192
War of the Copper Kings, The, by C. B. Glasscock, 258n
Warne, William, English agent, 48, 58, 71
Warner, W., 174
Waterhouse, Euclid, sells Callaway and Eureka Mines, 49, 67; buys Tennessee Mine, 63; interest in Callaway Mine, 73; mentioned, 50, 56, 144
Waterhouse Mining Co., incorporated, 51
Waters, Frank, 254
Waters, Joe, 238
Waters, John, farm of, 100; mentioned, 254
Waters, Samuel T., 73, 76, 119, 214
Waters, Thomas, 28
Waters family, 28
Weaver, A. J., ships ore, 45; loses life, 46; cabin of, 47; mentioned, 48, 57, 58
Weber. See Weaver
Webster, Thomas, 84, 222

Webster, Thomas, and Co., 146
Weeks, Drewry, 19
Weeks, E. M., 174
Weese family, 28
Wendt, Arthur F., 152
West, A. G., 174
Wetmore, Oliver, 50
Wetmore, Tennessee, 7, 23
Wheeler, Montague, 222
Whim, description of, 65-66
Whitney, J. D., geologist, 53, 54
Wiggins, William, 27
Wilder, General John T., 222
Williams, Black and Co., 168
Williams, Elizabeth, wife of Duvall, 157
Williams, Francis W., and Union Consolidated Mining Co. properties, 169; mentioned, 168
Williams, John, 23
Williams, John H., 156-57, 265
Williams, W. T., 137
Williams boy, stabbed, 99

Wilson, Johnson, 255
Wilson, Levi, 28
Wimberly, W. H., first lieutenant, 96; and Raht's lawsuit, 173, 175
Witherow, J. M., 174
Witherow family, 27
Witt, Bell, 157
Witt, Betty, 127
Witt, James B., 156, 208, 240
Witt, William R., 27
Wolf Creek, 2, 17
Wolf Creek Postoffice, 19
Womble, William, 26
Wood, George, 49, 71
Woodfolk Iron Co., 174
Worth County, Ga., 168, 190
Wyles, William H., 50

Yonce, William B., 246

Zion Iron Works, 253
Zisch, Henry, 149
Zodak, Jacob, 119

www.ingramcontent.com/pod-product-compliance
Lightning Source LLC
Chambersburg PA
CBHW021355290426
44108CB00010B/244